PRAISE FOR
FROM FAMILY COLLAPSE TO AMERICA'S DECLINE

"Political correctness leads some topics to be completely avoided, regardless of their importance. Family fragmentation is one of these, but Mitch Pearlstein has now broken it open. He makes a compelling case that we avoid problems of the family at our individual and national peril. Perhaps now that the topic has been so forcefully exposed, we as a nation can address the issues in a broad and constructive manner." —**Eric A. Hanushek**, Paul and Jean Hanna Senior Fellow in Education, Hoover Institution at Stanford University

"A shot across the bow of the national conversation on education and economic competitiveness. Pearlstein challenges both the left and right for an elephant-sized blind spot about the importance of family fragmentation in our persistent achievement gaps. He is appropriately humble about solutions, but argues convincingly that we can't hope to turn things around if we keep avoiding this uncomfortable conversation." —**William J. Doherty**, professor of family social science, University of Minnesota

"The public does not seem concerned that the American family is dissolving before our eyes. Yet children reared by lone mothers are more likely to have mental health problems, teen births, school failure, and several other afflictions than kids reared by married parents. America has too many adults making decisions about divorce and nonmarital childbearing to promote their own happiness rather than their children's well-being. This disturbing case is made in provocative and convincing fashion by Mitch Pearlstein in this remarkable volume. Anyone who reads it will come away alarmed by the costs being imposed on America by family dissolution." —**Ron Haskins**, codirector, Center on Children and Families, The Brookings Institution

"Conservative and liberal education reformers, for all their disagreements on policy, are united on one matter. Both camps maintain a studied silence regarding the greatest impediment to closing the achievement gap and improving U.S. educational performance: family breakdown. Mitch Pearlstein is determined to break that silence. Unless Americans can figure out how to stem the epidemic of out-of-wedlock births and divorce, he warns, the favorite educational nostrums of both left and right will have only limited effect in raising student achievement. Pearlstein readily admits that the antidotes to family disintegration are not obvious. But until the problem is recognized, there can be no hope for a solution. This clearly written, unblinkered book ought to trigger a long-overdue confrontation with what can rightly be called America's greatest civilizational threat." —**Heather Mac Donald**, senior fellow, Manhattan Institute

"This is a terrific book, a highly readable and profound account of a ticking time-bomb—family fragmentation. To this controversial subject, Mitch Pearlstein brings both passion and compassion, sprinkled throughout with wisdom and wit. Pearlstein shines a bright light of integrity on a crisis too-long ignored." —**David Lebedoff**, author, *The Uncivil War*

"This work of earnest policy reflection ought to arouse our moral indignation, as the educational and vocational futures of millions of children are being sacrificed at a cost none of them should bear. If we want to recover a vigorous economy and vibrant culture, those of us in education, religion, business, and policy-making must seriously heed what Mitch Pearlstein sagely writes about family and parenting failures. God forbid if we don't." —**Robert Osburn**, executive director, Wilberforce Academy

"This important volume should direct some much-needed attention to the fact that the United States now leads the world in fragmented families and the threat this poses to children, education, the economy, and the very welfare of the nation. Mitch Pearlstein documents the case well and even offers a little hope." —**Robert L. Woodson, Sr.**, founder and president, Center for Neighborhood Enterprise

"Mitch Pearlstein has a big idea. It's that today's family trends affect far more than our families. They affect how and whether our schools can teach, and how and whether our economy can grow. Written with a light touch and a sure hand, this book is a genuine, serious contribution to our national discussion. I particularly like the fact that Pearlstein does more than diagnose the problem. He also offers up a pail full of creative solutions." —**David Blankenhorn**, founder and president, Institute for American Values

"Parents are the first and most influential teachers that any child has and the family the first and most influential school. When those are in good shape and do their part, kids tend to fare well in education and in life. When those falter, great schools (and other key institutions) can help a lot—but never really substitute. Understanding—and trying to reverse—America's 'nuclear meltdown' is this thoughtful book's peerless contribution." —**Chester E. Finn, Jr.**, president, Thomas B. Fordham Institute

From Family Collapse to America's Decline

The Educational, Economic, and Social Costs of Family Fragmentation

New Frontiers in Education
A Rowman & Littlefield Education Series
Edited by Dr. Frederick M. Hess

Rowman & Littlefield Education series provides educational leaders, entrepreneurs, and researchers the opportunity to offer insights that stretch the boundaries of thinking on education.

Educational entrepreneurs and leaders have too rarely shared their experiences and insights. Research has too often been characterized by impenetrable jargon. This series aims to foster volumes that can inform, educate, and inspire aspiring reformers and allow them to learn from the trials of some of today's most dynamic doers; provide researchers with a platform for explaining their work in language that allows policymakers and practitioners to take full advantage of its insights; and establish a launch pad for fresh ideas and hard-won experience.

Whether an author is a prominent leader in education, a researcher, or an entrepreneur, the key criterion for inclusion in *New Frontiers in Education* is a willingness to challenge conventional wisdom and pat answers.

The series editor, Frederick M. Hess, is the director of education policy studies at the American Enterprise Institute and can be reached at rhess@aei.org or (202) 828-6030.

From Family Collapse to America's Decline

The Educational, Economic, and Social Costs of Family Fragmentation

Mitch Pearlstein

ROWMAN & LITTLEFIELD EDUCATION

A division of

ROWMAN & LITTLEFIELD PUBLISHERS, INC.
Lanham • New York • Toronto • Plymouth, UK

Published by Rowman & Littlefield Education
A division of Rowman & Littlefield Publishers, Inc.
A wholly owned subsidary of The Rowman & Littlefield Publishing Group, Inc.
4501 Forbes Boulevard, Suite 200, Lanham, Maryland 20706
http://www.rowmaneducation.com

Estover Road, Plymouth PL6 7PY, United Kingdom

British Library Cataloguing in Publication Information Available

Library of Congress Cataloging-in-Publication Data

Pearlstein, Mitchell B., 1948–
  From family collapse to America's decline : the educational, economic, and social costs
of family fragmentation / Mitch Pearlstein.
    p. cm.—(New frontiers in education)
  Summary: "Very high rates of family fragmentation in the United States are subtracting
from what very large numbers of students are learning in school and forever holding
them back in many other ways. This in turn is damaging the country economically by
making us less primed for innovation while also making millions of Americans less
competitive in an increasingly demanding worldwide marketplace. All of which is leading
to deepening class divisions in a nation which has never viewed itself or operated in such
splintered ways. What can be done to reverse these severely destructive trends, starting
with reducing the enormous number of children forced to grow up with only one parent
living under the same roof? What educational reforms are most likely to help under
such demanding circumstances? And as dangerous as the situation is, why do leaders
in education and other fields persist, for both understandable and less-worthy reasons,
in dancing around profoundly important questions of family breakdown to the point of
contortion and ultimately failure? Shortchanging Student Achievement looks at these
issues and more in an attempt to reconcile family and education"—Provided by publisher.
  ISBN 978-1-60709-361-9 (cloth : alk. paper)—ISBN 978-1-60709-362-6 (pbk. : alk.
paper)—ISBN 978-1-60709-363-3 (electronic)
  1. Home and school—United States. 2. Children with social disabilities—
Education—United States. 3. Dysfunctional families—United States. 4. Academic
achievement—United States. I. Title.
  LC225.3.P43 2011
371.19'20973—dc23
                                                                                2011016322

∞™ The paper used in this publication meets the minimum requirements of American
National Standard for Information Sciences—Permanence of Paper for Printed Library
Materials, ANSI/NISO Z39.48-1992.

Printed in the United States of America

With life-shaping gratitude for C. Peter Magrath, Albert H. Quie, the late Samuel H. Popper, and *all* my teachers.

Contents

Acknowledgments

Coming up with a tight but fair list of people to thank is difficult given that I started thinking about this book, or something akin to it, sometime between three years ago and the latter half of the 1970s. Knowing exactly when is a bit of fog, meaning it's not too much of an exaggeration to say I'm in debt to many scores of scholars, writers, analysts, public officials, and others who have shaped my thinking over a long stretch of time about a wide range of educational, familial, economic and others issues.

I pay special respects in the dedication to three of them: C. Peter Magrath, a brilliant and generous university president for whom I worked both at Binghamton University and the University of Minnesota, and whose embracing fascination with American higher education deepened mine; Albert H. Quie, a truly one-of-a-kind man and courageous governor for whom I also worked and whose biography, *Riding into the Sunrise*, I was entrusted to write; and the late Samuel H. Popper, the very definition of a learned doctoral adviser whose devotion to a universe of ideas was matched by his allegiance to his students and their more condensed worlds at the time. The three, moreover, stand in for all my teachers over the years, and insofar as I'm within a thousand days of collecting my first Social Security check, it's about time I thanked them in this way.

When it comes specifically to the tough issues discussed in *From Family Collapse to America's Decline*, to whom else do I owe scholarly thanks? I started typing out the roster only to have it begin looking like a midsized phone book. Suffice it to say it's a bountifully unwieldy list of remarkable men and women, so might I suggest that readers simply review the endnotes and index for a decent sense and sampling of who they are. Though, in keeping with the just-created tradition of picking three friends and colleagues to represent many others, it's with pleasure that I thank Chester E. Finn, Jr., from whom I've learned more about elementary and secondary education than anyone else. And David Blankenhorn and Wade Horn, with whom I coedited a vital book about the then-still-young fatherhood movement in 1998, and from whom, once again, I've gained much.

Back to the endnotes and index for a second: Please note there is no necessary reason to eliminate anyone from the Blue Chip List just because he or she shows up in the book for purposes of my disagreeing with them in a particular instance. No one fits this latter category better than Diane Ravitch, whose work I've admired since her earliest historian days.

I fortunately connected with Rowman & Littlefield Education via a couple of routes, including Rick Hess's recommendation that RLE's Tom Koerner consider the book, which in fact has come to be part of a series of studies coshaped by Rick, the prolific director of education studies for the American Enterprise Institute. At virtually the same time, my longtime friend Bob Brown of the University of St. Thomas also suggested that I pitch Tom, and as things have pleasantly turned out, I'm more than grateful that everyone recommended, urged and agreed as they did. Tom has been terrific to work with, joined by everyone else at Rowman & Littlefield Education, including Lindsey Schauer, Karin Cholak, and Julia Loy. Rick Hess's colleague Juliet Squire was also first-tier.

Hiding in a corner of one's home (or the Caribou at 46th and Nicollet in South Minneapolis, for that matter) so as to write can be an inconvenience not only one's family but also one's associates at work. Never once, I'm proud to say, did any of my colleagues at Center of the American Experiment raise a detectably skeptical eyebrow whenever I announced by phone or email that I'd be "working at home today, and probably tomorrow, too." I thank them enormously, as I do the center's directors, led by Chairman Chuck Spevacek, all of whom were equally accommodating. In particular, Britt Drake on staff did a wonderful job formatting the manuscript and doing any number of electronic things I know zero about, and Director Keith Kostuch helped me think through some of the economic ramifications of fragmenting families in an increasingly demanding marketplace. I'm likewise most grateful to the center's many donors who keep the organization funded and its employees fed, especially those who have generously supported this venture, notably the Greycoach and Chiariscuro foundations.

And then last yet always cardinal, there's my wife, the Rev. Diane Darby McGowan. In the aforementioned *Riding into the Sunrise*, I acknowledged how, after spending a lot of time thinking and writing about themes of love and devotion (Al Quie, as you may know, is a very loving and devoted person), it was impossible not to revere and give thanks for her even more. After now spending even more time delving into various themes which are both congruent with and radically opposite those in that previous book, let's just say it's even more impossible not to recognize how lucky I am.

The same applies when it comes to my life with everyone in my family: my daughter, stepsons, daughters-in-law, grandchildren, and so on. But given the tough subjects addressed in the pages ahead, permit me to add a few more words about my adult daughter and my three adult stepsons, the latter of whom were teenagers when I burst into their lives twenty-one years ago with what had to be an extraordinary and unsettling surprise.

Diane and I adopted Kaila—not her real name for reasons that will become increasingly clear—fifteen years ago, which was five years after she first came into this world in the most unlucky and damaging of ways. She somehow never drowned in that earlier brew, but her introduction to this world, it cannot be overstated, was terrible. And while it was more severely so than the starts experienced by most children talked about in this book, the tissue connecting their respective plights is often more sinewy than many would like to believe. We love Kaila and pray for good and healthy new days for her and her own new baby, just as we do for all children, no matter where along Lottery Road they begin.

As for my stepsons, reconfirmed in what follows is that successful stepfamilies are not easy to pull off. Frankly, I did not know two decades ago exactly what researchers already had found, and what they are still finding, about just how difficult stepfamily victories can be and how children growing up in such households often suffer educationally, emotionally, and in other ways. In my own family's situation, let's just say things have worked out better than what the heavy-duty literature might have predicted as well as better than what I could have hoped for, and for which I am eternally thankful once more, this time to Chris, Brian, and David for allowing me to share in their lives—and their mother's.

Mitch Pearlstein
Minneapolis
April 2011

Introduction

The argument that follows is straightforward. Very high rates of family fragmentation in the United States are subtracting from what very large numbers of students are learning in school and holding them back in other ways. This in turn is damaging the country economically by making us less hospitable to innovation while also making millions of Americans less competitive in an increasingly demanding worldwide marketplace. All of which is leading—and can only lead—to deepening class divisions in a nation which has never viewed itself or operated in such splintered ways.

"Family fragmentation" has come to be the favored term of the art for out-of-wedlock births, churning relationships, separations, and divorce. Suggestive of how many families never get to fully form in the first place, and perhaps promoted by some to connote less personal failure or societal danger than "family *breakdown*," the impossible-to-soften or redefine fact is that the United States continues to lead virtually the entire world in it. With a nonmarital birth rate of more than 40 percent (more than twice at high in many urban communities) and an overall divorce rate of close to 50 percent, no major nation in the world starts from as deep a deficit, as measured by instability on the most personal and formative of home fronts.

This is the case, in other words, when it comes to the not-short list of countries where students consistently and often significantly outperform their American counterparts academically. It's especially the case when it comes to our most potent economic competitors around the world. Fully taking into account that enormous numbers of young people in places like China and India are severely disadvantaged in other ways, there's no legitimate way of sidestepping the empirically demonstrated ways in which family fragmentation retards American kids educationally and the United States, therefore, economically.

Or more to an integral contention of the book, while there may be no acceptable way of skipping around the multiple and handicapping products of nonmarital births and divorce, that doesn't mean that otherwise trenchant leaders of mettle in a variety of fields aren't practiced in doing so. In education, for a prime example, try a quick experiment. Pull half-a-dozen books off your shelves that deal in one way or another with poor or otherwise disadvantaged boys and girls. Now go to their indexes and see how many times words such as "fathers," "marriage," or anything pertaining to what more frequently and offensively used to be called "illegitimacy" are cited. The number doubtless will be tiny, quite possibly zero. Now, it's understood that indexes don't capture everything found in preceding pages. But omissions like these, one can just about guarantee, are neither happenstance nor uninformative, as they suggest a fogged-in mountain of educational and, thereby, economic troubles.

Richard Rothstein, for instance, is one of the most important writers in the country arguing that significant progress in reducing achievement gaps is impossible so long as "lower-class" students (his term) face so many social and cultural obstacles, starting with poverty. More than a fair point, it's an acute one, and in significant ways a variation on what I've long claimed and do so here. But there is an enormous difference. Hardly ever, for example, in his influential book *Class and Schools*[1] does he begin to consider the fact of massive family fragmentation in the United State generally and inner cities particularly and how its connection to low incomes and other shortages and shortcomings is direct and powerful. Never does he hint at recognizing how rates of family disruption are higher in the United States than virtually anywhere else on planet. It's a remarkable omission, not that his blind spot—akin to missing pregnant elephants stomping around classrooms—is the least bit rare.

A case can be made, for example (I've regularly made it), that Diane Ravitch has been the most influential education historian of the last generation and rightfully so. But note what she *doesn't* say about the lives and situations of many children in a representative passage from her recent book, *The Death and Life of the Great American School System.* "As every educator knows," she writes, "families are children's first teachers," and that "on the very first day of school, there are wide differences in children's readiness to learn."

> Some children have educated parents, some do not. Some come from homes with books, newspapers, magazines, and other reading materials, some do not. Some parents encourage their children to do their homework and set aside a place and a time for them to study, some do not. Some parents take their

children to the library, zoo, museum, and other places of learning, while some do not. As a result of different experiences in early childhood, some children begin school with a large vocabulary, while others do not.[2]

Every assertion is correct, of course. But taken in sum they're also incomplete, as Ravitch strains—precisely in concert with Rothstein and others—to ignore an elephantine reason why many children are less likely to be taken to libraries, zoos, and museums, not to mention sufficiently supervised and inspired around kitchen tables reconfigured every evening as study carrels. In fact, the best I could tell, never in *Death and Life* does she ever say anything at all about children growing up with only one parent at home, even though immense majorities do so in many of the school settings she writes most forcefully about.

For another, albeit this time novel example, take *Organizing Schools for Improvement*, a methodologically sophisticated analysis of a major school decentralization initiative in Chicago, written by five current and past University of Chicago scholars under the leadership of Anthony S. Bryk, another first-tier scholar. To their credit, Bryk and his colleagues include a chapter titled "The Influences of Community Context." To their further credit, they raise matters like this:

> Almost by accident, one factor caught our attention: stagnating schools had a relatively high percentage of students "living with nonparental guardians" as recorded in CPS [Chicago Public Schools] records. This one piece of data, which we interpreted as a proxy for children living in a foster care arrangement, suggested another possibility. Might the concentration of students living under extraordinary circumstances—in foster care, homeless, neglected or abused, and/or living in a household marred by domestic violence—pose exceptional demands on schools that made attention to reform much harder to sustain?[3]

"Yes" is the manifestly obvious answer to a question that borders on the rhetorical. But again, note what's not spoken of here: At the risk of unattractive glibness, what's missing in this key excerpt, as well as throughout the chapter, is any reference whatsoever to broken families of a much more routine, even everyday sort. It's as if we've graduated to a new order of political correctness, one in which researchers, writers, and others are no longer silenced merely by intimidating cant and fear of ostracism, but rather by a now habitual, barely conscious acquiescence that children and fathers living separately is the new normal; one in which great cities are ground zero of an increasingly familiar to the point-of-invisible landscape. No longer is the remarkable deemed worthy of remarking, as deviancy continues being defined down, way down, as Daniel Patrick Moynihan might have put it.

Here's another variation on the theme, this time not regarding a book about education but an analysis of the very idea and practice of marriage over the eons by historian Stephanie Coontz. In many ways, *Marriage, a History* is a magnificent piece of scholarship, living up to its blurbs ("myth-shattering" and "endlessly fascinating," according to Oprah's magazine *O*). It's an unusually rich interpretation of how much of the west (not just the United States) has gotten to this stage of married life. And to the extent anyone conflates marriage as idyllically practiced by Beaver's parents for a few decades following the Second World War with "traditional" unions as known over centuries and millennia, Coontz effectively disabuses such silliness, as she well understands how marriage is a transforming institution in several senses of the term. Nevertheless, what she downplays to the point of near erasure is also endlessly fascinating.

Virtually the only thing Coontz has to say about the effects of marital breakup on kids comes in the next-to-last chapter when she acknowledges that divorce, in most cases is a "traumatic process that inflicts pain [and] sometimes long-lasting wounds on everyone involved," and that it can be "especially stressful for children." And while she contends that "75 to 80 percent of children recover well and function within normal ranges after divorce," to her credit she does note that boys and girls from divorced families "have twice the risk of developing behavioral and emotional problems as children from continuously married families."

A sentence later she's again correct in arguing that children in "high-conflict" marriages are often better served if their parents go their separate ways. But in the very next breath she writes that "children also suffer when exposed to constant and low-level friction" in a marriage.[4] Obviously, marital "friction" cannot be terrific, much less enjoyable, for children regardless of severity (at least if they actually notice, which is not always the case). But when it comes to children's health and well-being, there's generally a significant difference between growing up in high-conflict and low-conflict situations, with the former much harder and more damaging. Or from the flip side, getting divorced for low-conflict reasons is usually not in the best interests of kids, never mind rarely welcomed by them. Coontz, however, largely ignores the critical distinction.

Yet if Coontz sends late and less-than-emphatic signals about the effects of divorce on children, she is almost completely silent when it comes to the aftermaths of out-of-wedlock births. Best I could tell, she doesn't say a word about how growing up in neighborhoods containing barely a handful of married couples could ever be other than unhealthy or unwise. For that matter, while her analysis is unusually comprehensive as to assorted crosscurrents undermining marriage, she somehow manages to completely ignore the way in which the Great Society and continuing welfare programs have made it much more feasible than ever before in American history—and, therefore, more likely—for women to raise children without the economic help of a husband. As omissions go, color this one breathtaking.

Spurred by this observation about welfare as well by the connotative punch of "deviancy" in the Moynihan dictum above, this is an early and right time to acknowledge just how emotionally tough familial issues like these can be and how any serious discussion of them can scrape exposed nerve endings even rawer. So let me be as clear as I can, as I always try to be when dealing with this subject.

My aim is not to gang up on or hurt anyone: single parents—single mothers—wholly included. While I'm not without passion on the subject and I very much do believe that family fragmentation is the overwhelming social disaster of our times, I also recognize (paraphrasing another ameliorating phrase) that *stuff* happens. My wife of twenty years, for example, was a single mother with three young sons for a long time after her divorce many years ago. I'm also in my second marriage, or as I've learned to say, my second and "ultimate" marriage. (I used to say second and "last" marriage, but for some reason, Diane didn't like the locution.) Often overlooked, by the way, in analyses like this is the nation's significant number of single fathers, representing as they do about one-sixth of all single-parent households.[5]

When it comes to how children fare when two-parent families dissolve or never combine in the first place, this book wouldn't have amounted to even a gleam if the answer was just as well as other kids on average. This, however, is obviously not the case as boys and girls growing up in single-parent homes, once more generally speaking, do less well than young people growing up with their two biological parents by every important measure one can think of.

Before going much further, why in fact is this the case? In the tightest of abbreviations, what are the dynamics at play in undercutting kids in this way?

We'll return several times to large-scale and ongoing research sponsored by Princeton and Columbia universities, the Fragile Families and Child Wellbeing Study, which started in 1998. Three participating scholars, in 2010, cited "five key pathways through which family structure might influence child well-being": parental resources; parental mental health; parental relationship quality; parenting quality; and father involvement. The three researchers—Jane Waldfogel, Terry-Ann Craigie, and Jeanne Brooks-Gunn—cautioned that it's important to also consider the "selection of different types of men and women into different family types," as well as matters of family stability in thinking all this through. Still, they concluded, in customarily cautious academic language, "[A]nalysts remain uncertain how each of these elements shapes children's outcomes."[6]

To be fair and accurate, none of this is to say that millions of children growing up in single-parent situations aren't, in fact, doing very well, because they are. Or for that matter, it's not to say that millions of children growing up in seemingly ideal, two-parent situations aren't doing poorly, because they are indeed flailing. All that is complicated and nuanced about American lives as actually lived must be kept in mind. Nevertheless, the bottom line is a straight line: rampant family fragmentation subtracts from personal and societal success and well-being and does so not just a little, but a lot. And to be clearly understood as well as fair, our focus is not solely on dollar-poor adults and children, but on all social classes, with growing attention paid to the great American middle, which increasingly resembles those notches below them in income when it comes to bearing and raising children.

Before going on I'm also obliged to add here that while each of my three stepsons, all of whom are approaching 40, is doing great professionally and in other ways, as I was within months of finishing the first draft of this book, our then 19-year-old and still-unmarried daughter—in further and painful proof that stuff happens—became pregnant. I'll return to this anything but simple matter in Chapter Six.

From Family Collapse to America's Decline connects dots that have never been adequately connected before: family fragmentation . . . how that leads to educational weakness . . . how that, in turn, leads to economic weakness . . . how that results in a loss of U.S economic competitiveness . . . and how they all lead to growing and very disturbing class cleavages. It considers how, literally in the world, the United States can maintain its economic preeminence when, in addition to simply being massively out-peopled by several countries, so many American young people are held back and damaged by family problems. The book also discusses how we've fallen into this social, scholastic, and business hole and how we might climb our way out, albeit in no adequate way anytime soon, as deep cultural problems are largely bereft of fast and effective levers.

This latter point about the inherent limitation of policy approaches and remedies in such matters is likewise a central premise of the book, as is the driving assumption that unless we adequately repair American families it will be impossible to adequately repair American education. Yes, devoted educators, pursuing sound policies, can make real headway under rugged circumstances and many have. But it's exceedingly hard to imagine nearly enough students making nearly enough progress—no matter how many solid educational reforms are adopted—given the extent of familial corrosion. Never mind, moreover, the tantamount-to-insurmountable problem of bringing successful reforms and great programs to scale in any field, much less one in which human elements are so elementary.

Nevertheless, this book will have failed if it doesn't strike a constructive balance between a "can-do" spirit and a "what-in-the-world" skepticism. I likewise will have been unfair to many scholars and great numbers of other educators who are devoting their lives, often with wonderful progress, to improving learning for all American children under al circumstances. Still, as the following pages will continue to make clear, my ultimate bias and fear are that the educational and related problems our nation faces are worse than most people in and out of both education and public life generally acknowledge—at least publicly.

The argument continues like this.

Chapter One. How have we gotten to this juncture? Have we ever faced as severe a problem that we have addressed so obliquely and meekly? For those who think our sinful history of slavery and Jim Crow is a better answer, loud and perpetual controversies over the abolition movement, followed by the Civil War, followed by Reconstruction, followed by the civil rights movement, followed by ongoing and ceaseless disagreements all argue otherwise. Starting with what quickly became known as the "Moynihan Report" in 1965 and continuing through studies with names such as "My Daddy's Name is Donor," this chapter sets the recent historical stage by tracing upwards of a half-century of social and intellectual history via synopses of pivotal books such as Charles Murray's *Losing Ground* in 1984, television documentaries such as Bill Moyers' "The Vanishing Family—Crisis in Black America" in 1986, welfare reform in 1996, and other federal reports, articles, movements, and the like. It isn't an exhaustive roster obviously, but taken in sequence, it provides a useful motion picture of important stages of the story.

Chapter Two. As first reported to a mass audience by historian Barbara Dafoe Whitehead in her famous *Atlantic* magazine cover story in 1993, "Dan Quayle was Right," rigorous social science research has left no doubt that children growing up in fragmented families, on average, do less well than other boys and girls by every conceivable measure. In addition to educational performance (which will be dealt with at greater length in Chapter Three), the list includes mental illness, drug use, criminal activity, early sexual initiation, and new generations of nonmarital pregnancies. This chapter will trace now-copious lines of research, focusing on peer-reviewed findings released since 2000 so as not to simply re-run previous recitations and analyses. This is also where we will delve deeper into competing explanations and interpretations of how we've arrived at this point as well as take a quick look at complementary research and commentary on the personal and societal benefits of marriage more generally.

Chapter Three. What does research say about the effects of family fragmentation—what can be described in many instances as the deinstitutionalization of marriage—on educational achievement more specifically? Marriage problems are far from the only cause of educational problems, but they are also far from small factors. A main premise here is that there are more students in our country than we might believe or fear, growing up in family turmoil, for whom working consistently and effectively hard in school is just too hard, as they are not emotionally and mentally healthy enough. Conceded, such a view can be easily misinterpreted as being too quick to view the world through a therapeutic prism as well as with "making excuses" at the exact moment when both left and right are equally vocal in demanding they never be made again. Unquestionably, some educators and programs do succeed, remarkably so, even with the most at-risk boys and girls. Still, it's impossible to deny that large numbers of children start in debilitating holes of various kinds, dug deep from their first days, and from which their prospects for escape are harshly abridged.

Chapter Four. What are the economic costs of family fragmentation as measured in several ways, including the amount of public dollars spent on lifting single mothers and their children out of poverty, as well as the more important degree to which weak math and science skills, along with achievement gaps more broadly, curtail economic growth? Yet even if the United States as a whole somehow manages to remain at the economic pinnacle, what about very large numbers of inadequately skilled workers—which, is not to say, only "poor" people but middle-class men and women as well—who will be unable to keep up with increasingly demanding international competition? How can they possibly fare well? Americans don't like thinking about their country as a place in which groups and generations are locked into economic and social place. Yet given the way family breakdown is already making it hard for many citizens to do well enough educationally in an ever-tougher environment, it's hard to see how economic and social cleavages won't grow and how debates about class and even caste can be avoided.

Chapter Five. Given the often severe social problems described above, what kinds of educational reforms are necessary—which is not necessarily to say sufficient or readily scalable? As demonstrated by the inner-city successes of KIPP (Knowledge Is Power Program) and similar charter and other schools, instruction will need to be substantially more intensive than the norm. Or in the words of Patrick McCloskey in *The Street Stops Here*, a telling book about a Catholic high school in Harlem, if inner-city education is to succeed, it will need to effectively address the "father wound" suffered by so many kids.[7] And instead of fixating on "celebrating" an expanse of cultures, educators will need to *overcome* certain subcultures, as in what sociologist Elijah Anderson has called the "oppositional culture of the streets." Also required are more than scattered expansions of educational freedom, as research—going back to James Coleman's seminal work—has shown how many low-income and minority students do better in private schools, perhaps particularly in regards to graduation rates. And as argued persuasively by the likes of Clayton Christensen, Michael Horn, Curtis Johnson, Terry Moe, John Chubb, and Paul Peterson, enormous advances in educational technology are already customizing learning for students starting from different points and with different learning styles.

Chapter Six. Parallel to changing the educational landscape, what can be done to change marital and broader cultural landscapes; rocky locales where effective levers are hard to find much less manipulate. Beyond hoping that millions of mostly teenagers and young adults reconsider all these issues in new religious and spiritual lights (as in "Thou shalt nots"), what might work? No less important, what cultural and other barriers stand in the way? A large answer here is the degree to which marriage in the United States has become, in the words of Barbara Dafoe Whitehead and David Popenoe, less "child centered," and in those of Daniel Yankelovich, how the nation's "New Rules" have diminished adults' traditional sense of obligation to others, including children. In regards to potentially effective programs and routes, lessons are emerging, albeit not always encouraging ones, from scores of federally funded marriage education programs. As for other potentially useful approaches, focus is on ways to help boys and men (especially in regards to education) so they may be more attractive marriage partners; ways to help ex-offenders overcome their criminally stained names so they might build decent careers; and on a bolder than usual way of debating matters of family fragmentation by focusing more concertedly on how it hurts children and why the adults in their lives, thereby, are morally obliged to better sacrifice on their behalf.

Chapter Seven. And a concluding chapter will pull together and reinforce several themes and threads, and if I say it ends "divinely," it's not meant as a self-congratulatory pat. But for now, permit me to make a few more introductory points before moving on.

It would be a large mistake to assume that reducing family fragmentation more than fractionally, or increasing educationally achievement more than marginally, is other than treacherously difficult. Depending on whether one views the launch of current school reforming as the late 1970s when governors and business leaders started growing increasingly agitated, or twenty years prior when Sputnik launched, efforts to improve learning have been under way double-time for either three or five decades with less-than-impressive results for so much time and exertion. For a very large example in the specific matter of achievement gaps, political scientist Abigail Thernstrom and her historian husband Stephan Thernstrom, citing data from the National Assessment of

Educational Progress (NAEP), have written about how African Americans by the twelfth grade are "typically four years behind white and Asian students," with Hispanics doing only slightly better than black students.[8] Translated, this means that black and Hispanic students are finishing high school, on average, "with a junior high education." Never mind that extraordinary numbers of Americans—but especially blacks and Hispanics—don't finish high school to begin with. "Graduating high school with a regular diploma," political scientist Jay P. Greene has calculated, "is little more than a fifty-fifty proposition for African American and Hispanic students nationwide."[9] All this—and in some respects even *less*—after decades of decades of non-stop "reforming."

As for nonmarital births, while welfare reform at both the state and national levels in the 1990s has been exceedingly successful (some might say miraculously so) in reducing rolls, it has been basically impotent in increasing marriage rates, one of its other main aims. Likewise, while wide varieties of voices have been citing and celebrating the joys and contributions of fathers and fatherhood for a long time now, American men are still absent from the everyday lives of their children in stunningly sad numbers. All of which is to say, modesty is a good guide for much that follows.

In fact, I'm obliged to acknowledge that the more I've learned and pondered about the breakdown of marriage, both in America and elsewhere, the more I've come to increasingly appreciate just how deeply embedded and complex its causes are and how unlikely more than marginal progress in turning matters around will be made in any near term. More than a sobering thought, it's a depressing one, but not nearly a sufficient reason to back off or give up.

In explaining why so much about families has changed since the 1960s, especially since the War on Poverty picked up momentum, a common three-part approach has been to consider the respective roles of policy changes, economic changes, and cultural changes. As frames go, it's a satisfactory way of getting started, though as one might expect, the best analyses and interpretations both meld and add to these three strains. I'm thinking, for example, of acute ethnographies such as *Promises I Can Keep*[10] which show how lower-income women fundamentally embrace the *idea* of marriage but routinely stay clear of the institution in *practice* because of the shortcomings, often violent ones, of many of the men in their lives. All of which is to say, in the same way the best work in the field subtly blends, the intention here is the same.

A main premise of the book, as asserted more than once already, is that connections between family breakdown writ widespread and economic performance writ continent wide are inescapable. It would seem self-evident. But what if, getting right down to it, economic performance for the country as a whole is really much more dependent on a comparatively small (although still numerically large) number of truly creative and productive men and women rather than the population in toto? Simplifying matters sarcastically, what if we can continue to get by as an economic giant primarily via the talents of a relative handful of entrepreneurs, computer scientists, and stem cell mavens along with a few social scientists and art professors thrown in for broadening spice? Or getting to the non-facetious contrarian core of the matter, is it possible that the truly severe and ultimate problem posed by family disintegration does not pertain to the American economy *overall*, but instead to economic and social *cleavages* that are bound to grow unevenly and dangerously between and among discrete groups of citizens (and noncitizens)? This is a more pregnant than an idly speculative thought, and I'm surely not the first person for whom words like "caste" speed to mind when they think about America's marrying and non-marrying worlds and the frequent gulfs between.[11]

A guaranteed way of offending big portions of the country is to argue that too many adults over the last four or five decades have been overly interested in their own happiness and fulfillment but not nearly as occupied by the well-being of their children. I'm not completely comfortable in making the case, as it's easily interpretable as arrogant. Nevertheless, and for example, consider how actual babies and their futures routinely get lost in discussions about highest-tech ways of bringing boys and girls into a new world in which fathers—biological or otherwise—are *purposely* excluded from all pictures. At the risk of further rudeness, I would argue that a useful frame for understanding current family debates and departures—what's been called a "Revolution in Parenthood"—is that they often have at least as much to do with grown-up self-actualizing as with thinking hard and selflessly about best possible ways of raising and serving kids.[12]

While I'm in the midst of irritating, I also would argue that one of the unfortunate byproducts of the campaign for same-sex marriage is that commentators of all sorts often work overtime at avoiding words like "mother" or "father" when they can get by with the safer and all-encompassing "parents" instead. It's as if they fear supporters of same-sex marriage—be they gay or straight—are apt to be offended by the more gender-based terms, so they neutralize the two by generically combining them. Glossing over and sometimes denying the distinctive and vital contributions of men-as-fathers and women-as-mothers is an unfortunate idea whose time should not have arrived but has.

It would be presumptuous to think of this study as a first volley. For despite all that has *not* been written about the most politically sensitive aspects of the subjects at hand, a fair amount in fact has been by brave and brilliant scholars and others who, I am proud and thankful to say, often double as friends. So while the discussion to follow (pardon the expression) is not a maiden voyage, it does take a distinct and, and one hopes, helpful tack.

In concluding the Introduction, permit me to add two postscripts: the first one interesting but second one incumbent.

It's interesting and important to note that while family fragmentation as defined in these pages is less rampant in China,[13] great numbers of children there live apart from their parents in ways barely ever reported in the United States. The Chinese government itself has estimated that almost 20 percent of all children, including close to half in the countryside, were classified as "left-behind children." That comes to approximately 58 million boys and girls in all, as cited in 2011. As described by the *Financial Times*, these are youngsters of parents "who have decamped to the cities in order to earn a better living." Some live with grandparents, but "others are handed over to foster centres." An official of the All-China Women's Federation is quoted as saying not everything about the phenomenon is negative, as children learn to be independent. Nevertheless, she acknowledges, "[Y]ou can't deny they suffer. These children tend to have difficulty opening up emotionally. They run a higher risk of getting hurt due to lack of supervision. We also find that they run a higher risk of getting involved in illegal activities as teenagers."[14] It's also reasonably safe to predict they will wind up less educationally successful and economically productive, on average, than the other 80 percent of their fellow young people.

The second and final point has to do with abortion, about which the following pages have hardly anything at all to say. Yet in arguing as I do that Americans bring far too many children into this world sans marriage, I suspect it's not hard to infer that the book's implicitly recommended remedy in many instances is abortion. No it is not. Or, to borrow a recently popular expression, abortion is not my default position. Conceiving far fewer babies outside of marriage, in the first place, is. And yes, the great majority of Americans, both younger and older, really do know how to do so.

Notes

1. Richard Rothstein, *Class and Schools: Using Social, Economic, and Educational Reform to Close the Black-White Achievement Gap* (Economic Policy Institute: Washington, DC, 2004).

2. Diane Ravitch, *The Death and Life of the Great American School System: How Testing and Choice are Undermining Education* (New York: Basic Books, 2010), p. 239.

3. Anthony Bryk, Penny Bender Sebring, et al., *Organizing Schools for Improvement: Lessons from Chicago* (University of Chicago: Chicago, 2010), p. 168.

4. Stephanie Coontz, *Marriage, a History: How Love Conquered Marriage* (New York: Penguin, 2005), p. 297. For excellent discussions of the subtle but

large prices often paid by the children of divorce especially as they reach adulthood themselves, see: Elizabeth Marquardt, *Between Two Worlds: The Inner Lives of Children of Divorce* (New York: Crown, 2005); and Judith Wallerstein, Julia Lewis, and Sandra Blakeslee, *The Unexpected Legacy of Divorce: The 25 Year Landmark Study* (New York: Hyperion, 2000).

5. Thomas F Coleman, "Honoring Single Dads on Father's Day," *singlefather. org*, June 2006.

6. Jane Waldfogel, Terry-Ann Craigie, and Jeanne Brooks-Gunn, "Fragile Families and Child Wellbeing," *The Future of Children*, Vol. 20, Number 2, Fall 2010, p. 87.

7. Patrick J. McCloskey, *The Street Stops Here: A Year at a Catholic High School in Harlem* (Berkeley: University of California, 2008).

8. Abigail Thernstrom and Stephan Thernstrom, *No Excuses: Closing the Racial Gap in Learning* ((New York: Simon & Schuster, 2003), p. 2. These numbers don't seem to have changed much in the years since the Thernstroms noted them in 2003.

9. Jay P. Greene, *Education Myths: What Special-Interest Groups Want You to Believe About Our Schools—and Why It Isn't So* (Lanham, MD: Rowman & Littlefield, 2005), p. 96.

10. Kathryn Edin and Maria Kafalis, *Promises I Can Keep: Why Poor Women Put Motherhood before Marriage* (Berkeley: University of California, 2005).

11. For example, see Kay S. Hymowitz's perfectly on-target book, *Marriage and Caste in America: Separate and Unequal Families in a Post-Marital Age* (Chicago: Ivan R. Dee, 2006).

12. Three useful sources in regards to this last paragraph are Daniel Yankelovich, *New Rules: Searching for Self-Fulfillment in a World Turned Upside Down* (New York: Random House, 1981); "Making Marriage More Child Centered," a symposium edited by Barbara Dafoe Whitehead and David Popenoe, *American Experiment Quarterly*, Summer 2001; and *The Revolution in Parenthood: The Emerging Global Clash Between Adult Rights and Children's Needs*, Elizabeth Marquardt, principal investigator, Institute for American Values, 2006.

13. All one needs to know is in a news account and a survey. In a story with the headline "Online Debate Focuses on Punishment for Out-of-Wedlock Births in Chongqing [China]," an official with the "Population and Family Planning Council" there said the new rule was an "important measure to enforce the country's family planning policy." *Global Times*, September 17, 2010. As for India, in a 1997 Gallup Poll conducted in sixteen countries on four continents, respondents were asked "Do you think it is or is not morally wrong for a couple to have a baby if they are not married?" A greater proportion of people in India, 84 percent, said it was in fact morally wrong than in any of the sixteen nations. The second highest was Singapore, where 69 percent of respondents said it was wrong, a full 15 percentage points behind. The United States, actually, was fourth highest, with 47 percent saying it was wrong. In night-and-day contrast, 9 percent said so in Germany, 8 percent in France, and 3 percent in Iceland. "Family Values Differ Sharply Around the World," The Gallup Organization, November 7, 1997.

14. Kathrin Hille, "Love You and Leave You," *Financial Times Magazine*, February 4, 2011.

Chapter 1

From Moynihan to "My Goodness"[1]

No proposed solution in this book is equal to the central problem it aims to solve. There is no tax break, no welfare reform, no marriage education program, no public service campaign or anything of the sort that can reduce out-of-wedlock birth rates and divorce rates to what they were as recently as when the Everly Brothers beseeched "Little Suzy" to wake up lest their reputations get shot. Or when Diana Ross informed her boyfriend that while she surely wanted to please him, no way was she going to have sex with him and possibly conceive a "Love Child" like herself.

Intimately and intricately, family fragmentation has more to do with the cultural and spiritual air we breathe than with legislation we pass; more to do with what we believe to be right and wrong rather than with the economic return of this or that. It's not that economic and legal incentives and disincentives—the stuff of policy—don't matter; they can matter significantly. It's that they don't matter enough in this instance.

So what's to be said of a largely policy book on the topic?

A starting aim is to more completely grasp the connections between family breakdown and educational troubles, going beyond surface recitations of what is now well-documented (if downplayed) empirical evidence.

A following aim is to explore how such diminished academic performance is leading inescapably to diminished economic performance for the United States as a whole.

And a third goal is to show how such compromised economic strength is leading to a loss of economic competitiveness—including that on the part of individuals, not just the nation collectively—and how it is leading to deepening class divisions, once again inexorably.

What's the ultimate goal of this three-part construction? Drawing connections in this way may perhaps, just perhaps strike enough chords—both broadly public and deeply personal—so as to improve the way we bring children into the world and raise them, with educational and economic betterment only two among many benign results.

This chapter sets the mid-range historical stage for the next two, which discuss what several decades of research have concluded about the effects of nonmarital births, divorce, separation, cohabitation, fatherlessness, and motherlessness on the health and well-being of children and adults. The first of those succeeding chapters focuses on how family fragmentation increases the likelihood of a wide range of sad and destructive behaviors and conditions over and above educational and cognitive ones. The subsequent chapter hones in on those educational deficits and losses.

As for pages following most immediately, they trace—via synopses of about 15 defining books, articles, documentaries, speeches, movements, and the like—nearly a half-century of social currents and intellectual history which have animated the topics at hand. Accelerated though the exercise may be, it's illuminating, often painfully so. We lead off with the groundless commotion that saturated an admirable and brave act of research in 1965. It was a travesty that shaped, to the point of contorting and crippling, virtually everything in the field for decades.

The Moynihan Report. For a variety of reasons, the so-called "Moynihan Report," written in 1965, remains the most salient document since the New Frontier and the Great Society on family breakdown in the United States. This is so for both sound and unfair reasons; for what it actually argued as well as for the routinely confused way in which it was received.

The late Daniel Patrick Moynihan was a Democrat who wound up serving five terms as a United States Senator from New York before retiring and being succeeded by Hillary Rodham Clinton in 2000. A brilliant and catholic social scientist, he wrote the report—officially called *The Negro Family: The Case for National Action*—while an assistant secretary of labor in Lyndon Johnson's administration. In actuality, his less-than-50 pages of text and tables reported nothing dramatically new, as he wrote about the effects of family disintegration and its related problems in the tradition of distinguished black scholars such as E. Franklin Frazier and Kenneth Clark. Nonetheless, the uproar the report generated led directly to two decades of near public silence on the subject of fatherlessness generally and fatherlessness in the African American community most precisely.[2]

As we will see, much important empirical research on families was, in fact, conducted in that roughly 20-year period, from the mid-1960s to mid-1980s. But these activities—essential as they have proved to be—took place largely in offices and libraries behind the scenes. Few academics, elected officials, or other public figures went out of their way during this span to publicly address the topic, given the absurd charges of racism thrown at Moynihan, as well as the gross and routine misreading of his argument by many. He also was undercut by some of his own colleagues in the Johnson administration. What *did* Moynihan (who was white) write and advocate provoking all this?[3]

"At the heart of the deterioration of the fabric of Negro society," he wrote, "is the deterioration of the Negro family. It is the fundamental source of the weakness of the Negro community at the present time."[4]

According to Lee Rainwater and William Yancey, authors of the most detailed account of the episode, Moynihan "sought to present a sharply focused argument leading to the conclusion that the government's economic and social welfare programs, existing and prospective ones, should be systematically designed to encourage the stability of the Negro family." It was Moynihan's view, they wrote, that too many African American marriages broke up and too many African American children were born out of wedlock because of the "systematic weakening of the position of the Negro male."

> Slavery, reconstruction, urbanization, and unemployment [Rainwater and Yancey wrote in characterizing Moynihan's analysis] had produced a problem as "old as America and as new as the April unemployment rate." This problem of unstable families in turn was a central feature of the "tangle of pathology of the urban ghetto," involving problems of delinquency, crime, school dropouts, unemployment, and poverty.[5]

Citing census and other data, Moynihan noted that while one-tenth of all white children were living in "broken homes" in 1960, one-third of all "nonwhite" children were living in such situations.[6] Similarly, he showed how the nonwhite out-of-wedlock birth rate was almost eight times higher than the white rate in 1963: 23.6 percent compared to 3.1 percent.[7]

By contrast, out-of-wedlock birth rates in the United States now over 70 percent for black babies and about 30 percent for white babies. The figure for the country as a whole is about 40 percent.[8]

For all the discomfort and anger it engendered among progressives in government, universities, civil rights organizations, and the media, the Moynihan Report was an exquisitely progressive document. In no way did Moynihan put blame on African Americans themselves; in every way he indicted the nation's history of slavery and racism. And by focusing on the need to achieve equality of *results,* not just *opportunity,* the report also helped construct the very foundation for affirmative action.

Nevertheless, while some on the left did defend Moynihan—saying it was ridiculous to think of him as a bigot, and acknowledging that he really wasn't saying anything that hadn't already honorably been said by others[9]—criticism was often severe. William Ryan, a Boston psychologist and civil rights activist who would soon become better known for coining the phrase "blaming the victim," had representative things like this to say: "Unemployment, the new ideologists tell us, results from the breakdown of Negro family life; poor education of Negroes results from "cultural deprivation"; the slum conditions endured by so many Negro families is the result of lack of "acculturation" of Southern rural migrants."[10]

"We are in danger," Ryan concluded, "of being reduced into de-emphasizing discrimination as the overriding cause of the Negroes' current status of inequality."[11]

The very short answer to this last charge (which was consonant with other condemnations at the time) was obviously no: Moynihan had not de-emphasized discrimination at all. He had forcefully cited it as the prime reason for instability among black families—which, in turn, contributed to various "pathologies."

Yes, by current understandings, the Moynihan Report might be considered more of a conservative than liberal statement (in part, anyway), as it focused with unusual frankness on the kinds of statistical data about families that conservatives are more likely than liberals to publicize. In addition, it unhesitatingly recognized that fathers matter; once again, something that latter-day conservatives are more inclined than liberals to publicly acknowledge. But at the very same time, it was a clearly liberal or progressive document by both past and present definitions, as it spoke with not-yet-spoiled confidence about the capacity of government—particularly the federal government—to make the lives of African Americans measurably better via programs aimed at increasing employment, improving education, and the sort.

Many other useful things can be said about Moynihan's study (as well as his associated writing at the time), nearly a half-century later. The first has to do with his prescience. Something he wrote then about "inviting chaos" has come to be quoted frequently. Here is the full passage:

> From the wild Irish slums of the 19th century Eastern seaboard, to the riot-torn suburbs of Los Angeles, there is one unmistakable lesson in American history; a community that allows a large number of men to grow up in broken families, dominated by women, never acquiring any stable relationship to male authority, never acquiring any set of rational expectations about the future—that community asks for and gets chaos. Crime, violence, unrest, disorder—most particularly the furious, unrestrained lashing out at the whole social structure—that is not only to be expected; it is very near to inevitable. And it is richly deserved.[12]

As a sociologically inclined scholar, Moynihan naturally emphasized matters of family structure. But the primary prism through which he analyzed and prescribed in regards to *The Negro Family* was an economic one. Jobs—good jobs—for black men were critical if black families were to have a chance. Moreover, he wrote, government ought to actively see to it, one way or the other, that more African American men indeed had such opportunities. As with other parts and aspects of the report, these themes were misread and discounted, too.

The Moynihan Report, in fact, provided early guidance in understanding what was to develop into three different, albeit reinforcing ways of thinking about fatherlessness and poverty, especially in underclass communities.

One is an economic argument and contention: Marriage has deteriorated mainly because increasing numbers of men are incapable of earning decent incomes, with women consequently viewing them as less "marriageable." William Julius Wilson, interestingly also a sociologist, has been the leading scholar associated with this latter view, particularly as it applies to the loss of relatively good-paying jobs for low-skilled workers.[13]

A second argument is rooted in public policies: Welfare programs—especially the old Aid to Families with Dependent Children—have made matters worse by seducing recipients into undisciplined choices about sex, schooling and the like by driving down the personal prices to be paid for laxity and failure. Such programs, as compassionately intended as they may be, nonetheless subsidize the very problems they are (poorly) designed to fix. Political scientist and social critic Charles Murray has been the most rigorous proponent of this interpretation.[14]

The third leg is grounded in culture: What can anyone expect other than an increase in out-of-wedlock births and divorce, goes this argument, when the media, universities, churches, and other defenders of middle-class values lose their bearings and confidence; when basic rules—particularly those regarding sex and marriage—bend and break under counter-cultural assault, as in the 1960s and afterwards? Figures closely identified with this view include writers Heather Mac Donald and Myron Magnet.[15]

Another person theorizing in this vein—at least during a more right-of-center stage of his intellectual life—was economist Glenn Loury, who trenchantly wrote in 1995:[16]

> People are not automata; their behavior in matters sexual may not be easily manipulated by changing their marginal tax rates or their recipiency status under welfare programs. It is my conviction that the problem of illegitimacy and family breakdown are, at base, cultural and moral problems, which require broad societal action in addition to legislative change. . . . [I]n every community there

are agencies of moral and cultural development which seek to shape the ways in which individuals conceive of their duties to themselves, of their obligations to each other, and of their responsibilities before God. These mainly though not exclusively religious institutions are the natural sources of legitimate moral teaching—indeed, the only sources.[17]

Needless to say, none of these approaches stand alone, and while focusing on the economic dimension, Moynihan instructively dealt with all three.

A final point about the landmark report is in order before moving, more rapidly, through the decades which followed.

Was it really surprising that it caused the passionate and intimidating fight that it did? Of course not, as not only did Moynihan take on keenly sensitive questions of family life, he combined them with keenly sensitive questions of race. Yet it isn't as if the two could have been neatly separated, either then or now. For if American families in general have been flailing for decades, African American families have been in even greater trouble—for whatever reasons—over the period.

The Interregnum. Moving along more quickly now. I did not realize until after selecting most of the studies, television shows, and other events cited in the pages below that the gap between the first and second items stretched for almost 20 years. As noted, this is not to say that nothing of consequence happened regarding family breakdown and fatherlessness in the United States between the release of the Moynihan Report in 1965 and Charles Murray's *Losing Ground* in 1984; only that very little happened publicly.[18]

Or, more precisely, very little happened in terms of seriously questioning—aloud—the effects of exploding out-of-wedlock and divorce rates, especially on children. Not only was the spirit of the age far from conducive to such skepticism, it was decisively hostile to it, as it was during that period when "liberating" (and simultaneously cloistering) ideologies were remarkably successful in curtailing debate to their tastes. As Moynihan gave early evidence, to violate the rules of dogma and language of various movements then feverishly under way, was to invite great trouble.

Yet, as also suggested above, much of the empirical research that has come to be regularly cited as evidence of children being very poorly served by family deterioration took place during the 1970s and thereabouts. For instance, according to Barbara Dafoe Whitehead:

The National Survey on Children, conducted by the psychologist Nicholas Zill, had set out in 1976 to track a large sample of children aged seven to eleven. It also interviewed the children's parents and teachers. It surveyed its subjects again in 1981 and 1987. By the time of its third round of interviews the eleven-year-olds of 1976 were the twenty-two-year-olds of 1987. The California Children of Divorce Study, directed by Judith Wallerstein, a clinical psychologist, had also been going on for a decade. E. Mavis Hetherington, of the University of Virginia, was conducting a similar study of children from both intact and divorced families. For the first time it was possible to test the optimistic view against a large and longitudinal body of evidence.[19]

The results of this collective test were commonsensical: Kids (and their moms in particular) were being hurt. Whereas children had been imagined as unrealistically "adaptable," and whereas "optimistic" writers such as Carol Stack had argued (in Whitehead's words) that "the single-mother family is an economically resourceful and socially embedded institution," it was now objectively clear that the opposite was true. Off-stage, scholars such as Zill, Wallerstein, Sara McLanahan and Irwin Garfinkel[44] had put the "interregnum" to good use, making it much more difficult down the road for Pollyannish strictures to reign and rule.[20]

As we will see shortly, historian Whitehead played an almost iconic role in 1993 in making sense of this train of research and, just as importantly, its frequent train wreck of a reception. Child psychologist Wade Horn, to whom we'll return to later as well, has elucidated similarly over the years; more specifically for our purposes, arguing that the two decades following the Moynhian Report, and not just then, are best understood as periods featuring "dual histories."[21]

The first history, he writes, developed out of the research community. For most of the 20th century, researchers "assumed the value of family structure and concentrated on researching parenting behaviors and their impact on child development." However, most of this work was done focusing on mothers, as fathers were manly considered economic providers, and at any rate, they generally weren't available or willing to participate in research. "But that did not mean," Horn makes clear, "researchers thought fathers were superfluous. Indeed, the superiority of families headed by both a mom and dad was simply assumed." That changed in the 1970s, he notes, perhaps in partial reaction to the Moynihan Report, although as a graduate student during the period he allows he never even heard of it. More specifically, it was during the '70s that interest in the effects of poverty on the well-being of children "exploded."

Researchers like Sara McLanahan, he writes, set out to "prove" that the negative effects of single parenting were "really all about the money." But what they kept finding was that while, yes, money mattered, so did family structure, and "they were honest enough to report so—and without much real controversy" (see below). So the 1980s and early 1990s saw the publication of a substantial amount scholarship showing the superiority of two-parent families, although poverty was naturally seen as important as well. "Indeed," Horn writes, "except for some ideologues in academia, the importance of family structure in the academic research literature was a largely settled question by the early '90s, with some caveats, of course."[22]

The distinction Horn draws here between serious scholars on the one hand, and "radical leftist ideologues" on the other, is a critical one. While the former essentially came to appreciate the importance of fathers (if they ever thought otherwise), the latter were quick and determined to teach and write that family structure was irrelevant. But as nonsensical as this dismissal was, it found a credulous audience among many cultural and other elites, and it was in their arenas, both in and out of the academy, where the idea of extraneous fathers took root and where dissenting opinions were often belittled and suppressed with politically correct fervor. This is what Horn means by a "second history."

While P.C. persists, the silliness has grown less heavy duty when it comes to family makeup. Horn's analysis here turns to "connectors," politically astute public intellectuals who, starting in the late-'80s, re-sculpted the debate by mining and interpreting the scholarly literature—which by then was sensibly and persuasively settled—for both elite and more popular audiences. He refers to men and women such as David Blankenhorn, Chester E. Finn, Jr., Bill Galston, and Barbara Dafoe Whitehead, all of whom we'll hear from shortly. Needless to say, Horn himself was a prime member and mover of the group.

Is Wade Horn's analysis of all of this on target? Bull's-eye.

Losing Ground. More potently than any other document ever, *Losing Ground* (subtitled *American Social Policy, 1950–1980*) argued that not only were welfare-state programs ineffective in alleviating social problems, but that they tended to actually make matters worse. "I will suggest," Murray wrote "that changes in incentives that occurred between 1960 and 1970 may be used to explain many of the [deleterious] trends we have been discussing. . . . All were results that could have been predicted (indeed, in some instances were predicted) from the changes that social policy made in the rewards and penalties, carrots and sticks, that govern human behavior."[23]

Exactly what kinds of rewards and penalties, carrots and sticks did he refer to in this book, released in 1984? In addition to grounding his argument in detailed statistical analysis, Murray used two imaginary characters, "Harold" and "Phyllis," to speculate about how poor people with "few chips" might take advantage of their available options. Here's an example:

> The bottom line is this [in 1970 compared to 1960, when governmental programs were less generous]: Harold can get married and work forty hours a week in a hot, tiresome job; or he can live with Phyllis and their baby without getting married, not work and have more disposable income [because of welfare]. From

an economic point of view, getting married is dumb. From a noneconomic point of view, it involves him in a legal relationship that has no payoff for him. If he thinks he may sometime tire of Phyllis and fatherhood, the 1970 rules thus provide a further incentive for keeping the relationship off the books.

Of Phyllis' possibilities, and those of young women in similar circumstances, Murray similarly wrote:

It is commonly written that poor teenaged girls have babies so that they will have someone to love them. This may be true for some. But one *need* not look for psychological explanations. Under the rules of 1970, it was rational on grounds of dollars and cents for a poor unmarried woman who found herself to be pregnant to have and keep the baby even if she did not particularly want a child. . . .

If Phyllis and Harry marry and he is employed, she will lose her AFDC benefits. His minimum wage job at the laundry will produce no more income than she can make [through welfare], and, not incidentally, he, not she, will have control of the check. In exchange for giving up this degree of independence, she gains no real security. Harold's job is not nearly as stable as the welfare system.[24]

It goes without saying that Murray was not well-received across the spectrum. He was vigorously accused by many on the left as not only distorting the analysis and numbers, but doing so in mean-spirited and perhaps racist ways.[25] Charles Murray is as well-practiced as anyone in American intellectual life in defending himself; he needs no extra bolstering here. But fact is, in no way was he guilty of such transgressions, and the line between his critique of the American welfare system in the 1980s and major welfare reform in the 1990s proved to be virtually straight.

The Vanishing Family—Crisis in Black America. If *Losing Ground* was a breakthrough in intellectual and nearby circles, Bill Moyers' 1986 television documentary, "The Vanishing Family—Crisis in Black America," was a watershed in broader circles.[26] Prior to each, obviously, lips hadn't been clenched entirely. But these two "events"—one a learned book and the other a network TV show—not only increased the salience of such tough issues, but also made it more acceptable for scholars as well as other citizens to talk more openly about them. They did so—a bit, anyway.

Moyers had come to network television unconventionally, by way of a 1960s stint in the White House. A very senior assistant in the Johnson administration, he had been "fascinated" back then by the Moynihan Report.[27] This is how two writers described his two-hour portrait of young African American men and women in Newark, New Jersey, first broadcast in January 1986. The first excerpts are by theologian and sociologist Michael Novak.[28]

"According to one of the bravest TV documentaries ever made . . . there is a crisis in black America. . . . Only a tiny fraction of black children born in America has a father at home during all 16 years of childhood. Nearly 60 percent are born out of wedlock. Such matriarchy is proving colossally destructive."

Novak quoted Timothy, then 26, who had already fathered six children by four different women. "Well," he said, "the majority of the mothers are on welfare. . . . What I'm not doing, the government does." This didn't seem to bother Timothy at all.[29]

Clarinda, then 15, is quoted for good measure: "I wouldn't want no man holding me down, because I think I could make it as a single parent"—as her mother had tried, as well as her grandmother.

Newsweek, for its part, called "The Vanishing Family" perhaps "the most important documentary in recent memory."[30] Among other things, the brief review noted how "Mother's Day" in one woman's Newark neighborhood (according to the program) came not only in May, but every month when welfare checks arrive.

Moyers' television documentary and Moynihan's government report were separated by two decades. They also were two fundamentally different enterprises. But whereas the Moynihan Report was contorted into a barrier to further public consideration, "The Vanishing Family" seemed to serve a constructively opposite end. Again, this is not to say that debate became safely and comfortably freewheeling; just better than it was. A kind of ice age had been broken. As for why the improvement, two thoughts are persuasive.

Moynihan was relatively unknown in 1965, meaning that many had not yet come to accept his good intentions as a given. Moyers, on the other hand, was a certified liberal (meaning that he was comparatively okay on racial issues), and had been thought as such for more than 20 years.

Of probably greater consequence, however, is that by the mid-1980s, familial conditions in the United States—particularly but not solely among African-Americans—had ruptured badly enough so that evasion began to give way to modest candor. Enough people were finally afraid enough.

A Liberal-Democratic Case for the Two-Parent Family. An exchange of complimentary notes about what the other had written in early 1990s, between a former assistant secretary of education in the Reagan Administration, Chester E. Finn, Jr., and the man who would turn out to be one of President Clinton's major advisers, William A. Galston, was illustrative of a this then-emerging, very rough consensus about family failure.

Republican Finn, in an essay about endangered families and children, had written in 1990:

We know that a well-functioning society must condemn behavior that results in people having children who are not prepared to be good parents. I find it astonishing that, in the fact of that knowledge, today we seem to attach more opprobrium to dropping out of school, experimenting on a cat, or uttering nasty remarks on campus than we do to giving birth to what, not so many years ago, were called "illegitimate" children. . . . Children fare better in some circumstances than others, and no decent society will remain silent when it comes to pointing out which circumstances are which.[31]

Democrat Galston wrote similarly at about the same time:

A healthy liberal democracy, I suggest, is more than an artful arrangement of institutional devices. It requires, as well, the right kinds of citizens, possessing the virtues appropriate to a liberal democratic community. A growing body of empirical evidence developed over the past generation supports the proposition that a stable, intact family makes an irreplaceable contribution to the creation of such citizens, and thus to promoting both individual and social well-being. For that reason, among others, the community as a whole has a legitimate interest in promoting the formation and sustaining the stability of such families.[32]

In the exchange of letters, Finn essentially told Galston that he liked his paper, and Galston returned the salute. This was an encouraging symbolic event given the extent to which leading Democrats and others on the political left were still muffling themselves on "traditional" family questions.

Galston's paper was very much a breakthrough. As we will see below, a slightly different version of it[33] was key in persuading Democratic members (plus staffers) of the National Commission on Children, in 1991, to endorse unusually direct language on the importance of two-parent families. Similarly, if not the paper itself, then certainly Galston himself and his circle of colleagues, were influential in shaping candidate Bill Clinton's successful 1992 campaign rhetoric about paternal responsibility and welfare reform, among other things.[34] At root, "A Liberal-Democratic Case" gave essential and welcome cover to men and women on the left side of the continuum who had perhaps long shared the paper's ideas, but who had been reluctant for all the aforementioned reasons to speak out. In addition to the just-cited paragraph, what else did Galston, a political theorist, say?

Of poverty, he argued that "after a decade-long economic expansion," the poverty rate for children was almost twice as high as it was among elderly Americans, and that it was no overstatement to say that, *"the best anti-poverty program for children is a stable, intact family."* (Emphasis in the original.)[35]

Yet if the "economic effects of breakdown are clear," he wrote, the "noneconomic effects are just now coming into focus." Here, Galston noted that

while "scholars over the past generation have disagreed over the consequences of divorce, work done during the 1980s has on balance reinforced
the view that children of broken families labor under major non-economic
disadvantages."[36] He quoted Karl Zinsmeister (who was to serve as a senior
policy adviser to President George W. Bush) on this "emerging consensus":

> There is a mountain of scientific evidence showing that when families
> disintegrate, children often end up with intellectual, physical, and emotional
> scars that persist for life. . . . We talk about the drug crisis, the education crisis,
> and the problems of teen pregnancy and juvenile crime. But all these ills trace
> back predominantly to one source: broken families.[37]

Of the "education crisis," more specifically, Galston contended that "recent
studies confirm" what many educators had suspected for a while: *"[T]he dis-
integrating American family is at the root of America's declining educational
achievement."* (Emphasis in the original.)[38]

In light of all this, Galston was nonetheless and appropriately compelled to
caution that a "general preference" for two-parent families does not mean that
all marriages ought to survive, or that "endorsement of the two-parent family" be confused for "nostalgia for the single-breadwinner 'traditional' family
of the 1950s." His left flank thus partially protected, Galston went on to say
the following in perhaps the essay's most important passage:

> Having entered these disclaimers, I want to stress that my approach is frankly
> normative. The focus is on what must be a key objective of our society: raising
> children who are prepared intellectually, physically, morally, and emotionally—
> to take their place as law-abiding and independent members of the community,
> able to sustain themselves and their families and to perform their duties as
> citizens. Available evidence supports the conclusion that on balance, the in-
> tact two-parent family is best suited to this task. *We must then resist the easy
> relativism of the proposition that different family structures represent nothing
> more than "alternative life-styles"*—a belief that undermined the Carter ad-
> ministration's efforts to develop a coherent family policy and that continues to
> cloud the debate even today. (Emphasis again in the original.)[39]

This takes us to the previously mentioned National Commission on Children, more commonly known as the "Rockefeller Commission on Children,"
after its chairman, Sen. Jay D. Rockefeller IV of West Virginia.

The National Commission on Children. It should not constitute anything
remarkable to declare that fathers matter. But it was remarkable—which is to
say it was big news on television talk shows and the like—when a 34-member
federal panel, with more liberal than conservative members, unanimously
endorsed language like this in 1991: "Children do best when they have the

personal involvement and material support of a father and a mother and when both parents fulfill their responsibility to be loving providers."[40]

Suffice it to say that chances would have been slim for such a straightforward proposition to have been included in any similar federal report any time earlier in the period under review. Also suffice it to say that few report writers would have ever considered the need for such a statement any time prior to 1965, as no one had yet seriously proposed that fathers were superfluous. But along with a recommendation to allocate $40 billion in the first year for a refundable child tax credit, the report's most noted portion was its strong endorsement of two-parent families. "There can be little doubt," it said,

> that having both parents living and working together in a stable marriage can shield children from a variety of risk. Rising rates of divorce, out-of-wedlock childbearing, and absent parents are not just manifestations of alternative lifestyles, they are patterns of adult behavior that increase children's risks of negative consequences. Although in some cases divorce is the least harmful outcome of a troubled marriage, today's high rate of family breakdown is troubling.[41]

Naturally, the report also said that the nation "must never fail to reach out and protect single-parent families as well," and that, "Many single parents make extraordinary efforts to raise children in difficult circumstances."[42] Yet such boilerplate—necessary and gracious as it was—could not subtract from the significant step forward represented by the unambiguous as well as culturally and politically pregnant passage right before it: The one about two-parent families being important. As we quickly will see, this advance did not necessarily clear the way for Vice President Dan Quayle to speak safely on the question of single parenthood during the 1992 presidential campaign, but it was, all things and history considered, real progress.[43]

Murphy Brown. Right before the (real) Mother's Day in May 1992, Barbara Dafoe Whitehead wrote a syndicated newspaper column about the impending birth of a baby to a fictional, unmarried television character, Murphy Brown, the star of a successful comedy series of the same name. Whitehead was neither amused nor impressed. "Baby Brown," she wrote, "points to our society's acceptance of out-of-wedlock childbirth. Certainly over the past several decades, the shame and blame attached to unmarried pregnancy has steadily eroded. But with Murphy Brown, unwed childbearing becomes positively appealing."[44]

Very shortly afterwards, and inspired by Whitehead's column, Vice President Dan Quayle delivered what came to be known as his "Murphy Brown speech," although its specific reference to the show consisted of only one sentence and a grand total of 39 words. "It doesn't help matters," Quayle said in a re-election campaign speech, "when prime time TV has Murphy Brown—a character who supposedly epitomizes today's intelligent, highly paid, professional woman—mocking the importance of fathers, by bearing a child alone, and calling it just another 'lifestyle choice.'"[45]

At which point a fair amount of hell—and mocking hilarity—broke loose.[46]

It's of course true that if someone other than the routinely belittled Quayle had said what he had said about Murphy Brown the reaction might have been more sober. Commentators might even have paid more than passing attention to other things he said in what was a substantial speech about families, poverty, values and, most immediately, the Los Angeles riots which had erupted just weeks earlier. "I believe," the vice president said, "the lawless social anarchy which we saw is directly related to the breakdown of family structure, personal responsibility and social order in too many areas of our society." He also said:

Children need love and discipline. They need mothers and fathers. A welfare check is not a husband. The state is not a father. It is from parents that children learn how to behave in society; it is from parents above all that children come to understand values and themselves as men and women, mothers and fathers. . . . Ultimately . . . marriage is a moral issue that requires cultural consensus, and the use of social sanctions. Bearing babies irresponsibly is, simply, wrong. Failing to support children one has fathered is wrong. We must be unequivocal about this. . . . Now is the time to make the discussion [about values] public.

First reactions by President George H. W. Bush and his senior aides reflected the deep and continuing ambivalence and political nervousness implicit in the issue. "Quayle was not helped," a reporter wrote a few days after the speech, "by the uncertain reaction from the White House, where press secretary Marlin Fitzwater and then President Bush himself seemed hesitant to join the vice president in his assault on Hollywood." Aides traveling with Quayle were said have spent much of the morning after the speech on the phone trying to convince colleagues back at the White House that the vice president had not committed a serious mistake.[47]

As for the issue of fatherlessness itself, the *Murphy Brown* episode demonstrated that while progress continued to be made in discussing it with a measure of frankness, both at the upper reaches of government and portions of the nation more widely, the topic remained an exceptionally tough and divisive one. It was in this context that Whitehead, in April 1993, published the most compelling *popular* review of the scholarly literature on absent fathers up until then. That it was titled "Dan Quayle Was Right"[71] and ran in a venerable mainline magazine—*The Atlantic Monthly*—only showcased it better.

Dan Quayle Was Right. Whitehead opened by offering a sampling of a "growing body of social-scientific evidence" showing that children in families disrupted by divorce and out-of-wedlock births, generally speaking, do worse than other children on various measures of well-being. For instance, 22 percent of children in one-parent families tended to suffer poverty during their childhoods for seven years or more versus only 2 percent for children in intact families; or that children in disrupted families were at much higher risk of physical and sexual abuse. Yet despite this increasing evidence, "it is nearly impossible," Whitehead argued "to discuss changes in family structure without provoking angry protest."

Many people, she said, view such discussions as little more than attacks on single mothers and their children, while others believe that major changes in family structure, though "regrettable," are impossible to reverse, and hence society is obliged to adapt accordingly. The debate, she wrote,

> is not simply about the social-scientific evidence, although that is surely an important part of the discussion. It is also a debate over deeply held and often conflicting values. How do we begin to reconcile our long-standing belief in equality and diversity with an impressive body of evidence that suggests that not all family structures produce equal outcomes for children? . . . How do we uphold the freedom of adults to pursue individual happiness in their private relationships and at the same time respond to the needs of children for stability, security, and permanence in their family lives?[48]

This is why, she wrote (referring to the Dan Quayle–Murphy Brown altercation of a year earlier) that, "every time the issue of family structure has been raised, the response has been first controversy, then retreat, and finally silence."[49]

From another angle, Whitehead asked why, given the power of the evidence, had rampant family disruption not come to be viewed as a "national crisis"? Here she talked of a "shift in the social metric," from child well-being to adult well-being. However difficult divorce and out-of-wedlock births may be, "both of these behaviors can hold out the promise of greater adult choice, freedom, and happiness."[50]

Much of "Dan Quayle Was Right" is devoted to three "bold new assumptions" about family change that Whitehead argued took hold in the 1970s—but which subsequent research refuted.

First assumption: Women are now financially able to be mothers without being wives.

Second assumption: Family disruption does not cause lasting harm to children—in fact, it can actually enrich their lives.

Third assumption: Such new family forms and "diversity" will make America a better place.

Her key summarizing paragraph is worth quoting at length:

> Not a single one of the assumptions underlying [the view that such family change has led to social progress] can be sustained against the empirical evidence. Single-parent families are not able to do well economically on a mother's income. In fact, most teeter on the economic brink, and many fall into poverty and welfare dependency. Growing up in a disrupted family does not enrich a child's life or expand the number of adults committed to the child's well-being. In fact disrupted families threaten the psychological well-being of children and diminish the investment of adult time and money in them. Family diversity in the form of increasing numbers of single-parent and stepparent families does not strengthen the social fabric. It dramatically weakens and undermines society, placing new burdens on schools, courts, prisons, and the welfare system.[51]

Whitehead's frequently cited essay increased popular understanding of father absence. It also modestly defused the subject, making it fitter for public conversation in the first place. But maybe most beneficially, "Dan Quayle Was Right" made it more difficult for academics, journalists, politicians, and others to plead continued ignorance about the demonstrated effects of fatherlessness.

The Coming White Underclass. Yet if it was Whitehead who succeeded in further showing that the problem posed by father absence was real and large, it was Charles Murray who most dramatically encapsulated just how immense it really was. "Every once in a while" he wrote in the *Wall Street Journal* in 1993, the "sky really is falling, and this seems to be the case with the latest national figures on illegitimacy."[52] Using data which had just been made available, he noted that 1.2 million American children had been born out of wedlock in 1991, which was "within a hair" of 30 percent of all live births. Out-of-wedlock births to black women, he reported, had reached 68 percent in 1991, with the figure "typically" in excess of 80 percent in inner cities.

"But the black story, however dismaying," Murray wrote, "is old news. The trend that threatens the U.S. is white illegitimacy. Matters have not yet gotten out of hand, but they are on the brink. If we want to act, now is the time."

More than 700,000 babies, he wrote, were born to single white women in 1991, representing 22 percent of all white births. (Recall that the out-of-wedlock birth rate reported by Moynihan for African American women less than 30 years earlier in 1963 was just over 23 percent.) Murray argued that "elite wisdom" held that this trend in white births was cutting across social classes, "as if the increase in Murphy Browns were pushing the trendline." But such a view was inaccurate, he said. Instead, women with college degrees contributed only 4 percent of white nonmarital births, while women with high school educations or less contributed 82 percent. Likewise, women with family incomes of $75,000 or more contributed but 1 percent of out-of-wedlock births, while women with family incomes under $20,000 contributed 69 percent of them. "White illegitimacy," Murray wrote, is "overwhelmingly a lower-class phenomenon," which "brings us to the emergence of a white underclass"—something that the United States has never had.

Why, exactly, did he see this as a huge problem? "As the spatial concentration of illegitimacy reaches critical mass," he wrote, "we should expect the deterioration to be as fast among low-income whites in the 1990s as it was among low-income blacks in the 1960s." He contended that illegitimacy was the "single most important social problem of our time," more important than crime, drugs, homelessness, and the rest "because it drives everything else."

While acknowledging that the "steep climb" in black nonmarital births had been "calamitous" for African Americans, he said that the "brutal truth is that American society as a whole could survive when illegitimacy became epidemic within a relatively small ethnic community."[53] The nation as a whole, he concluded, could not survive a similar same epidemic among whites.

As one might expect, this warning made an impression. And as a sign that Americans were increasingly prepared to address the problem of fatherlessness, Murray subsequently reported that the piece had not led critics to vilify him in the way he thought they might—and as they did after *Losing Ground,* and as they would again after *The Bell Curve.* Instead, he was interviewed a lot and invited to speak frequently.

Growing Up with a Single Parent. Growing Up with a Single Parent: What Hurts, What Helps, by sociologists Sara McLanahan and Gary Sandefur, was the first book-length, quantitatively grounded study by respected, mainstream scholars that refuted the frequently expressed view that children really weren't hurt—or at least hurt all that much—by family breakdown.[54] In an opening chapter titled "Why We Care about Single Parenthood," McLanahan and Sandefur get right to it. "We have been studying this question for ten years, and in our opinion the evidence is quite clear."

> Children who grow up in a household with only one biological parent are worse off, on average, than children who grow up in a household with both of their biological parents, regardless of the parents' race or educational background, regardless of whether the parents are married when the child is born, and regardless of whether the resident parent remarries.

Drawing on four major data bases, three of which were longitudinal, McLanahan and Sandefur made sure to say that single motherhood and father absence were not the root cause of child poverty, school failure, and juvenile delinquency. Growing up with only one parent at home, they wrote, is "just one of many factors that put children at risk of failure, just as lack of exercise is only one among many factors that put people at risk of heart disease."

Still, they did critically conclude that adolescents who lived with only one of their biological parents for some portion of their childhood, were "twice as likely to drop out of high school, twice as likely to have a child before age twenty, and one and a half times as likely to be 'idle,'" which they defined as being both out of school and out of work in one's late teens and early twenties.

Growing Up with a Single Parent was a further breakthrough, this one emerging valuably from deep within the academy itself, as the two authors credited the esteemed Institute for Research on Poverty at the University of Wisconsin as their "primary intellectual home." (McLanahan currently holds an endowed chair at Princeton and Sandefur is dean of the College of Letters and Science at Wisconsin.)

A begged question: Why hadn't many other scholars addressed similar matters with equally open minds? McLanahan and Sandefur's recital of their own route is telling.

"Our investigation," they wrote, "was stimulated by a series of articles on the 'underclass' by Ken Auletta which first appeared in the *New Yorker* in 1981." What caught their attention was the fact that a large proportion of the clients in a particular program had grown up in single-parent families, the essay's implication being that single-mother families "were somehow responsible" for the growth of the underclass. But the very idea that family breakdown had key things to do with crime, drugs, and the like seemed "wrongheaded" to them, given what they had learned as graduate students in the 1970s; namely, that the negative effects sometimes attributed to family makeup were *really* the product of poverty and discrimination? Or, "So we thought when we began our study."

Fatherless America. If Murray's "The Coming White Underclass" was unusually pointed, and if McLanahan and Sandefur's *Growing Up with a Single Parent* was quantitatively exacting, David Blankenhorn's *Fatherless America: Confronting Our Most Urgent Social Problem,* published in 1995, was interpretively rich.[55] Blankenhorn did not deal with questions out-of-wedlock births, divorce, separation, desertion and such narrowly. Instead, he discussed the ways in which the very idea of fatherhood in the United States had been deconstructed (which, is to say, emasculated) as a cultural fact and principle. He wrote, for example:

> Men in general, and fathers in particular, are increasingly viewed as superfluous to family life: either expendable or as part of the problem. Masculinity itself,

understood as anything other than a rejection of what it has traditionally meant to be male, is typically treated with suspicion and even hostility in our cultural discourse. Consequently, our society is now manifestly unable to sustain, or even find reason to believe in, fatherhood as a distinctive domain of male activity.[56]

Does every child deserve a father? Blankenhorn said the answer at the time hovered someplace between "no" and "not necessarily."[57] In contrast, he described the length to which the federal government tried *not* to draft men with children during World War II, as it was commonly understood 50 years previously that fathers were, in fact, very important in the lives of their sons and daughters.

Blankenhorn contended the "principal" cause of fatherlessness in the mid-'90s was "paternal choice." In contrast, a century earlier, middle-aged widowed men surpassed middle-aged divorced men by more than 20 to 1.[58]

In language akin to Murray's, Blankenhorn argued that the "most urgent domestic challenge facing the United States at the close of the twentieth century is the re-creation of fatherhood as a vital social role for men." For unless Americans reversed course, he argued, "no other set of accomplishments—not economic growth or prison construction or welfare reform or better schools—will succeed in arresting the decline of child well-being and the spread of male violence."[59]

Fatherless America was a key catalyst in the growth of what was coming to be known as the fatherhood movement.[60] Blankenhorn, in fact, was the first chairman—and Dr. Horn the first president—of the National Fatherhood Initiative, a thriving organization headquartered in Maryland. Though, as is the case with any continental effort, the fatherhood movement's real strength continues to lie in hundreds, perhaps thousands of small, hands-on programs across the country, whose principal focus is on helping men become more involved, committed, and responsible fathers.

Joining the fatherhood movement, more or less as the millennium turned, was the emergence of a mostly complementary marriage movement, which has aimed to strengthen that institution largely by dramatically expanding marriage education programs for all Americans, especially low-income men and women.[61] Its proponents had a lot to do, for instance, with the (second) Bush administration's successful passage of a "Healthy Marriage Initiative."

TANF and Healthy Marriage Initiative. The federal government's Healthy Marriage Initiative is best understood as the product of two major movements: one, as just mentioned, in celebration and service of marriage itself; with a second, an integral part of the drive for welfare reform. The initiative, in fact, was adopted by Congress as part of its 2005 reauthorization of watershed welfare reform legislation.[62] That bill, originally passed in 1996, had abolished the rampantly exploited Aid to Families with Dependent Children (AFDC), replacing it with the more stringent demands of Temporary Assistance to Needy Families (TANF).

As first pursued in states like Wisconsin under Gov. Tommy Thompson, and cities like New York under Mayor Rudy Guiliani, getting welfare recipients into the work force was a major aim of welfare reformers in the early 1990s. But reducing out-of-wedlock births also took increasingly firm root as a central goal, especially by Republicans, who gained control of both the Senate and House in 1995. Ron Haskins, who was staff director of the key House Ways and Means subcommittee during this period, has written what almost certainly will remain the definitive history of the extraordinarily complicated passage of TANF: the comparably detailed *Work over Welfare: The Inside Story of the 1996 Welfare Reform Law.*[63]

Births outside of marriage, Haskins argued early in the book, had come to rival welfare dependency itself in the "Republican hierarchy of social ills." At the heart of the conservative position was the way in which not only cash benefits, but also food stamps, Medicaid, housing assistance, and various other welfare programs "helped lead young men and women to a reduced state of vigilance in avoiding pregnancy before marriage." Conservatives, of course, were not the only ones of this mind, or were they the only ones for whom "the value issue was central." For example, according to Haskins, Bill Clinton

> had been more outspoken than any other president about the tragedy of illegitimacy; he was even given to stating flatly that it was "wrong" for young people to have children outside of marriage whom they could not support. Speaking to the National Baptist Convention in 1994, Clinton said, "[too many] babies will be born where there was never a marriage. That is a disaster. It is wrong. And someone has to say, again, it is simply not right. You shouldn't have a baby before you're ready, and you shouldn't have a baby when you're not married. You just have to stop it. We've got to turn it around.[64]

The 1996 law contained explicit assertions such as "Marriage is the foundation of a successful society," and "Marriage is an essential institution of a successful society which promotes the interests of children." Building on this, and due in large measure to the tenacity of the ubiquitous Wade Horn, President George W. Bush's assistant secretary for children and families in the Department of Health and Human Services, the 2005 law provided funding and matching grants of $150 million annually for competitive research and demonstration projects aimed at testing promising ways of encouraging healthy marriages and responsible fatherhood.

Persistence was in order as opposition to the initiative came from eclectic directions. Not a few on the left, especially organized feminists charged that the government was intent on pushing and/or keeping women in dangerous marriages. While not a few on the right argued that marriage promotion wasn't part of the government's job description to begin with.

In response to liberal objections, the addition of the prefix "healthy" to the program's title was no rhetorical accident. And the promulgated list of activities that the initiative is *not* about is clear-cut, including *not* coercing anyone to marry or remain in unhealthy relationships; *not* withdrawing support for single parents or diminishing the importance of their work; and most surely *not* running a federal dating service.

In response to conservative objections regarding taxpayer involvement, the most potent arguments were likely those of Robert Rector of the likewise conservative Heritage Foundation, who has spent years itemizing and illustrating how family breakdown is an immensely powerful cause of very expensive governmental spending on scores of anti-poverty and other social welfare programs. Government, he has long written, has a very large stake in strengthening marriage.[65] "The Bush marriage initiative," two other veteran Washington players have written, "is one of the few strikingly new directions in American social policy (along with Child Support Enforcement, the Earned Income Tax Credit, and mandatory work programs) since the outpouring of innovation at the beginning of the War on Poverty."[66]

Same-Sex Marriage and The Revolution in Parenthood. It's incomplete to close this history brief without including a few words about the religiously and emotionally saturated question of same-sex marriage, as well as what might fairly be described as a culturally radical and often high-tech-propelled "revolution in parenthood." To be clear, whatever the manner of adult relationships, the principal focus here is on the children involved: Most specifically, are they simply expected—without anyone's objections or qualms—to grow up minus a father, or maybe a mother, and without everyone living under the same roof?

By definition, supporters of same-sex marriage (and sometimes same-sex adoption, for that matter) argue that boys and girls neither deserve nor need what has been assumed a birthright almost always: a mother and a father. Whatever one thinks about same-sex marriage—and millions of very good people think it's a great and necessary idea—it's striking how several decades of progress in better appreciating the specific contributions of men as fathers (as opposed to adults as all-purpose parents) is effectively gainsaid and ignored by those advocating the idea.

Perhaps sometime in the future researchers will persuasively conclude, controlling for everything that needs controlling, that children raised by two men or two women succeed just as well, by a range of measures, as kids growing up in traditional homes. Then, again, perhaps answers will be no better than mixed. Despite regular claims, it's still far too early to know any of this for sure, though findings discussed in the next two chapters are not suggestive of human beings as interchangeable parts.

But whatever various answers turn out to be, one of the undeniable byproducts of the same-sex marriage debate is that many people who would be otherwise inclined, even eager, to write and talk about the unique importance of fathers and mothers are opting instead for silence, lest they do damage to rationales for same-sex unions. (In Spain, where same-sex marriage was legalized several years ago, birth certificates for all children now read "Progenitor A" and "Progenitor B" instead of "mother" and "father."[67])

In regard to changes in parenthood made possible by scientific and technological marvels, my intent is to be neither outlandish nor unkind. But society is increasingly obliged to address the wisdom of arrangements and possibilities like the following, as reported by Elizabeth Marquardt of the Institute for American Values in 2006:

> Headlines recently announced research at leading universities in Britain and New Zealand that could enable same-sex couples or single people to procreate. In Britain, scientists were granted permission to create embryos with three genetic parents. Stem cell research has introduced the very real possibility that a cloned child could be born—the man who pioneered in vitro fertilization (IVF) treatment has already said that cloning should be offered to childless couples who have exhausted other options. The list goes on.[68]

It's not hard to ferret out a common denominator in much of this: a preoccupation with adult happiness—their "self-actualization," as Abraham Maslow might have put it—with the happiness of children, along with their prospects, coming in no better than second.

A not-happy concluding question and answer: After decades of intellectual and policy gyrations, which in large part have been in the beneficial direction of recognizing the importance of family stability, what kind of on-the-ground progress have we, in actual fact, made? Desperately sadly, we're in much worse shape now than we were when Moynihan sounded alarms in 1965. Yes, some numbers and trends have stopped deteriorating, and in some instances they've actually improved.[69] But on balance and by any sensible reading, they're still terrible and destructive, and for anyone to argue otherwise is to beckon another seminal work by Moynihan, his famous 1993 essay, "Defining Deviancy Down."[70]

Precisely how does severe family fragmentation affect young and not-so-young people, particularly in terms of their educational achievements and eventual contributions to the nation's economic vitality? We start answering those very big questions more directly now.

Notes

1. The chapter heading is the same as that of an essay I wrote in 1995, a substantial portion of which is adapted and updated in this first chapter. "From Moynihan to 'My Goodness': Tracing Three Decades of Fatherlessness in the United States, 1965–1995," Center of the American Experiment, August 1995.

2. Glenn Loury has written: "Those committed to the silencing of Moynihan, and to the banishment of the topic of behavioral pathology in the ghetto from public discussion, managed to have their way. A dear price was paid for this indulgence, although it was not paid by those responsible for it." *One by One from the Inside Out* (New York: Free Press, 1995), p. 257.

3. I am indebted, as I was more than 30 years ago when I first wrote about this subject, to *The Moynihan Report and the Politics of Controversy,* by Lee Rainwater and William L. Yancey (Cambridge, MA: M.I.T. Press, 1967). This analysis of after-effects, published two years after the Moynihan Report was released, also contains a full copy of the report itself: *The Negro Family: The Case for National Action* (Washington: DC: Office of Policy Planning and Research, U.S. Department of Labor, March 1965).

4. *The Negro Family,* p. 5.

5. *The Moynihan Report and the Politics of Controversy,* pp. 27–28.

6. *The Negro Family,* p. 18.

7. Ibid., p. 8.

8. "NCHS Data Brief," National Center for Health Statistics, Number 18, May 2009. "National Vital Statistics Reports," Centers for Disease Control and Prevention, Vol. 59, Number 1, December 2010.

9. For example, psychologist Kenneth Clark, whose work had been cited by the U.S. Supreme Court in its 1954 *Brown v. Board of Education* decision outlawing officially segregated schools, said: "It's kind of a wolf pack operating in a very undignified way. If Pat is a racist, I am. He highlights the total pattern of segregation and discrimination. Is a doctor responsible for a disease simply because he diagnoses it?" *The Moynihan Report and the Politics of Controversy,* p. 263.

10. Ibid., pp. 197–98.

11. Ibid., p. 199.

12. Daniel P. Moynihan, "A Family Policy for the Nation," *America* (September 18, 1965).

13. William Julius Wilson, *The Truly Disadvantaged: The Inner City, the Underclass, and Public Policy* (Chicago: University of Chicago Press, 1987).

14. For example, see: Charles Murray, *Losing Ground: American Social Policy, 1950–1980* (New York: Basic Books, 1984); David Frum, *Dead Right* (New York: Basic Books, 1994); and George Gilder, "End Welfare Reform as We Know It," *The American Spectator,* June 1995, pp. 24–27.

15. For example, see: Heather Mac Donald, *The Burden of Bad Ideas: How Modern Intellectuals Misshape Our Society* (Chicago: Ivan R. Dee, 2000); and Myron Magnet, *The Dream and the Nightmare: The Sixties Legacy to the Underclass* (New York: William Morrow, 1993).

16. For example, see: William J. Bennett, *The Devaluing of America: The Fight for Our Culture and Our Children* (New York: Summit Books, 1992); several things by Glenn C. Loury, including his previously cited *One by One from the Inside Out;* and his "Ghetto Poverty and the Power of Faith," Center of the American Experiment," Minneapolis, MN, December 1993. From a different angle, see Kathryn Edin and Maria Kafalas, *Promises I Can Keep: Why Poor Women Put Motherhood Before Marriage* (University of California: Berkeley, 2005).

17. Glenn C. Loury, testimony before the Human Resources Committee of the U.S. House of Representatives' Ways and Means Committee, Washington, DC, January 20, 1995.

18. President Carter did convene a "White House Conference on Families" in 1980, but in the words of Barbara Dafoe Whitehead, "The result was a prolonged, publicly subsidized quarrel over the definition of 'family.' No President since has tried to hold a national family conference." "Dan Quayle Was Right," *The Atlantic Monthly*, April 1993, p. 48.

19. "Dan Quayle Was Right," p. 61.

20. For example, this is what Barbara G. Cashion wrote, almost sunnily, in 1982: "The two-parent family is hierarchical with mother and father playing powerful roles and children playing subordinate roles. In the female-headed family there is no such division. Women and children forgo much of the hierarchy and share more in their relationships. . . . Single mothers report that they enjoy their ability to set norms and make decisions about time schedules and routines that suit their own and their children's needs. There is general lack of conflict, and decisions are made more easily and quickly, provided resources are adequate." Barbara G. Cashion, "Female-Headed Families: Effects on Children and Clinical Implications," *Journal of Marital and Family Therapy,* 8, No. 2, April 1982, p. 80. David Blankenhorn calls Cashion's qualifier, "provided resources are adequate," an "inspired touch."

21. Wade S. Horn, personal email correspondence, May 20, 2009.

22. For example, see the *Father Facts* series published by the National Fatherhood Initiative in Gaithersburg, MD.

23. *Losing Ground,* pp. 154–55.

24. Ibid., pp. 160–61.

25. One such critic (all things considered, an exceptionally moderate one) wrote: "The intellectual establishment, particularly the liberal intellectual establishment, has been quick to criticize Murray's work, and these attacks have cast considerable doubt on the credibility of his conclusions. But what is often missed in this frenzy is that

although Murray is almost certainly wrong in blaming the social welfare system for a large part of the predicament of the poor, he is almost certainly correct in stating that welfare does not reflect or reinforce out most basic values. He is also correct in stating that no amount of tinkering with benefit levels or work rules will change that." David T. Ellwood, *Poor Support: Poverty in the American Family* (New York: Basic Books, 1988), p. 6.

26. The documentary aired January 25, 1986, on CBS.

27. *The Moynihan Report and the Politics of Controversy,* p. 376. Rainwater and Yancey describe Moyers on the same page as Johnson's "chief policy factotum."

28. Michael Novak, "The Content of Their Character," *National Review,* February 28, 1986, p. 47.

29. In an essay analyzing the socialization of young black men in light of America's history of slavery and discrimination, sociologist Orlando Patterson sums up this way with brutal directness: "This, then, is what we have inherited: a lower class with gender attitudes and behaviors that are emotionally and socially brutalizing and physically self-destructive. The posturing, pathological narcissism of 'cool pose' masculinity with its predatory, antimaternal sexuality, self-healing addictions, and murderous, self-loathing displacements; the daily and nightly carnage on the streets of the inner cities; the grim statistics on child and spousal abuse, rape, poverty, illiteracy, and suicide—these are the gruesome manifestations of this historically, sociologically, and psychologically engendered tragedy." "Blacklash: The Crisis of Gender Relations Among African-Americans," *Transition,* No. 62, 1993, p. 25.

30. "Bill Moyers Examines the Black Family," *Newsweek,* January 27, 1986, p. 58. Also see: Mitchell B. Pearlstein, "Crime and Marriage: If Wedding Rings Help Break Vicious and Violent Cycles, What's Impeding Them from Doing So More Often?" *American Experiment Quarterly,* Fall 2005.

31. Chester E. Finn, Jr., "Ten Tentative Truths," Center of the American Experiment, Minneapolis, MN, June 1990, p. 5.

32. William A. Galston, "A Liberal-Democratic Case for the Two-Parent Family," *The Responsive Community,* Winter 1990–91, p. 14.

33. Elaine C. Kamarck and William A. Galston, "Putting Children First: A Progressive Family Policy for the 1990's," Progressive Policy Institute, Washington, DC, 1990.

34. Galston was a leader of the Progressive Policy Institute. The Washington-based PPI might best be described as a "neoliberal" think tank associated with the Democratic Leadership Council, the group of moderate Democratic politicians formerly led by Gov. Bill Clinton of Arkansas. Galston served as deputy assistant to the president from the beginning of Mr. Clinton's administration in January 1993 until May 1995, when he returned to the University of Maryland for family reasons of his own (i.e., he wanted to spend more time with his wife and son).

35. "A Liberal-Democratic Case for the Two-Parent Family," pp. 16–17.

36. As argued, I would expand this reference to read both the 1980s and 1970s.

37. This is how Rutgers University sociologist David Popenoe put it in a 1992 op-ed: "Of course, social science research is almost never conclusive. There are

always methodological difficulties and stones left unturned. Yet in three decades of work as a social scientist, I know of few other bodies of data in which the weight of evidence is so decisively on one side of the issue: on the whole, for children, two-parent families are preferable to single-parent families and stepfamilies. . . . Sure nontradtional families can be successful, and they deserve our support. But here is what social scientists call a confirmed empirical generalization: these families are not as successful as conventional two-parent families. Want further confirmation? Ask any child which kind of family he or she prefers." "The Controversial Truth: Two Parent Families Are Better," *New York Times,* December 26, 1992, p. 21.

38. "A Liberal-Democratic Case for the Two-Parent Family," p. 18.

39. Ibid., p. 20.

40. *Beyond Rhetoric: A New American Agenda for Children and Families: Final Report of the National Commission on Children* (summary), (Washington, DC: U.S. Government Printing Office, 1991), p. 18. The commission was established by Public Law 100–203 "to serve as a forum on behalf of the children of the nation." Its 34 bipartisan members were appointed by the president, the president *pro tempore* of the U.S. Senate, and the Speaker of the House of Representatives.

41. Ibid.

42. Ibid.

43. While I've come to understand that members of the Rockefeller commission never actually talked about the Kamarck-Galston paper during their meetings, according to one source, the paper was nevertheless very useful in persuading the panel's majority of liberal members to subscribe to its thesis precisely because its messengers were not conservative. The commission's staff, moreover, borrowed freely from "Putting Children First" in drafting the final report. A case also can be made that Chairman Rockefeller put unusual pressure on commission members to reach unanimity insofar as we was thinking about running for president in 1992 and he saw such across-the-board agreement as helpful. Even so, the report's two-parent language was a major departure for a federal document. A final note: Then-Gov. Bill Clinton was a member of the commission, though he may never have attended any of its meetings from 1989 to 1991.

44. Barbara Dafoe Whitehead, "What is Murphy Brown Saying?" *The Washington Post,* May 10, 1992.

45. Vice President Dan Quayle, remarks delivered in San Francisco to the Commonwealth Club of California, May 19, 1992.

46. *The Wall Street Journal* editorialized: "The day-after press coverage of the Vice President's speech was remarkably tendentious, even by current standards." May 21, 1992.

47. John E. Yang, "Quayle Sums Up Trip: 'It Worked Out Well," *The Washington Post,* May 22, 1992. As witness presidential candidate Bob Dole's subsequent criticism of the popular culture, politicians became less nervous about blasting Hollywood than they had been a short time earlier. Much of this credit went to film critic Michael Medved and his 1992 breakthrough book, *Hollywood Vs. America: Popular Culture and the War on Traditional Values* (HarperCollins). Of interest, Medved, an observant Jew, frequently has been ridiculed and dismissed as a "right-wing Christian."

48. "Dan Quayle Was Right," pp. 47–84.

49. Ibid., p. 48.

50. Ibid., p. 52.

51. Ibid., pp. 60; 79–80.

52. "The Coming White Underclass." Syndicated columnist Suzanne Fields described Murray's column as the "most faxed op-ed of the year" in a speech, in Minneapolis, sponsored by Center of the American Experiment, June 9, 1994.

53. Blacks comprised 12.4 percent of the U.S. population in 1991. *Statistical Abstract of the United States, 1993: The National Data Book* (Washington, DC: U.S. Department of Commerce, 1993), p. 14.

54. Sara McLanahan and Gary Sandefur, *Growing Up with a Single Parent: What Hurts, What Helps* (Cambridge, MA: Harvard, 1994).

55. For a much briefer treatment of Blankenhorn's argument, see his oral essay, "Fatherless America," Center of the American Experiment, Minneapolis, MN, April 1993.

56. *Fatherless America: Confronting Our Most Urgent Social Problem.*, p. 2.

57. Ibid., p. 222.

58. Ibid., p. 22.

59. Ibid., p. 222.

60. For example, see: Wade S. Horn, David Blankenhorn, and Mitchell B. Pearlstein, *The Fatherhood Movement: A Call to Action* (Lexington Books: Lanham Maryland, 1998).

61. For example, see: "What's Next for the Marriage Movement?: A Strategic Discussion, *American Experiment Quarterly*, Summer 2002. For a scholarly review of the benefits of marriage, see: Linda J. Waite and Maggie Gallagher, *The Case for Marriage: Why Married People are Happier, Healthier, and Better Off Financially* (Broadway: New York, 2001).

62. For basic information on the Healthy Marriage Initiative, see: www.acf.hhs. gov/healthymarriage/.

63. Ron Haskins, *Work over Welfare: The Inside Story of the 1996 Welfare Reform Law* (Washington, DC: Brookings Institution, 2006).

64. *Public Papers of the Presidents of the United States: William J. Clinton, 1994*, vol. 2 (Government Printing Office, 1995), p. 1529.

65. For example, see: Robert Rector, *America's Failed War on Poverty* (Heritage Foundation: Washington, DC, 1995.)

66. Ron Haskins and Isabel Sawhill, *Creating an Opportunity Society* (Washington, DC: Brookings Institution, 2009), p. 262.

67. Elizabeth Marquardt, *The Revolution in Parenthood: The Emerging Global Clash Between Adult Rights and Children's Needs*, Institute for American Values, 2006.

68. Ibid.

69. The rate of births per 1,000 teenage girls has actually gone down, although the proportion of teenage births occurring outside of marriage remains stratospheric. And after spiking in the 1980s, divorce rates have more or less leveled off.

70. Daniel Patrick Moynihan, "Defining Deviancy Down," *American Scholar* (Winter 1993).

Chapter 2

Fragmentation's Effects on "Every Conceivable Measure"

Newspaper anecdotes can capture a lot, especially those which by historical standards are hard to conceive, as in the 2010 courtroom comments by a Minnesota woman whose son had been murdered.

The story is both extra sad and complicated, involving the sentencing of a teenager who had shot and killed her own teenage son—a kid who, only a year prior, had shot and wounded the kid now being sentenced. The second shooting, in other words, was in retribution of the first. For good measure, the mother herself, a woman named Stephanie Moreland, was in prison for forgery. In speaking of her child—her second son to be murdered—she said that he had worked two jobs and received his high school diploma posthumously. After saying that she never had a chance to see him graduate, she added this stunner: "I am never going to see him come home and say, 'Mama, I got some girl pregnant.'"

I double checked with the reporter to make certain I had interpreted what Moreland said accurately; that she had, in fact, intended the term "Mama, I got some girl pregnant" to convey the same kind of joy parents traditionally have derived from hearing their married children and spouses announce in celebration: "Mom and Dad, *we're* going to have a baby." Or more up to date: "Mom and Dad, *we're* pregnant." Yes, I was told, I had interpreted her lament correctly, as she mourned not only her son's death, but how he never would impregnate *some* girl.[1]

When I mentioned this story, or perhaps a similar one (I don't recall which exactly), to a pastor friend of mine whose ministry has long been in poor neighborhoods, suffice it to say he betrayed not the smallest surprise. Sadness yes, but surprise no, as he noted there's a "parallel universe" out there when it comes to matters like these that most Americans simply don't know very much about.

Numbers and hard data also can amaze in this arena, and we'll start getting to some hard-to-fathom ones shortly. But as a head's up of what's to come afterwards, whereas the previous chapter focused on how Americans have debated—or have determinedly declined to debate—matters of family fragmentation, this one deals more directly, albeit also quickly, with a variety of hypotheses as to why family fragmentation exploded in the first place. From there, we will review what researchers continue to learn about the actual effects of family fragmentation on children in terms of their economic impoverishment, mental health, drug use, criminal behavior, early sexual initiation, their later married (or unmarried) lives and the like. We'll save an examination of what researchers say more specifically about family breakdown and its bearing on educational achievement and subsequent career prospects for Chapter Three.

Though by way of one more piece of prologue, I should note that my operative view of fatherhood, perhaps surprisingly, is a rather minimalist and non-romanticized one, in that I don't argue or even hope for fathers being immersed in their children's live in the kinds of intense ways some seek. If it doesn't upset their wives too much, I don't see it as required, for instance, that they ever change a diaper. It surely would be nice if they did, but it's not imperative they actually do so. They can even pass on coaching soccer as well as carving out chunks of "quality time," especially if their paying jobs don't lend themselves to such flexibility. Instead and generally speaking, American children would be much better off than they currently are if millions of fathers who are currently absent (really absent) in one physical or emotional way or another upped their ante by taking seriously Woody Allen's simple rule about how "eighty percent of life is showing up." In other words, dads simply need to *be there*, they need to be around—not all the time, not always thoroughly engaged, and frankly not even eighty percent of the time. But they do have to be there *enough*.

What's an example of *not* enough? By age five, nearly two-fifths of boys and girls of unwed parents had no regular contact with their fathers over the previous two years.[2] It's granted, by the way, that Allen hasn't been the best person in the world to quote about responsible fatherhood ever since he ran away with girlfriend's daughter, but his axiom is useful.

Any credible roster of the most important marriage scholars of the last generation would have to include sociologist Andrew Cherlin. In an important 2009 book which (it's fair to say) subscribes neither to the wisdom nor efficacy of Bush-era policies aimed at strengthening the institution, he nonetheless acknowledges international comparisons, drawn mostly from surveys of women in the mid-1990s, like these[3]:

- Marriages and cohabiting relationships in the United States are much more fragile than elsewhere in the world. After only five years, more than one-fifth of Americans who married had separated or divorced as opposed to half that many or fewer in other Western countries.
- Because of such fragile partnerships, American children born to married or cohabiting parents are more likely to see their parents' partnerships break apart than are children most anywhere else. In fact, children born to *married* parents in the United States were more likely to experience their parents' breakup than were boys and girls born to *cohabiting* parents in Sweden. (Similarly, in an anthology coedited by Daniel Patrick Moynhian and released after his death in 2003, it was reported that from 1989 to 1995, more children were born to consensual unions than to single mothers in every country surveyed except the United States.[4])
- American women give birth at earlier ages and are much more likely to spend time as lone parents while still in their teens or twenties than are women in Western Europe. By age 30, one-third of American women had spent time as lone mothers; comparable proportions in France, Sweden, and the western part of Germany were half as large or even less.

What statistics like these mean, Cherlin sums up still early in the book, is that family life here "involves more transitions than anywhere else."

> There is more marriage but also more divorce. There are more lone parents but also more repartnering. Cohabitating relationships are shorter. Over the course of people's adult lives, there is more movement into and out of marriages and cohabiting relationships than in other countries. The sheer number of partners people experience during their lives is greater. . . . [I]n the United States, 10 percent of women had three or more husbands or live-in partners by age thirty-five, more than twice the percentage in Sweden and New Zealand and several times the percentage anywhere else.

In a comparative analysis of 15 European nations and the United States, and relying on similar sources, Gunnar Andersson, a Swedish demographer, concludes similarly: "The USA stands out as an extreme case with its very high proportion of children born to a lone mother, with a higher probability that children experience a union disruption than anywhere else, and with many children having the experience of living in a stepfamily." The "vast majority" of children in Europe, he writes, spend the entirety of their childhoods living with both of their biological parents. Interestingly (some might say benignly predictably), he adds that the most stable family patterns in Europe are found in countries "strongly dominated by the Catholic confession."[5] When thinking, by the way, about the implications of frequent transitions, keep in mind that a great amount of research makes clear that growing up in stepfamilies, on average, tends to be at least as tough on children as growing up in single-parent households.

Key questions: How has the United States come to be an outlier when it comes to affording children a fighting chance of reaching maturity free of major familial disruptions? How have we come to part company (in both senses of the term) with the rest of the world? We're more unsecured at home than even Sweden, where just about everyone (goes the stereotype) lives in what used to be called "sin." Might our loose ties have something to do with heavy doses of centrifugal freedom, expressive individualism, with a little religious hypocrisy added to the cracked pot? As for this last point, how is it that citizens of one of the most religious nations of the 16 studied by Andersson have the hardest time living up to the most sacred vows they're ever likely to make?

Or have other things been going on and eating away? Not just human frailties, bur rather, economic, sociological, and additional dynamics more powerful than any plausible public policies or programs could ever compensate for, as well as much more potent than any earnest call for the pulling up of a nation's moral socks could ever be? Yes, all of the above are the answers— although sometimes the best answer is much less grand and complicated, as when pedestrian sexual irresponsibility is dressed up as reflecting something epochal. To the mix, of course, many would add too much free marketing and too-thin safety nets, resulting in too many very poor people *and* too many very rich ones.

The strongest of scholarly explanations, regardless of their philosophical or ideological assumptions, are persuasive when it comes to how and why the ground underneath marriage and childbearing has been shaking. This is even more the case when such theories are considered in sum, as it's clear that tectonic plates truly have been shifting. Whether one reaches back to the 1960s or a century before that, big and basic changes in how we live and love and take care of one another continue. And save for the relatively few transformations that are the direct result of legislative votes or judicial rulings (think of the Great Society and Roe v. Wade, for example), they're pretty much beyond the ken of politicians and other individuals to sculpt or re-sculpt.

A concluding chapter, for instance, in historian Stephanie Coontz's *Marriage, a History* is aptly titled "The Perfect Storm." A great range of changes, she writes, similar in force to the industrial revolution "have profoundly and irreversibly transformed modern marriage." And not just in the United States, as virtually all industrial countries are living through similar upheavals despite significant cultural and other differences among them. This is the case even in nations she describes as original holdouts from the 1980s and early 1990s such as Spain, Italy, and Japan. The number of two-earner marriages in the three countries has increased markedly since the mid-'90s, and although divorce remains stigmatized in each of them, there has been a huge fall in marriage rates in each of them as well, suggesting, she contends, "a massive historical tide" which when "blocked in one direction [low divorce rates], seeks another place to flow [high non-marriage rates]."[6]

It's easy to see why researchers and other smart observers routinely accept (some might say bow to) trends they judge overpowering. Metaphorically, it's accurate to say they equate resistance with squeezing toothpaste back in tubes. They also have no interesting in playing King Canute. Fair enough. Still, it's striking the degree to which the well-being of children—as well as the health of society as a whole—is so frequently treated no better than sub-plots. This is the case, for example, even though, as of 2008, less than half of U.S. teenagers between 15 and 17—only 45 percent—had spent their lives living continuously with both their birth mother and biological father. Meaning, 55 percent—a decided majority—had not.[7]

What are the main components of analyses of how we've gotten to this stage?

The subtitle of Coontz's book is *How Love Conquered Marriage*, meaning that deciding whom to marry, or whether to divorce, or whether to marry in the first place, has come to have much less to do with maintaining family dynasties in Europe, or assuring extra hands to milk cows on the prairie, or simply putting food on a woman's table and feeding her children, and instead much more to do with never-known-before freedom to make the most personal of lifelong decisions on the most intimate of grounds. Yet whatever benefits have been wrought by these fundamental changes over recent centuries and decades—and they've been huge—stability has not been one of them. What's the Carol King lyric about no one staying in one place anymore?"

In addition to freedom, key words and terms in the literature describing the remaking of marriage include the likes of "individualism," "fairness," and "self-expression," all meant in the sense of affording men and women, although especially women, much more latitude than they've ever enjoyed before. Completing more of the circle, such options and opportunities have been the product not just of the benign churn of centuries, but of enormously consequential economic, technological, legal, normative, and other changes originating and taking hold, in the grand scheme of things, rather recently. Say, only since Dobie Gillis proclaimed his many televised loves in the 1950s, which turned out to be but relative moments before millions of flower children began proclaiming their many and often profligate affections in the 1960s.

Let's start with two different types of economic change, with it understood that almost everything about this analytic sketch swirls together like a marble wedding cake. "Economic" phenomena, in other words, are by no means economic alone. We'll go quickly, insofar as our constrained aim here is to provide context for more detailed discussion about some of the specific effects of family disruption. Much of this backdrop, moreover, is well known to the point of cliché.

More women, both in the United States and many other places around the world, are better equipped to be economically self-sufficient than ever before. By no stretch is this to say that large numbers of women have been working "outside of the home" only since a renewed feminist movement emerged in the late 1960s. An armed Rosie the Riveter and millions of other women who helped win a world war in the 1940s might object. But it is true that the proportion of women working for income has exploded. Here's just one set of data.

In 1968, less than a quarter of married women whose youngest son or daughter was not yet six were working for dollars. Even for mothers whose youngest child was already in elementary school, only about 40 percent of them worked, and not nearly all fulltime, of course. By 2000, approximately two-thirds of all married mothers with children younger than five years were working, with percentages even higher for mothers with older children. From under a quarter of all married mothers with pre-school children working for money to about two-thirds; that's an immense jump over any length of time, but especially a lone generation.[8] Moreover, this is the same exact period, for foreshadowing example, during which the enrollment of women in college and key professional programs began surpassing that of men.

As for men, this is also the same exact period during which those with little education and limited skills found it harder and harder to support themselves, much less a wife and kids. Framing matters in a more positive light (not that many low-income men would agree with the vantage point), one could argue that a significant dynamic at play was the rapid rise in the premium derived from a college degree. But no matter how the picture was drawn, it often was not a pretty one for men who came to be described by sociologist William Julius Wilson and others as "unmarriageable."

But before getting to Wilson's research, a quick point about men as well women who aren't accurately thought of as low-income, but rather, who have been described by Brad Wilcox and Elizabeth Marquardt as "moderately educated" members of the middle class. As the two have written, among Americans holding high school diplomas but less than four-year college degrees, out-of-wedlock birth rates and divorce rates are rising measurably. This is no small slice of the citizenry, but rather a strong majority, a full 58 percent of the adult population. Nevertheless, this pattern represents the "newest and perhaps most consequential marriage trend of our time," concerning as it does, the "broad center of our society," where marriage has been an iconic institution.[9] This is bad news with bad implications, which we'll return to in Chapter Four.

Back to Wilson, whose notion of unmarriageable men is most immediately associated with inner-city males whose chances for decent-paying jobs, goes his argument, vanished as factories and other businesses requiring lots of low-skilled workers vamoosed to suburbs, exurbs, rural communities, as well as other countries—to the decreasing extent such manual jobs continue to exist at all, regardless of location. But as sociologists Kathryn Edin and Maria Kafalis have written, the term also has come to apply to men who are routinely viewed as problematic marriage prospects for other reasons. Given the array of men "in the neighborhood partner pool," they write, the only ones that low-income women can reasonably expect to attract "are of fairly uniformly low quality." What do Edin and Kafalis mean by the uncommonly acerbic stricture for an academic study of "low-quality" men? "It's the drug and alcohol abuse, the criminal behavior and consequent incarceration, the repeated infidelity, and the patterns of intimate violence that are the villains looming largest in poor mothers' accounts of relational failure."[10]

Edin and Kafalis withstanding, rarely is enough attention paid to the poisonous role played by criminal and kindred behavior and colossal increases in incarceration rates when it comes to the disintegration of marriage across the country. We'll return to the subject in greater length in Chapter Six, but studies have shown, for example, that more than 40 percent of low-income men who father a child out of wedlock have already been in jail or prison by the time their first son or daughter is born. In another study, while more than half of male inmates were found to have children under eighteen, only about a fifth of them were found to be married.[11] A further piece of research from about decade ago estimated over 12 million ex-felons living in the United States, representing about 8 percent of the nation's working-age population at the time. That latter proportion, of course, is much higher in some communities than others, with "communities" defined in geographic, ethnic, and racial terms.[12] With findings like these, how can adequately larger numbers of men, particularly in inner cities, succeed well enough occupationally and in building careers so they may be seen by many more women as attractive and reassuring partners for life? The short answer is they can't. Much of this, one must add, is of a piece with the kind of equally poisonous mistrust that historically has characterized female-male relationships among African Americans in particular, and as examined with care and courage by sociologist Orlando Paterson in particular.[13] This might be the most difficult of all subjects to talk about, much less resolve.

From the world of science, it's difficult to overstate the importance of The Pill in providing women with more control than ever before in controlling their reproduction, and hence how they choose to live their lives and (getting to the germane core of the matter) with whom. Infinitely more contentiously, the legalization abortion in 1973 has done much the same. As did the rapid-fire adoption of no-fault divorce laws by all 50 states, with Ronald Reagan (some might think ironically) signing the very first one as governor of California in 1969.

All of these threads—be they thought of as economic, technological, or jurisprudential at root—entwine with cultural changes, often of a revolutionary sort, reflected in survey and other data like these:

- While divorce rates in the United States have been essentially stable since Reagan's subsequent days in the White House, they more than doubled between 1960 and 1980. According to one study, in 1962, half of survey respondents disagreed with the idea that parents should stay together for the sake of their kids even if they didn't get along. By 1977, just fifteen years later, over 80 percent had come to disagree.[14]
- Starting in the mid-to-late 1970s, national samples of high school seniors were asked if they agreed that "having a child without being married is experimenting with a worthwhile lifestyle and not affecting anyone else?" By 2001–03, the proportion of boys concurring with the claim had grown to 56 percent, up from 41 percent in the late '70s. For girls, the rise was even steeper, rising to 55 percent from 33 percent over the same period. It's understandable that seventeen- and eighteen-year-old kids are not familiar with arcane research about families. But what media and other cultural messages does one need to absorb in order to believe that nonmarital births don't affect *anyone*?[15] Incidentally or not, the out-of-wedlock birth rate in 2004 for women ages 20 to 24 was 55 percent.

We'll be citing plenty of studies and numbers as we go along, so no need to add much right now to these two illustrative sets in making the case for changes in cultural attitudes having been deep and wide other than to note that it's just as easy to find poll results in which people actually say very distinctly favorable things about marriage. For example, 81 percent of respondents in a survey published in 2005 said that marriage was, in fact, a lifelong commitment, with a full 71 percent disagreeing with the statement: "Either spouse should be allowed to terminate a marriage at any time for any reason."[16]

In regards to this last sentence, and as further proof that ambivalence and paradoxes abound, please note that ending a marriage "any time for any reason" is exactly what entrenched no-fault divorce laws allow. The failure of "covenant marriages" to take hold anywhere in the United States—unions in which new husbands and wives commit themselves to higher bars if they ever choose to divorce—is tangible evidence that Americans like no-fault laws just the way they are.

Edin and Kafalis brilliantly capture how mixed emotions and beliefs like these play out among low-income women—white, black, and Hispanic—when they write about how such women routinely like the idea of marriage, often to the point of idealization, but how they also view childlessness "as one of the greatest tragedies in life." The two scholars refer to surveys that show female high school dropouts to be more than *five* times as likely (and male high school dropouts more than *four* times as likely) than college-educated counterparts to say that childless men and women "lead empty lives." Or as they sum up, alluding back to an often severe lack of promising marriage partners in their neighborhoods and other circles, "[P]oor women consider marriage a luxury—one they desire and hope someday to attain, but can live without if they must. Children, on the other hand, are a necessity."[17]

It's fair to assume Edin and Kafalis would have heard and found different things—different cultural artifacts, if you will—if they had been pursuing their ethnographic work in the Philadelphia field, not in the late 1990s, but only a relatively small number of years earlier when "Ozzie and Harriet" reruns were still running.

Other than quick references to abortion and no-fault divorce, we've said hardly anything in this chapter about the role of public policy in the decline of marriage and upsurge in nonmarital births. Funny, but neither do many observers if by "public policy" the reference is to the emergence of an expanse of welfare programs since the kick-off of the War on Poverty. Once again, the silence of many can be loud. Then, again, it's fair to say that many other observers spend quite a bit of energy on the subject; one might even say too much on occasion. How the disparity? At the risk of rough and off-putting ideological distinctions, commentators and others on the left tend to fall into the former category; commentators and others on the right into the latter.

I've never met Stephanie Coontz, and as noted last chapter, I found her to be a more reasonable, even compelling writer than I thought I would. Yet never once in *Marriage, a History* does she even acknowledge how the enormous growth of financial and other supports for single women and their children—well-intended as they invariably were—may have contributed to family breakdown, doing so by making it more possible than ever before for women and especially mothers to get by without the economic help of husbands or other men in their lives. This is not a small omission.

As also cited last chapter, the most obvious scholarly rejoinder to Coontz's blind spot would be Charles Murray's *Losing Ground*. Heavy-duty researchers may still be arguing legitimately over whether he overstated the impact of welfare on family fragmentation, but there's no question that he was fundamentally on-target when it comes to the ways in which welfare programs, at the very least, *enable* many women to raise babies alone and for many men to abandon their heretofore life-shaping responsibilities. "Life-shaping," I should add, for themselves as well as their children. Yet while Murray might be the most obvious public intellectual to cite in rebuttal, perhaps the most fascinating by his prescience was philosopher Bertrand Russell, who wrote in 1929 about how, "with a slight change in our economic institutions," it would be possible to have families composed of mothers only. "It may be—and indeed I think it far from improbable— that the father will be completely eliminated before long, except among the rich." In such cases, the British Russell concluded, "women will share their children with the state, not with an individual father."[18] For American (and British) purposes, by "slight change in our economic institutions," read the kind of welfare state which has come to pass.

Bringing this section to a close, it's clear that for many powerful cultural, economic, political and other reasons, women of all stations no longer neces- sarily need what husbands have traditionally brought to the table financially— putting aside whether enough potential husbands are still in a position to provide in such traditional ways in the first place. As a result, many women are going without and many men have been successfully staying clear and wiggling off hooks. What does sophisticated, usually quantitative research say about how kids have been faring in this new world?

As you read the quick review that starts immediately below and which focuses on areas other than academic achievement, ask yourself how aca- demic performance is, nonetheless, almost inevitably diminished in both direct and roundabout ways. For example, given that family fragmentation is correlated with increased drug use and crime, would not such behavior gener- ally make it harder for young people to study hard, complete their homework, and to do well in school? One would certainly think so and that's exactly what the research says. Here, for example, is a generational example how everything ties together.

There's research showing that maternal grandmothers of the most success- ful children (as measured educationally) are more likely to have graduated high school, as well as less likely to have started their own families as teen- agers, than the maternal grandmothers of the least successful children. But doesn't it stand to reason, in even earlier turn, that the grandmothers with the least amount of education and earliest births were themselves the daughters of women most likely to have had out-of-wedlock children while still children themselves? One would think so."[19]

Then there's poverty. Even scholars and others who downplay the effects of fragmentation per se on children's well-being invariably acknowledge that poverty matters.[20] Yet in so doing, they rarely adequately acknowledge the obvious: that large numbers of families are poor precisely because of a missing parent. Please also note that all studies referenced in this next section have been published since 2000. A number of scholars and other writers, essentially going back to Barbara Whitehead's "Dan Quayle Was Right" in 1993, have pulled together quite useful summaries and reviews of what has been learned about the effects of family fragmentation, but they have relied disproportionately on research that's now decades old.[21] So as not to simply repeat those exercises, the handful of studies cited here, while often not as well known as earlier investigations and constituting well short of comprehensive sampling, have the virtue of relative newness. Suffice it to say they all reinforce the main style and thrust of earlier research: Meaning, while they're replete with scholarly cautions and caveats, they clearly demonstrate that growing up in the same household with one's married biological mother and father is most conducive to childhood and adult success—always on average, of course. Also suffice it to say, all articles in this next portion either appeared in refereed journals or were released by the Center for Research on Child Wellbeing, the home of the respected Fragile Families and Child Wellbeing Study, jointly housed at Princeton and Columbia universities.

Let's start with a study which addresses not only a number of important behaviors and outcomes, but also covers *all* young people in a nation, not just a sample of them. Sweden is often cited as country in which kids are doing just fine, never mind that marriage there has come to be a downplayed institution. But in what's known as a "population study"—meaning a whole population or subpopulation is examined—researchers found that Swedish children living with single parents showed increased risks of "psychiatric disease, suicide or suicide attempt, injury, and addiction." Lack of household resources, Gunilla Ringback Weitoft and her colleagues acknowledged, play a "major part in household risks." Yet even when all the demographic and socioeconomic factors that call for controlling were, it was found that children of single parents "still have increased risks of mortality, severe morbidity, and injury."[22]

It needs to be noted that while the study covered almost a million children and adolescents, only about 65,000 lived with only one parent at the time, usually their mother, of course. All the rest, more than 920,000, lived with two parents, a great number of whom, again of course, were not married, but rather cohabiting, as is common practice in Sweden.

All to which a critic of this book's thrust might politely note: See, marriage itself is really not all that important, as just living together suffices. This claim might hold up better in the United States than it does in fact if cohabitation as actually practiced by Americans was as stable as practiced by Swedes, but it's not nearly. For example, approximately a third of all American children currently live apart from their father,[23] a statistic that's telling about relationships in general, not just cohabitation.

Sandra L. Hofferth set out to discover how young children, ages 3–12, living in five different household arrangements fared in comparison with counterparts living with their two married biological parents. Variations included boys and girls living with their two biological but unmarried parents; their biological mother and stepfather; their biological mother and her unmarried partner; their biological father and their stepmother; or their father alone. Given the number of categories as well as Hofferth's interest in matters of both achievement and behavior, suffice it to say some findings are perhaps more surprising than others. For example, and wholly expected, children growing up with their biological fathers scored higher on achievement tests than those growing up with stepfathers. But Hofferth's data also resulted in a finding she described as "novel": Children of biological albeit *unmarried* parents experienced higher levels of behavioral problems than those of biological *and married* husbands and wives.

"The biological relationship between father and child," she rightly and self-evidently concludes, "is well established in the literature as a basis for paternal investment and, therefore, child well-being." The idea, however, that the *legal* relationship between parents is also tied to how children do "is a relatively new and important discovery."[24]

Granted, when it comes to social science research, one should never invest complete trust in a new finding, especially one described as novel. But that's not to say this one about the intrinsic value of marriage isn't intriguing.

Staying with threads of cohabitation, Susan L. Brown, in a study of several different kinds of familial and household transitions faced by adolescents, unsurprisingly found that stable cohabiting families are associated with lower levels of child well-being than are stable married stepfamilies. Yet perhaps indeed surprisingly, "formalization" of a cohabiting stepfamily by means of marriage "did not translate into any appreciable benefits for adolescent well-being."[25] Cohabitation and its reach, in other words, can be tough on kids.

"How about two unmarried adults," Chester E. Finn has asked, "one (or both) of whom has young children on site?" How might the young ones fare? Things can work out, he argued in a symposium on making marriage more child centered, if the "adult-to-adult relationship is durable, loving, and sharing." But how often does that really happen? How often do the children "get what they need from the second adult by way of love, attention, guidance, and role modeling?"[26]

Whereas most divorce- and separation-related research has focused on "the amount of damage . . . done to children after such disruption occurs," Yongmen Sun's focus was on how kids fare in the period prior. In findings that aren't the least bit surprising once one envisions what life may well be like in households ready to meltdown or explode, he writes of how, even before actual breakups, both male and female adolescents in such situations "exhibit more academic, psychological, and behavioral problems than peers whose parents remain married." Once more, this is wholly unsurprising given that families on the verge of falling apart are more likely, Sun continues, to be characterized by less intimate parent-parent and parent-child relationships, less parental commitment to their children's education, and less substantial economic, human, and other resources.[27]

How might the children of divorce do when it comes to the success or failure of their own marriages later on?

As with many others, Terry Teachman, writes of how the "children of divorce are "certainly" more likely to see their own marriages eventually end in divorce than is the case with counterparts whose parents' marriages remained intact. But he also writes of how kids growing up in homes in which their parents never married in the first place "experience a *very* high risk of marital disruption [emphasis supplied]."[28]

Then there is the question of whether all children, categorized in this instance by race, suffer the same because of divorce? If the measure is economic, then the answer, on average, is no. According to Marianne E. Page and Ann Huff Stevens, in the first two years after a divorce, the family income of white boys and girls drops by about 31percent compared to what it would have been if the divorce had not happened. In contrast, family income for black children falls by about 53 percent. The large discrepancy, Page and Stevens write is a result of white mothers being "much more likely than black mothers to increase their labor supply after divorce," along with the stunning fact that white families receive "over ten times as much child support as black families."[29]

This is an apt time to draw on three studies, all by Sara McLanahan and all published this millennium. As noted last chapter, McLanahan is a critically important scholar not only because of the sheer and continuing volume of her work, but also because she was one of the most persuasive academic voices last millennium in making the case that out-of-wedlock births and divorce, generally speaking, aren't very good for kids. Though having rightfully saluted her in this way, it nonetheless says something about a certain lack of conviction in the field that she and coauthor Irwin Garfinkel felt compelled to hedge thus as late as 2000: "Nonmarital childbearing is important because it is increasing and because there is concern (and some evidence) that it is damaging to children and perhaps parents as well."[30] *Some* evidence?

"In addition to high poverty rates," McLanahan did write four years later, "single motherhood is a proxy for multiple risk factors that do not bode well for children." Results from the ongoing Fragile Family and Child Wellbeing Study, she went on to say, showed that unmarried mothers with low education (defined as a high school degree or less) are more likely to suffer clinical depression and to have used drugs and alcohol while pregnant than married mothers with similar levels of education. The fathers of their children, moreover, also have more problems, including higher substance abuse, disability, violence, and incarceration rates. In a sample, for example, of mothers with high school educations or less, those who were single were more than eight times more likely to use drugs while pregnant than were mothers who were married at the time.[31]

In another paper, McLanahan writes of how "unmarried parents are clearly very different from married parents in terms of their capabilities." And while many unmarried parents have "high hopes" for a future together, very few actually wind up marrying, with nearly two-thirds ending their relationship by the time their son or daughter is five years old. Following such breakups, children in these families routinely contend with "partnership instability and household complexity" as their mothers form new partnerships and have children with other men. "These findings," McLanahan concludes, "underscore the fact that children born into fragile families are disadvantaged relative to other children in terms of both parents' capabilities and social capital."[32]

And then she found the following and further splintering dynamic: Demographic changes associated with *increases* in children's resources are occurring fastest among children in the top socioeconomic strata, while changes associated with *decreases* in resources are occurring fastest among children in the bottom strata. "These trends," McLanahan concludes, "are leading to greater disparities in children's resources, measured as parents' time and money."[33]

It stands to reason, of course, that children are generally financially better off in households in which both of their parents live for the simple reason that both may work for income. But there's also quite pertinent research showing that marriage provides husbands with incentives to work harder and more remuneratively than if they were still single.[34]

Let's close this chapter by citing other pertinent findings from the prodigious and influential Fragile Families and Child Wellbeing Study, co-founded by Sara McLanahan, which relies on a data set following a cohort of about 5,000 children born between 1998 and 2000 in medium-to-large American cities. Approximately 3,700 of the boys and girls were born to unmarried mothers and about 1,300 to married mothers. In a useful 2010 review of major findings from the study's first decade, Jane Waldfogel, Terry-Ann Craigie, and Jeanne Brooks-Gunn,[35] drawing also on findings of their own, concluded that the "relative importance of family structure versus family instability matters differently for behavior problems than it does for cognitive or health outcomes."

More specifically, instability at home appears to matter more than family structure when it comes to children's health and cognitive growth, whereas growing up with a single mother (whether her romantic situation is stable or not over time) appears to matter more than instability on the home front when it comes to behavior problems. Or, for our purposes at the moment, kids in single-parenthood households have a greater tendency to "act out" and otherwise misbehave than do most other kids.

For example, Jane Waldfogel et al. cited Cynthia Osborne et al., who found that "children living with cohabiting parents have more externalizing and internalizing behavioral problems than children living with married parents, *even at age three* [emphasis supplied]."[36] Waldfogel and her colleagues note that one explanation for this may be the "preexisting risks that accompany nontraditional families." This is a necessary caveat, as are concerns more generally about selection effects. (Extra-troubled people and potentially bad parents, for example, are less likely than others to find someone to marry them in the first place, and hence they remain single, perhaps cohabitating along the way.) Still, the finding that children growing up in single-parent homes are more likely to suffer behavioral problems runs throughout the literature, and on top of that, passes all tests of everyday observation and common sense.

In another study, the just-mentioned Osborne and the frequently mentioned McLanahan showed that "behavioral problems are intensified with each additional change in family structure the child experiences"; for example, changing from a single-parent to a cohabiting parent situation, or from a cohabiting to single-parent arrangement.[37] And in terms of health, further studies have shown that children living with single mothers have worse health "across a range of outcomes" than children living with married parents, even after controlling for mothers' age, education, race and the like. The "range" of health outcomes, more precisely, includes whether a child is overweight or obese; whether he or she has ever been diagnosed with asthma; the mother's overall assessment of her child's health; whether the child was hospitalized over the previous year; and whether he or she had any accidents or injuries over that period.[38]

So much for a sampling of findings—snippets, really—on family fragmentation's effects on the out-of-school and non-cognitive lives of children. Or to be more accurate, various family-related findings that may not pertain to a child's education directly, but one way or another, impinge on it, leading directly to an assertion:

If the United States is to continue leading the world economically, it will have to rely on something other than the educational wherewithal of its rank and file citizens. Family breakdown, obviously, is by no means the lone reason why Americans on the whole are underperforming academically. But severely compounding matters is the unlikelihood of significantly improving learning as long as nonmarital birth rates and divorce rates remain essentially where they are. The same unreality applies to adequately shrinking immense achievement gaps as long as the health and well-being of marriage remain, not merely terrible but calamitous, in many American communities. These are the tough subjects to which we now turn, starting with what first-tier research says about the ties between family makeup and both academic success and failure.

Notes

1. Rochelle Olson, "'I'm really suffering for taking your son's life,' killer says." (Minneapolis) *Star Tribune*, January 22, 2010, p. B4.

2. Jane Waldfogel, Terry-Ann Craigie, and Jeanne Brooks-Gunn, "Fragile Families and Child Wellbeing, *The Future of Children*, Vol. 20, Number 2, Fall 2010, p. 92.

3. Andrew J. Cherlin, *The Marriage-Go-Round: The State of Marriage and the Family in America Today* (New York: Alfred A. Knopf, 2009). The bulleted examples, plus excerpted passage, are found on pp. 17–19.

4. Daniel P. Moynihan, Timothy M. Smeeding, and Lee Rainwater (eds.), *The Future of the Family* (New York: Russell Sage), p. 9.

5. Gunnar Andersson, "Children's Experience of Family Disruption and Family Formation: Evidence from 16 FFS Countries," *Demographic Research*, Vol. 7, Article 7, August 14, 2002.

6. Stephanie Coontz, Marriage, a History: How Love Conquered Marriage (Penguin: New York, 2005), p. 277.

7. Patrick Fagan, *The U.S. Index of Belonging and Rejection*, Family Research Council, December 2010. Findings are based on the Census Bureau's 2008 American Community Service public use files.

8. David T. Ellwood and Christopher Jencks, "The Spread of Single-Parent Families in the United States since 1960," John F. Kennedy School of Government, Harvard University, 2002, p. 31.

9. W. Bradford Wilcox and Elizabeth Marquardt, *When Marriage Disappears: The Retreat from Marriage in Middle America*, The National Marriage Project and the Institute for American Values, December 2010.

10. Kathryn Edin and Maria Kafalis, *Promises I Can Keep: Why Poor Women Put Motherhood Before Marriage* (Berkeley: University of California, 2005), p. 81.

11. Ibid, p. 2.

12. Devah Pager, The Mark of a Criminal Record," *American Journal of Sociology*, Vol. 108, No. 5 (March 2003), p. 937.

13. See for example, Orlando Patterson's *Rituals of Blood* (Washington, DC: Civitas/Counterpoint, 1998).

14. Arland Thornton, "Changing Attitudes toward Family Issues in the United States," *Journal of Marriage and the Family*, No. 51, November 1989, pp. 873–93.

15. David Popenoe and Barbara Dafoe Whitehead, *The State of Our Unions 2005: The Social Health of Marriage in America*, The National Marriage Project, Rutgers University, p. 27.

16. *With This Ring . . . : A National Survey on Marriage in America*, National Fatherhood Initiative, Gaithersburg, MD, 2005: 4.

17. Edin and Kafalis, pp. 204; 210.

18. Bertrand Russell, *Marriage and Morals* (1929) (London: Allen & Unwin, 1976). As cited in Brenda Almond, *The Fragmenting Family* (Oxford: Oxford University, 2006), p. 61.

19. Tom Luster, Laura Bates, Hiram Fitzgerald, and Marcia Vandenbelt, "Factors Related to Successful Outcomes Among Preschool Children Born to Low-Income Adolescent Mothers," *Journal of Marriage and the Family*, 62, February 2000), pp. 133–146.

20. While they're certainly not ones to gainsay the importance of fragmentation on academic achievement, Paul E. Barton and Richard J. Coley do note that "Research identifies about half of the adverse effect of fatherlessness as coming from the lower incomes that result. The other half of the adverse effects [is] from not having both parents raising the children." *The Black-White Achievement Gap: When Progress Stopped*, Policy Information Report, Educational Testing Service, July 2010, p. 24.

21. See, for example, Wendy Sigle-Rushton and Sara McLanahan, "Father Absence and Child Well-Being: A Critical Review," in *The Future of the Family*, Daniel P. Moynihan, Timothy M. Smeeding, and Lee Rainwater, eds. (Russell Sage: New York, 2004), pp. 116–155.

22. Gunilla Ringback Weitoft, Anders Hjern, Bengt Haglund, Mans Rosen, "Mortality, Severe Morbidity, and Injury in Children Living with Single Parents in Sweden: A Population Study," *The Lancet*, Vol. 361, January 25, 2003.

23. Congressional Research Service tabulations of the March 2009 Annual Social and Economic Supplement of the Current Population Survey.

24. Sandra L. Hofferth, "Residential Father Type and Child Well-Being: Investment versus Selection," *Demography*, Vol. 43, Number 1, February 2006.

25. Susan L. Brown, "Family Structure Transitions and Adolescent Well-Being," *Demography*, Vol. 43, Number 3, August 2006, pp. 447–61.

26. Chester E. Finn, Jr., "Public Policy and Private Suasion," *American Experiment Quarterly*, Vol. 4, No. 2, Summer 2001, p. 19.

27. Yongmen Sun, "Family Environment and Adolescents' Well-Being Before and After Parents' Marital Disruption: A Longitudinal Analysis," *Journal of Marriage and the Family*, 63 (August 2001), pp. 697–713.

28. Jay D. Teachman, " Childhood Living Arrangements and the Intergenerational Transmission of Divorce," *Journal of Marriage and Family*, 64, August 2002, pp. 717–29.

29. Marianne E. Page and Ann Huff Stevens, "Understanding Racial Differences in the Economic Costs of Growing Up in a Single-Parent Family," *Demography*, Vol. 42, Number 1, February 2005, pp. 75–90.

30. Sara McLanahan and Irwin Garfinkel, "The Fragile Families and Child Wellbeing Study: Questions, Design, and a Few Preliminary Results," Center for Research on Child Wellbeing, Working Paper #00–07, May 2000, p. 3.

31. Sara McLanahan, "Children and the Second Demographic Transition," *Demography*, Vol. 41, No. 4, November 2004, p. 621.

32. Sara McLanahan, "Children in Fragile Families," Center for Research on Child Wellbeing, Working Paper #09–16-FF.

33. Sara McLanahan, "Diverging Destinies: How Children are Faring in the Second Demographic Transition," *Demography*, Vol. 41, No. 4, November 2004, p. 614.

34. Ayner Ahituv and Robert L. Lerman. "How Do Marital Status, Wage Rates, and Work Commitment Interact?" IZA Discussion Paper No. 1688, Bonn, Germany: Institute for the Study of Labor, 2005.

35. Waldfogel, Craigie, and Brooks-Gunn.

36. Cynthia Osborne, Sara McLanahan, and Jeanne Brooks-Gunn, "Young Children's Behavioral Problems in Married and Cohabiting Families," Working Paper 03–09-FF, Center for Research on Child Wellbeing, September 2004. The quote ("relative importance of family structure. . . .") is actually that of Waldfogel and her two collaborators, reporting on this paper.

37. Cynthia Osborne and Sara McLanahan, "Partnership Instability and Child Wellbeing," *Journal of Marriage and Family* 69 (2007), pp. 1065–83.

38. Waldfogel, Craigie, and Gunn here cite another review of the research by Sharon Bzostek and Audrey Beck, "Family Structure and Child Health Outcomes in Fragile Families," Working Paper 08–11-FF, Center for Research on Child Wellbeing, 2008.

Chapter 3

Fragmentation's Effects on Educational Performance

"It is very hard," two sober scholars whom we'll return to later in the chapter concluded in a 2010 Educational Testing Service report, "to imagine progress resuming in reducing the education attainment and achievement gap without turning these family trends around," by which they meant "increasing marriage rates and getting fathers back into the business of nurturing children." The very idea, they said, of a "substitute for the institution of marriage for raising children is almost unthinkable," although they did add that "stronger support for the family is not."[1]

But doesn't such a view radically differ from those of many smart and good people, both left and right, who are quick to declare "No Excuses" when it comes to expectations that all kids can indeed learn at high levels, regardless of their home circumstances, and that it's primarily the fault of inferior schools and teaching if they don't? Big time is the answer, as their exaggerated confidence—be it real or postured—is reflective of another major gap, this time with educators and other observers not as sanguine about the power of mere schools to overcome virtually all.

Before going any further, we need to assure exactness regarding verbs like "close," "reduce," and "narrow" when used in conjunction with the word "gaps," as in *achievement* gaps. The meaning of "reducing" or "narrowing" them is clear; it's to say they've become smaller yet persist to some degree. "Closing" gaps, however, can mean both things: Perhaps they've been eliminated completely, or maybe they're just smaller than they used to be. As often as not, precise meanings are difficult to decipher, especially in headlines.

A perfect example was in a 2010 *Education Week* e-story about achievement gaps in Gwinnett County, Georgia, outside of Atlanta.[2] After the headline announced that the district had won a $1 million prize from the Broad Foundation, the subhead read: "Cited for *closing* the achievement gap, the 161,000-student urban district will receive $1 million in college scholarships for the class of 2011 [emphasis supplied]." The second sentence in the story itself, however, read: "The annual award, announced today, honors large urban school systems that demonstrate the strongest student achievement and improvement while *narrowing* performance gaps between different groups based on family income and ethnicity [emphasis supplied again]." Which one was it: Are achievement gaps a thing of the past in Gwinnett County, or did they just shrink? The answer is obviously the latter, as the main text doubtless would have used a more victorious term than "narrowing" if gaps had been erased entirely. But the only way of knowing that from the headline and its use of the word "closing" is to be familiar enough with the field to know that income-based and ethnicity-based achievement gaps are prototypically stubborn. All such words will be used with care in the chapters going forward.

Back to excuse-making and unmaking. Without paradoxically picking on him, as I write this I'm at an airport, having just come from hearing former Florida Governor Jeb Bush—the most successful "Education Governor" we've had in decades—give a strong luncheon speech in which he repeated the "No Excuse" mantra. True, he never specifically said all kids could learn at *high* levels, but he emphatically did say, correctly so in almost all cases, that they could learn a lot more than they currently do, regardless of their circumstance. Yet also true, and truly not surprisingly, was how he never once mentioned fragmentation or fatherlessness as one of those handicapping circumstances—not that he's the only conservative or Republican in public settings ever to ignore elephants in such family ways. Though in fairness, he has written how "Florida's story dispels common myths about education," and how his state has "proved that poverty, an absence of parental involvement, language barriers, disabilities, broken homes, even catastrophic natural disasters like hurricanes, are not valid excuses for a lack of learning in the classroom."[3]

We'll return to Governor Bush's very real accomplishments in Florida later in Chapter Five, but for now, take the Heritage Foundation, a terrific organization that I hold in superior regard, just as I do the governor himself. "Apologists," Samuel Casey Carter wrote in the think tank's aptly named 2000 publication, *No Excuses: Lessons from 21 High-Performing, High-Poverty Schools*, "claim that the legacies of poverty, racism, and broken families cannot be overcome when it comes to educating our nation's neediest. They are wrong."[4] Of course such skeptics are wrong if what they really mean is that hardly any kids growing up in distressed homes could ever do well, and that no schools or teachers, no matter how talented and devoted, could ever help them soar. But few if any people are saying that. Or at the very least, I'm not. Rather, the argument is that the odds against such boys and girls doing great are often great themselves, and to expect regular and mass replication of the stunningly good and life-changing schools that Carter celebrates is to expect the impossible. In no sphere are brilliant and outlying programs brought to continent-wide scale, and to predicate substantial academic improvements on such organizational improbabilities, especially when the children involved are disproportionately troubled, is simply and starkly not going to work. Though in complete fairness, Jeb Bush can point to quite impressive progress for younger black and Latino students in Florida during his watch.[5]

It's entirely unsurprising that at the root of conservative analysis is the view that as long as teacher unions, administrator organizations, colleges of education, and the rest of the educational establishment hold oligopolistic sway, American education in general and inner-city education in particular will continue to founder and poor kids will fail. What *is* surprising—though perhaps really not given the gritty ways reform efforts inescapably play out political-ly—is the right's seeming confidence that public governmental institutions and endeavors can do a solid job fixing what, in large measure, are deeply personal, social, and not unreasonably defined spiritual problems. "The message of this book," Adam Meyerson writes in the foreword of Heritage's *No Excuses*, "is that there is no excuse for this tragedy. All children can learn. The principals and schools profiled in this book have overcome the bureaucratic and cultural obstacles that keep low-income children behind in most public schools. No Excuse schools have created a culture of achievement among children whom most public schools would condemn to a life of failure."[6]

Liberal and progressive critics routinely expand the failure-inviting mix by adding racism, along with allegedly shredded safety nets, severely unequal personal and household incomes and wealth, and what they also claim is similarly skewed spending on schools attended by rich and poor children. But they also can sound much like those conservatives who contend that public schools—if run properly—can nevertheless get close to overcoming what everything else in a kid's life has badly wrought. Though, I should add here, to the extent conservatives concern themselves with improving public schools, as opposed to pursuing vouchers for private and religious schools, their focus tends to be on creating and strengthening charter schools and not refiguring conventional "district" ones. For that matter, many activists and others to their left seem to be recalibrating their focus, increasingly intrigued by the latitude and new beginnings afforded by charter schools.

Presuming that their politics are not right-wing, Geoffrey Canada, the remark-able founder and leader of the Harlem Children's Zone, and Roland Fryer, the

Harvard economist, are two classic examples of liberally inclined reformers who have come to recognize the liberating possibility of charter schools. They also brook no excuse whatsoever when it comes to poor kids excelling.

In an Aspen Institute conversation in summer of 2010,[7] later carried by C-SPAN, Canada said things like, "If you allow excuses in this business, you will fail." And, "If children don't learn, it's our fault." Fryer added that we do, in fact, know how to make schools work for all kids, more than suggesting there's no excuse if we don't do so. "We can create a vaccine for education," he said, one that would get all kids to grade level, making it possible to "solve" our education ills "in the next five to ten years." What makes Canada and Fryer's assertions and confidence even more impressive (it that's the right word) is that neither shies away from acknowledging the scope of single parenthood, poverty, and similar problems.

Along with observers all across the spectrum, Canada and Fryer draw heavily on what's known as "effective schools" research; a line of scholarship and recommended practices going back to the 1970s and updated more recently by high-tech breakthroughs which, for example, make data-driven assessment, teaching, and remediation much more possible.[8] "We already know what works, so let's get on with it," Canada and Fryer, in effect, say. "No excuses," accentuated.

To which I say, yes, great educators and great schools make enormous differences in the lives of all kinds of students—from the most fortunate to the least—every period of every day. Nothing that I've already said or will say subtracts from that fact of thanksgiving. And yes, while they are relatively small in number, truly terrific and successful schools of all kinds, public and otherwise, really do exist across the country and they're not usually state secrets, as books have been known to glorify them. They are both examples to learn from and proof that major progress is possible. And also yes, an across-the-board and across-the-country commitment to flat-out refusing to fail is precisely the kind of obsessive drive the toughest of jobs require. "*No blasted excuses*," it would please me mightily to declare in concert . . . but.

As teased in the Introduction, I start from the premise there are many more kids out there than we either assume or fear who, because of the holes and disorganization of their home lives, find it too hard to concentrate and work hard enough so as to perform well enough academically (leaving the definition of "well enough" unanswered for a while). Or, if they are in fact equipped to pass and perhaps even excel in their studies, I would argue there are more boys and girls throughout the country than we seem to think or acknowledge who are nonetheless unmotivated to break scholastic sweats in good measure because of their fractured home lives. Or viewing matters less individually and more communally (as in largely fatherless *communities*, of which we have vast numbers), I work from the evidence-based assumption that neighborhoods in which sizably more than 80 percent of children are born outside of marriage, and where divorce ends a large proportion of marriages that do manage to exist, are not particularly conducive places for high or often even middling achievement. Peer pressures confronted by kids in such situations (picking just one crippler) are almost always more perverse than those faced by other kids in more benign circumstances and settings.

After spending an ethnographic year in a Catholic high school in Harlem, journalist Peter McCloskey wrote of how its "difficult for inner-city minority youngsters to focus on academics," citing a freshman in one illustrative instance. "Eric McBride [possibly not his real name] attended a junior high school in Harlem where he was threatened every day for trying to do school work in class. His peers warned that they would beat him up after school if he dared to study and thus 'act white.' The young man invented circuitous routes from the school to his home in a housing project on what used to be the Polo Grounds, where the New York Giants and Mets baseball teams originally played."[9] Later in the book, McCloskey wrote of how Rice students "walk a thin line between self-defense and self-destruction," as teenage boys from other schools often try to pick fights with them. "They inspire resentment from public school peers since their school is both one of the top basketball schools in the country and an academy where minority boys go on to college."[10] Sociologist Elijah Anderson has written similarly about an African American boy who felt compelled to hide his books in his jacket on his way to school in the morning and then on his way back home in the afternoon, not that his report or McCloskey's is a rarity.[11]

Less in terms of peer pressures, more in terms of his emotional makeup, young McBride also has "never had to pay attention for an entire forty-seven-minute period and seems unable to focus without being harassed" With the "harassers" this time and for entirely different reasons, being teachers, with some driven to distraction themselves.

For the sake of argument let's assume that McCloskey's intention was not to attribute the difficulties many kids have in paying attention to fatherlessness in any direct way, but to the poverty endemic to inner cities more broadly. That wasn't his blind-eye aim, mind you, but let's assume for a moment it was, just as many skeptics over the years have argued that the real problem in such situations is not the makeup of families, but their lack of money instead. Fine, but the question then beseeched is: How and why are so many parents poor to begin with? Might it have to do with disproportionate numbers of households in distressed neighborhoods having only one wage earner, if that? Needless to say, poverty in the United States is not caused by family fragmentation alone. But also needless to say, a great deal of it is.

Or consider not just unremarkable ants in pants, but the specific matter of Attention Deficit/Hyperactivity Disorder, a serious affliction that affects not a large proportion of people but a large number of them. If reasonably narrowly defined, researchers estimate that anywhere from 2 percent to 10 percent of the population is affected. Many are also of the mind that ADHD's fundamental causes are genetic, not anything social such as AWOL parents and other unusual pressures at home.[12] Fine again. But isn't it true that constant pressures and accompanying crises—the very kinds often entwined with family fragmentation—can trigger and ignite genetic predispositions exactly like those associated with ADHD, bringing them to scattering life? Psychiatrist Kathleen Kovner Kline and her colleagues make a related point when they write that, "Nurturing environments, or lack of them, affect gene transcription and the development of brain circuitry." And, likewise, that the old "nature versus nurture debate," which focuses on whether heredity or environment is the main determinant of human conduct, "is no longer relevant to serious discussions of child well-being and youth programming."[13]

Whether it's ADHD as strictly defined that's at root in any individual situation, or whether it's another state of mind with fewer if any explanatory pages in any psychiatric or psychological textbook, I have no problem arguing that a sizable number of children have an extra hard time concentrating on their schoolwork, as well as loads of other things in their lives, in substantial measure because of unfilled holes and other tensions at home.

Do I recognize that such contentions invite any number of objections, the most pointed ones rooted in allegations that I really *am* making excuses? Keenly, I do. But while acutely recognizing the risks of arguing this way, I'm afraid, getting right down to it, I'm fundamentally right. For reinforcement, I can't recall any educator, or anyone else for that matter, ever disagreeing when I've expanded on the case with the care and nuance it demands. Drawing on Professor Berra, they all have observed a lot by just watching.

On the one hand, goes the preamble to the fuller discussion, viewing the world too much through a therapeutic prism does a much better job of demeaning young people and curtailing their prospects rather than helping them. Same thing with setting bars too low, as it does students the opposite of favors. Talented and devoted educators, moreover make a real difference in how well kids do every day and over lifetimes, with even the toughest urban landscapes dotted with truly, life-changing programs and schools.

Yet on another, more clenched hand, reams of empirical research are definitive that boys and girls growing up in fragmenting and fragmented families, on average, do less well academically and in other vital ways than other children. While great schools demand and propel many students into doing better than they otherwise might, that's not to say they wind up doing nearly well enough when measured against reasonable national, much less international standards. Replicating such schools and bringing them to scale, moreover, will continue proving impossible for a host of reasons, starting with the fact that exceptional programs are usually the inspiration and handiwork of exceptional and sometimes brilliant leaders; men and women who, by definition, are neither mass trained nor hired in bulk.

This may be the best time to cite two passages from a book and follow-up essay about the adoption of special needs children, each with the jarring but self-explanatory title of *The Limits of Hope*, by Ann Kimble Loux, an adoptive mother of two very troubled, now-adult daughters. As asides and stretches go, consider this one central and short.

A literary scholar, Loux has written with great insight and not a little courage about how men and women who adopt at-risk and (it's more than accurate to say) damaged children need to have "realistic expectations" for them. "A way to best help adoptive parents," she argued, "might well be to discourage them from regarding an adoptive child as a blank slate with infinite potential. . . . Although many of us yearn to defy the laws of nature, we also understand that without a strong wind an apple does not fall far from the tree."[14] One of her more germane points for our purposes was how her two adopted children (whose backgrounds were terrible) just couldn't compete with her three birth children (whose father and Loux's former husband also was an academic). "Sandy [one of Loux's adopted daughters] told me many things I'll never forget," one of which was how "she couldn't be the best of anything in our family, but she could be the worst."[15]

We'll return to the themes like these in this and later chapters, but before going further, let's briefly sample the scholarly literature for what is empirically known about the many connections between family fragmentation and learning. As was the case last chapter, the following summary (miles from a comprehensive review) relies exclusively on peer-reviewed studies, all published since 2000. It also looks to an exceptionally important 2010 report of the Educational Testing Service.

Let's start with that ETS document, *The Black-White Achievement Gap: When Progress Stopped*, by Paul E. Barton and Richard J. Coley.[16] Not at all incidentally, the former writer was the Labor Department official who, back in 1965, did much of the number crunching for the now-universally validated "Moynihan Report" on family breakdown among African Americans. Concentrated in this new report's 40 pages is a substantial and balanced analysis of why the gulf between black and white academic achievement is as large as it is, paying full respect to historical and more recent economic, political and other conditions and constraints that have hurt some groups more than others. For example, Barton and Coley line up squarely with William Julius Wilson and others who argue that severe concentrations poverty lead inescapably to severely self-destructive pathologies.

"Are strong neighborhood churches," they ask, "still available to the community or has their prevalence and impact waned? Are there safe and well-maintained community playgrounds where children and parents can gather? Do neighbors interact and support one another, and do they look out for neighborhood children? Does fear of crime in the neighborhood keep children indoors? Are libraries safely accessible and do they have programs for children? In short, is there a neighborhood and community?"

Barton and Coley also say important things about incarceration, poisonous music, fears of "acting white," and more than most, they recognize that when talking about economic differences among groups, it's essential to consider not just disparities in income, but also those in wealth, which are routinely much bigger. They draw on some of these factors in trying to understand why, after nearly a full century of movement in the right direction, progress in reducing academic gaps between blacks and whites stalled around 1980, then resumed briefly around the turn of the millennium, only to stall again. They pay particular attention here to two possible "shocks," the first being the continuation of huge differences in the rate of black and white children born into and growing up in highly disadvantaged communities. On average, they note, children in such neighborhoods are "impaired in their development, lack family capital, and face hostile neighborhood environments. They are also likely to attend lower-quality schools staffed by lower-quality teachers." While in them, moreover, they confront greater violence, disruption, and fear. "Children growing up in these places are hit with a triple whammy in the home, neighborhood, and school."

All true, and those (particularly on the right) who dwell on family fragmentation as a major cause of academic and other troubles without being similarly scrupulous in explanatory breadth make major and unhelpful mistakes. It's precisely Barton and Coley's argument's full context that makes their description of family breakdown as the second giant disruption and impediment that much more persuasive. "If we are looking," they write, for a 'shock' that roughly coincides with the end of the long-term relative economic and educational gain for Black children described earlier in the report, [the] steep rise in children being raised without fathers, and mostly without the benefit of earnings, coincides with the overall scenario of curtailed progress in narrowing the achievement gap."

The percentage of black children living with only one parent or zero parents grew from 33 percent in 1960 to 67 percent in 1995—from one-third to a full two-thirds of all African American boys and girls.[17] The first number, from a half-century ago, was already enormous enough to provoke Moynihan to weigh in. The second and twice-as-extraordinary number (which has decreased only marginally since the '90s) begs the question: With proportions like these, how can teaching and learning *not* be much more problematic than "No Excuse" partisans routinely and seemingly confidently claim? For that matter, is it realistic to expect schools which serve communities where children born to married parents are anomalies to have test scores and graduation rates akin to those serving communities where intact families are not just more likely, but multiply so?

For ideological or other reasons, some of the scholars responsible for the findings discussed immediately below might well resist my own claim about the extent to which family fragmentation regularly undermines academic success. But their rigorous studies, as well as others like them, do more to reinforce my contention than weaken it. Following up on several transnational comparisons last chapter dealing with fragmentation's *non*-education-related fallout, let's start with a couple of international studies that look at education specifically.

In a 2003 study of eleven nations, the appropriately multicultural team of Suet-Ling Pong, Jaap Dronkers, and Gillian Hampden-Thompson investigated math and science achievement among third- and fourth-graders living in single-parent homes versus two-parent homes. Getting right to the disconcerting nub, they found that gaps between the two groups were larger in the United States and New Zealand than any other place. Especially in the case of our country, this turned out not to be surprising, as they also found that such differentials are "greatest in countries where single-parent families are more prevalent."

Yet the three scholars also found something of particular interest to observers and advocates here who favor increased intervention by Washington and other levels of government in ameliorating the effects of growing up in lone-parent settings. "Following a multilevel analysis," they wrote, we find that single-parent families to be less detrimental when family policies equalize resources between single- and two-parent families. . . . We conclude that national family policies can offset the negative academic outcomes of single parenthood."[18]

If that's what they conclude, that's what they conclude. But putting aside whether "offset" is taken to mean making plausibly modest dents in reducing differences, or much larger successes in heroic contrast, let me suggest a single-sentence thought experiment: Can you imagine any new or more generous set of public programs and subsidies that would more than marginally improve the academic performance of American boys and girls living in often seriously troubled single-parent (as well as no-parent) situations? I, for one cannot, especially considering all that has been tried and all the trillions spent on similar programs since the 1960s. Likewise, I cannot conceive of any large-scale effort that doesn't result in unintended consequences of seriously counterproductive sorts—again, mirroring the pattern of the last half-century.[19]

A year before, in 2002, another team of scholars with aptly diverse names—Kathryn S. Schiller, Vladimir T. Khmelkov, and Xiao-Qing Wang—unsurprisingly concluded that the educational levels of parents, on the one hand, and the mathematical achievement of their middle-school students, on the other hand, were positively and consistently correlated across 34 nations.[20] In fact, they described the relationship as "remarkably" consistent. The three researchers also considered whether or not mothers and fathers were married and living with their children when the latter were tested as part of the Third International Mathematics and Science Study (TIMSS). This time, matters were mixed and I concede surprising, as they found that the "relative advantage of living in a traditional family for mathematics achievement varies systematically between nations," with the boost being "significantly greater in those with stronger economies." In other words, they argued that the "effect of family structure was significantly stronger in nations with higher GDPs." Or, as they might have put it in the language of the book: While growing up in a single-parent home is less advantageous (always on average) than growing up in a two-parent home in most places on the planet, it's particularly so in affluent places, of which the United States is Exhibit Number One.

"The greater relative advantage of living with two parents in more developed nations," the researchers persuasively go on, "suggests an increasing importance of parents' strategic investments of time and attention for their children's academic success. . . . The demands single and remarried parents have on their time and energy may cause these intangible resources to be especially lacking in nontraditional families in these nations."

These are important findings, which (one might think) would persuade the authors (all of whom work in American universities) *not* to somehow conclude: "In less developed nations, children's academic performance does not appear to be related to the type of family in which they live. *This finding suggests to us that concerns that the rising number of single parents [is] a cause for the relatively poor academic performance of American adolescents are misplaced* [emphasis supplied]. The problem," they continue, "is more likely related to larger cultural and demographic trends associated with economic development that create difficulties for adolescents regardless of whether they are living in a nontraditional family or not." The evasive leaps continue to abound.

Then there are studies that do not focus on nonmarital births and single-parenthood as such, but rather, on statuses and conditions disproportionately tied to them. For example, in a 2009 study, two University of Nebraska researchers, Bridget J. Goosby and Jacob Cheadle, concluded that "smaller birth weight is associated with lower math and reading scores at age five," and that "findings painted a complex picture of disadvantage, beginning in the womb and extending through a variety of mechanisms into adolescence." And while they found that such birth-weight-related achievement gaps did not grow significantly after age five, they tended not to shrink either. "Much of the birth weight gap in early childhood," they write, "at least for reading comprehension, appears to be at least partly explained by the racial background of smaller babies, to less favorable home lives, and disadvantaged characteristics of their mothers. This pattern of findings paints the picture of a complex gestalt of disadvantage, one that begins in the womb and persists across childhood into adolescence."[21]

The obvious dots, of course, in need of connecting are those having to do with birth weight and marital status. More precisely, are babies born out of wedlock more likely to be low weight (defined by the authors as less than 2,500 grams, or 5.5 pounds) than babies born within marriage? The short answer, according to three scholars we met last chapter, is yes, as "studies have consistently found that children born to unwed parents are at higher risk" of arriving tiny. Reasons include the greater likelihood of unmarried girls and women smoking cigarettes and using illicit drugs during pregnancy and their smaller likelihood of receiving prenatal care anytime in their first trimester.[22]

Goosby and Cheadle note that 11.3 percent of all white babies born in 2003 were low-birth-weight as opposed to 17.8 percent of all black babies. This is not a small gap in size, just as lifetime reading difficulties are not small problems. Reinforcing the point, the U.S. Department of Health and Human Services, in a 2010 study, reported that 24 percent of *very*-low-birth-weight babies (less than 1,500 grams), born in 2006, did not survive their first year of life. The proportion was hugely lower for "moderate low" birth weight babies, at 1.4 percent—but that was still *seven times* higher than for heavier infants, at 0.2 percent. Beyond death, the HHS study concluded that low-birth-weight babies, especially those who come into this life at very low weights, are also at higher risk of various neonatal and long-term morbidities "even into adulthood."[23]

Doris R. Entwisle, Karl L. Alexander, and Linda Steffel Olson also write about perverse persistence, this time in a Baltimore-based study that connected the socioeconomic environments of first graders to their educational success as 22 year olds, 16 years later. Much research, they write, pertaining to the stubbornness of social stratification relies on student experiences in high school. Their lead finding, however, was that first grade experiences are essentially as predictive, insofar as "social contexts and personal resources explain educational attainment levels in early adulthood about as well as do similar resources measured in adolescence." Meaning and reconfirming that millions of kids are handicapped from earliest days by the kinds of social, economic, cultural, and interpersonal environments that are disproportionately synonymous with lone-parent households. "The correlations between social class and children's marks or test scores," the authors correspondingly write, "are a product of life experiences *outside* the classroom and, for this reason, strongly reflect SES differences [emphasis in the original]."[24]

Let's return to *The Street Stops Here* and Patrick McCloskey's argument that "father wounds" have a lot to do with the severe academic, discipline, and other problems of the inner-city African American and Hispanic students he observed for a year at a Catholic high school in Harlem. It's readily granted that McCloskey studied only one school and not a representative sample of them; that he's trained not as a scholar but as a journalist; and topping it all he's a passionate believer in Catholic schools, in whatever kindly or prejudicial way some public school partisans and others might interpret that devotion. But his hundreds of descriptions of daily life at Rice High School, including the extraordinarily tough dilemmas and frustrations faced every day by educators, are by no means novel as they all ring familiar and true. As in this episode in which "Ricky," a freshmen who has just completed detention and is meeting with the dean of students, Christopher Abbasse, saying he wants to transfer to another school.

> "People are gonna get hurt if I stays here," he seethes.
> "Cut the crap, Ricky," Abbasse counters. "You're looking up at most of the students here."
> Ricky recounts several fights at his junior high where he beat up bigger boys.
> "How much bigger?" Abbasse asks.
> "I don't trust nobody," Ricky shoots back. His neck muscles look like steel cables and his skin turns an intoxicating burgundy. "I'm going to put somebody in the hospital."
> "One more word," Abbasse warns.
> "Just kick me out!" Ricky jumps up and screams. "A'ight. Just kick me out!"
> Abbasse leans forward to tell Ricky to sit down. According to the street code that socialized the youngsters, a man never backs down—an ethos that often escalates minor conflicts into violent confrontations. Worse, Ricky's temper is acting like an accelerant of its own.

"I can't deal with this place, man," Ricky says. "You always on my back, yo."

"I'm trying to get you to follow the rules," Abbasse explains warmly, trying to turn the confrontation into a conversation. "Every place has rules, Ricky."

"This school gots too many," Ricky exclaims.

"The National Basketball [Association] has a whole book full," Abbassee reminds him. "How are you ever going to make it to the pros?"

"I don't care, yo," Ricky answers, then switches to Standard English to articulate with precision. "I'm used to being myself at public school. There were girls there, and I didn't have to worry about getting a 70, or rules about behavior and dress code. We have to talk a certain way at Rice. Damn, we have to watch out for the N-word and be on time. There I could show up when I wanted and say whatever. At Rice, there's demands every minute and I don't know how to handle them all."

Abbasse, at this point assures Ricky that he can in fact make it, to which he responds, just like a billion other teenagers have melodramatically cried out, "Nobody cares about me." But in this instance the conversation turns to a home life in a high-crime neighborhood in which Ricky's single mother is trying hard to keep him free of dangerous involvements with both gangs and girls—too hard and restrictively, by Ricky's figuring. And all the while his father, who lives in the Dominican Republic, and who (according to Ricky) keeps promising to call and visit yet never does.

Abbasse, McCloskey wrote, listened quietly, having previously reached the same conclusion as Rice's very strong principal, Orlando Gober, that the "missing father's legacy fuels most behavioral problems and that it is almost impossible to get an estranged father to deal properly with his son."[25]

The fact that McCloskey wrote admiringly of a visit to Rice by the afore-mentioned Geoffrey Canada of the Harlem Children's Zone highlights the nuanced and largely unacknowledged complexity of "no excuses" as an idea and expectation. This is the case even though Canada's call for it, as we've seen, is unwavering and seemingly free of doubt, with exactly the same deservedly said about the late Gober. "Stop coddling them," the extra-tough but also extra-nurturing Gober lectured parents (mostly mothers) regarding their children. The setting was an orientation session. "Stop making excuses for them, and you do it all the time. You still wake them up in the morning and make their beds: Stop babying them! . . . You're not teaching them responsibility. Mothers, cut them lose. . . . Stop crippling them. If the young men happen to fall, pick them up and brush them off and let them keep on going. I say this every year because I see it so much. Let them grow up and be men."[26] His regular messages to faculty regarding academic matters were thematically consonant.

In a seminar for Rice faculty, Canada talked about how traumatized and "re-traumatized" inner-city students are by violence and from very early ages. As paraphrased by McCloskey, he said it is crucially important to provide safe spaces "where youngsters aren't looking over their shoulders in the hallway or worrying about getting jumped by classmates on their way home just because they do their homework." Canada finished off by noting how "nothing could be more insane than the oppressive and anti-intellectualism of hip-hop culture, which glorifies criminality, setting up a youngster for a lifetime of victimizing and victimization."

"Now I understand," one of the teachers said after the session, "why some students act so immaturely in class. They weren't able to have a normal childhood and it gets worse, but they're safe here so it comes out."[27] Another Rice teacher is quoted as saying about parent-teacher conferences: "You see it coming through the door when the parents arrive. They've abdicated their responsibilities and put their kids up for adoption at school."[28]

Given anti-learning pressures as described here as well as other poor but less treacherous environments, a fair question needs answering: As exceptional as Gober was and as exceptional Canada still is, and while fully recognizing how they've been far from alone in their skilled and passionate allegiance to all American children, does it really make sense to declare, from political and other mountaintops, that no truck be afforded to *any* condition or *any* explanation resembling an "excuse" whenever students fail, as many inevitably will, even under the best of circumstances? Or would it be infinitely fairer and more credible if the idea of "no excuses" was understood not as an iron code of teaching conduct, as it's employed by proponents, but as a pedagogical approach aligned, in equal measures, with on-the-ground reality and our most decent and demanding hopes?

All the above are ways of saying that culture and psychology among other elusive variables are just as important as politics and policies in determining how well children do in school. To further the case, permit me to revert to seventh grade.

I was a terrible junior high school student, and then for the next three years, a terrible high school student. I'm fond of saying it was because I had burned out after a particularly energetic and draining sixth grade performance, but realize that most people don't buy it. So why did I mess up so badly for six consecutive years? In the spirit and content of the book, it wasn't because my parents had split up, because they hadn't. But was I nevertheless *troubled* in some way? I guess so, though I wouldn't take that too far, as my problems might not have been anything more dramatic than a superior penchant for mundane procrastination, especially my failure to do much homework. All of which begs very good questions about the effective reach of political and educational leaders in getting me to shape up and buckle down.

More specifically, I (somehow) graduated high school in 1966; a year after the federal government significantly upped its involvement in elementary and secondary education in 1965 with passage of the first Elementary and Secondary School Act. Was there anything in that legislation that spurred me to responsibility, at least for a final few months? Was there anything President Johnson inspirationally said at the big signing ceremony that got my attention and shamed me to scholarship? Evidently not, I gather, in both cases. I lived in New York at the time and Nelson Rockefeller was governor for my entire junior high and high school careers. Was there anything he could have done to get me to do algebra rather than watch Ed Sullivan and then "Death Valley Days" on Sunday nights? Was there any law or "reform" the legislature in Albany could have passed? Was there anything the New York City Board of Education could have done? What about my principals? What about my teachers? Actually, the latter had a lot more leverage than everyone else, but beyond giving me stern looks and lousy grades, what could they really do? Once more, the only answer was effectively nothing. And remember, I grew up in an intact, un-poor, two-parent family. Not one, to be sure, free of all consequential tensions, but far from the kind of shredded environments other young people are forced to navigate—the kinds of kids for whom "no excuses" has come to be obligatory marching orders for their teachers. What makes anyone think that truly distressed boys and girls will prove any less resistant to best and sincere efforts than I was? I might add I wound up doing very well as a freshman at a community college, though far more out of a surplus of fear than self-esteem, as I assumed that was my last chance, at the tender age of 18, for a good career and life. It wasn't, of course, in this nation of multiple chances, but it was wonderfully beneficial that I mistakenly thought it was.[29]

Beyond re-reading James Coleman, one way of grasping just how poorly armed school can be in the battle for children's hearts and minds is to calculate, as Chester E. Finn, Jr. has done, just how relatively little time kids spend in school. A child who turns 18, he writes, will have been alive for about 158,000 hours since birth. Assuming she has attended for six hours a day, for 180 days a year, for thirteen years—never once missing a class—she will have spent a grand total of about 14,000 hours in school. While that's significantly fewer hours than had she grown up in many other places in the world with longer school years, it's still not a tiny amount of time to get serious work done. Still, 14,000 hours is but 9 percent of 158,000 hours. "Consider," Finn writes, "what this means in terms of the leverage of formal education, if much of what goes on during the other 91 percent is at cross purposes to the values and lessons of school." It's a cliché to talk about how schools are asked to do more than they realistically can.[30] This is one of the more vivid ways of quantifying and driving the point home.

It goes without saying that plenty of scholars and other observers have researched and written brilliantly about the kinds of environmental constraints on learning focused on here. And while they have indeed been attended to in various ways, it's hard not to conclude that many in positions of leadership nevertheless and routinely turn blind eyes to their disfavored findings and insights, hoping against hope to dismiss them away.

Why, for example, are reformers so seemingly oblivious to Coleman's central finding in the seminal study commissioned by a provision of the Civil Rights Act of 1964, about how unequally equipped families (putting matters crudely) generally matter more than unequally equipped and funded schools?[31] This is not to suggest that Coleman and his colleagues didn't have more nuanced and qualified things to say along the way in their mammoth report. It's also not to say, once more, that really good schools can't make big differences in the lives of unlucky kids, because they demonstrably can and do and every day. It is to say, however, that it's impossible to square Coleman's pivotal and on-target contribution—reinforced by decades of subsequent research—with serious people taking pronouncements about leaving *no* children behind seriously to the point of literalness.

Before his assumption-changing "Report" on equal educational opportunities in 1966, James Coleman had come to scholarly attention in large part because of his work on the power of peer pressures.[32] Writing more recently about such pressures in ways pertinent to issues at hand, sociologist Laurence Steinberg and his colleagues, drawing on surveys and interviews with more than 20,000 students (and often their parents) in nine diverse high schools in Wisconsin and California, concluded in 1996 that the cliques and crowds students were most likely to hang with went a very long way in explaining why boys and girls of Asian background were doing better academically than white kids, who were doing consistently better than Hispanic kids, who were doing consistently better than black kids. This was the result, more specifically, of Asian students being much more likely to have friends who celebrate and reinforce academic values, as opposed to black teenagers, at the other extreme, who were more likely to have friends who actively disparaged and discouraged academic success. Tying these inherently non-policy ingredients together was the scholars' no-leap contention that doing well in school and being "strongly engaged in school emotionally" are highly correlated. "School reform," they wrote, would continue to fail as long as we continue focus was on how schools work rather than how our culture does.[33]

Another commonsense but important finding from their Wisconsin-California investigation is that students who recognized the importance of effort (as opposed to luck, fate, or discrimination) in determining their success in life tended to do better than students who were less persuaded that hard work matters. A superb cross-national study making a similar point contrasted how mothers in the United States, China, and Taiwan comprehend their children's success or failure in school. In simplest terms, if an American mother was asked why her child was doing well, say, in math, she was apt to say it was because her son or daughter was good at it. Or conversely, if her son or daughter was doing poorly in math, it was because that just wasn't one of her better subjects. Chinese and Taiwanese mothers, on the other hand, were more likely to attribute their children's academic success to burning lots of late-night oil—and lesser performances to burning a lot less of it.[34]

Just think through the implications of such a cultural difference when it comes to learning more and getting better. Whereas American kids wrestling with algebra might infer from their parents that conceding is genetically justifiable, their Asian counterparts with similar "x" and "y" problems are more likely to be informed (by their more likely *two* parents) to quit whining and get to it. On first reading of this study in the *New York Times* in about 1983, I immediately, albeit once again, concluded that until cultural gaps like these shrank significantly, academic gaps between the United States and an increasing number of nations around the world wouldn't shrink nearly enough. For exactly the same reasons, I also once again concluded that policy-driven stabs at "reform" just couldn't and wouldn't cut it. Nothing, I'm afraid, in the nearly three decades since has caused me to change my view.

Back to the role of money in determining how children do. We've seen how researchers disagree over the relative degree to which children in fragmented families are hurt by the actual absence of a parent as opposed to the loss or lack of income which disproportionately afflicts single-parent households. It's an important argument although proponents of the money side of the equation, as noted before, seem habitually reluctant to acknowledge the obvious fact that households in which one adult lives will always, on average, have less money than households where two adults—a mother and father for our purposes—live. But be that as it may, does higher household income necessarily translate into improved academic performance (among other good results) by boys and girls growing up poor? The short answer according to Susan Mayer, a University of Chicago scholar, is "no," though as she honorably notes as a political progressive, she very much had hoped that her adroit quantitative research would demonstrate quite the opposite. "As it turned out," she writes, "the relationship between parental income and children's outcomes is more complicated than I first imagined."[35]

Mayer, whose 1997 book *What Money Can't Buy* still warrants more attention than it has ever received, argues that when parental income goes up, children's "material standard of living" goes up, too. "But this improvement has little influence on children's test scores or behavior, on their education attainment or labor-market success, or on teenage girls' chances of having a baby or becoming a single mother." Mattering more than policies aimed solely at increasing income for poor families, Mayer writes, are parental characteristics of the kind valued by employers, including enthusiasm, dependability, hard work, requisite skills, and what she calls "social adjustment." Without outside assistance (by which she means help other than just money), "parents who rank low on these characteristics find it hard to create an environment conducive to children's success." To illustrate the point, Mayer quotes a teacher:

> There are all kinds of poor. We have a lot of children of graduate students. They are poor in the economic sense only. They are rich in so many ways. We have the poor of Mexico and that is a lot poorer than anything here. Some of these kids have had nothing—no shoes, no clothes, no food. They move here when they are ten or so and they have had nothing, not even the most basic things. They are so poor they can be crammed twenty in a trailer with no food and babies all over the place, but they have a family unit. That's a different kind of poor than having no one there.[36]

Let's begin to close this chapter by returning and in many ways concurring with (some of) the insights of another observer from the left side of the aisle, Richard Rothstein.

As you may recall from the Introduction, I saluted Rothstein for making a compelling case that as long as so many black children were forced to grow up under often severe duress, there essentially was no chance that programs like No Child Left Behind could succeed as advertised.[37] Many of his points already have been made here, including one about crucial differences between income and wealth (whites have more of the former but a *lot* more of the latter), as well as a point I perhaps should have spent more time on by now, such as the much more enriching and educative ways higher-income parents tend to communicate with their children, including how babies and toddlers growing up in more affluent homes tend to hear *millions* of more words by the time they're three and four than do children growing up in lower-income homes.[38] But it's certainly fair to say that Rothstein discusses several impediments to learning, some bigger than others, that deserve more attention than they usually receive. Take matters of hearing and oral health, for example.

Lower-class boys and girls, he writes, have more hearing problems than other children. These may be the product of more ear infections suffered by children whose overall health is less robust. "But though ear infections are easily treatable for middle-class children with access to good pediatric care, lower-class children whose hearing is less acute will achieve less, on average, in school." If poor kids, he concludes, had as much treatment for ear infections as other kids, "they could pay better attention and the achievement gap would narrow a bit."

He makes a similar case for dental care: Since untreated cavities, Rothstein writes, are three times as prevalent among poor kids as middle-class ones, they are more likely to suffer toothaches. "Children with toothaches, even minor ones, pay less attention in class and are distracted more during tests, on average, than children with healthy teeth," thus contributing "another bit" to achievement gaps.

While hearing and dental problems are presumably not as detrimental overall as other obstacles, such as repeated school-year moves from one apartment and neighborhood to another (a subject Rothstein of course deals with), they are not trivial. For proof, imagine trying to master mysterious subjects with a throbbing pain that just doesn't go away. Yet rarely does Rothstein say anything (and then only peripherally) about how family fragmentation is connected to the increased probability of such academically depressing conditions, relying on diffuse and less instructive terms such as "poverty" and "socioeconomic status."

Rothstein, in other words, is abundantly right that culture, poverty and other beyond-school constellations matter and matter greatly when it comes to educational success and failure. In this sense, his contribution is invaluable. But as long as he and other observers refuse to adequately contend with how extraordinary family fragmentation rates seriously compound and worsen all of this bad news, not nearly enough children will do better, much less well enough.

Notes

1. Paul E. Barton and Richard J. Coley, *The Black-White Achievement Gap: When Progress Stopped*, Policy Information Report, Educational Testing Service, July 2010, p. 35. Sociologist David Armor, in 2004, calculated how long it would take for 100 percent of American students (an original No Child Left Behind goal) to reach "proficiency" as defined by the National Assessment for Educational Progress if eighth grade students across the nation continued to raise their achievement levels at the same rate as they had during the previous decade. The answer was 61 years for white students and 180 years for black students. David Whitman, *Sweating the Small Stuff: Inner-City Schools and the New Paternalism* (Washington, DC: Thomas Fordham Institute, 2009), p. 13.

2. "Gwinnett County, GA., Wins $1 M Broad Prize," *EdWeek Update*, October 19, 2010.

3. Jeb Bush, "Success in Florida Schools: Reforms, Refusal to Accept Excuses for Not Learning Play Major Roles," *The Arizona Republic*, February 12, 2010.

4. Samuel Casey Carter, *No Excuses: Lessons from 21 High-Performing, High-Poverty Schools*, Heritage Foundation, 2000.

5. According to the Phoenix-based Goldwater Institute, low-income Hispanic students in Florida have outperformed the general student population in several states. "Governor Jeb Bush Discusses Florida's Education Reforms," Heritage Foundation, July 22, 2008.

6. Samuel Casey Carter.

7. July 9, 2010.

8. For example, see Stewart C. Purkey and Marshall S. Smith, "Effective Schools: A Review," *The Elementary School Journal*, Vol. 83, Number 4, 1983. In regards to data-driven assessment and other activities, see Terry M. Moe and John E. Chubb, *Liberating Learning: Technology, Politics, and the Future of American Education* (San Francisco: Jossey-Bass, 2009; and Clayton M. Christensen, Michael B. Horn, and Curtis W. Johnson, *Disrupting Class: How Disruptive Innovation will Change the Way the World Learns* (New York: McGraw Hill, 2008).

9. Patrick J. McCloskey, *The Street Stops Here: A Year at a Catholic High School in Harlem* (Berkeley: University of California, 2008), p. 55.

10. Ibid., p. 125.

11. Elijah Anderson, *Code of the Street: Decency, Violence, and the Moral Life of the Inner City* (New York: W. W. Norton, 1999).

12. Katie Kelland, "Study Finds First Evidence that ADHD is Genetic," *Reuters*, September 30, 2010. "British scientists have found the first direct evidence attention deficit/hyperactivity disorder (ADHD) is a genetic disorder and say their research could eventually lead to better treatments for the condition. Researchers who scanned the gene maps of more than 1,400 children found that those with ADHD were more likely than others to have small chunks of their DNA duplicated or missing."

13. *Hardwired to Connect: The New Scientific Case for Authoritative Communities*, Institute for American Values, New York, 2003, pp. 17–21.

14. Ann Kimble Loux, *The Limits of Hope: An Adoptive Mother's Story* (Charlottesville: University of Virgina, 1997), p. 28. It's not irrelevant to note here that my wife Diane and I adopted a special needs little girl in 1996 (the now-20-year-old pregnant woman teased in the Introduction), as that experience, along with the reinforcing fact that Diane used to run homeless programs, have had something to do with many of my views expressed in this book. My wife and I are also in a distinctively good position to vouch that *The Limits of Hope* is a remarkably, even scarily perceptive analysis.

15. Ann Kimble Loux, "The Limits of Hope: Notes from an Adoptive Parent Advocate," *American Experiment Quarterly*, Vol. 1, No. 4, Winter, 1998–99, pp. 58–59.

16. Barton and Coley.

17. Ibid., p. 23.

18. Suet-Ling Pong, Jaap Dronkers, and Gillian Hampden-Thompson, "Family Policies and Children's School Achievement in Single- Versus Two-Parent Families," *Journal of Marriage and Family*, 65 (August 2003), p. 681. In addition to the United States and New Zealand, the other nine countries (or parts of countries) in the study were Australia, Austria, Canada, England, Iceland, Ireland, the Netherlands, Norway, and Scotland.

19. In fairness again, Pong et al. do claim that there are no academic gaps to speak of between children growing up in single-parent and two-parent homes in Austria and Iceland.

20. Kathryn S. Schiller, Vladimir T. Khmelkov, and Xiao-Qing Wang, "Economic Development and the Effects of Family Characteristics on Mathematics Achievement," *Journal of Marriage and Family*, 64 (August 2002), pp. 730–742.

21. Bridget J. Goosby and Jacob E. Cheadle, "Birth Weight, Math and Reading Achievement Growth: A Multilevel Between-Sibling, Between-Families Approach," *Social Forces* (87)3, March 2009, pp. 1291–1320.

22. Jane Waldfogel, Terry-Ann Craigie, and Jeanne Brooks-Gunn, "Fragile Families and Child Wellbeing," *The Future of Children*, Volume 20, Number 2, Fall 2010, pp. 99.

23. Joyce A. Martin, Brady E. Hamilton, et al., *Births: Final Data for 2007*, National Vital Statistics Reports, Vol. 58, No. 24, U.S. Department of Health and Human Services, August 2010, p. 28.

24. Doris R. Entwisle, Karl L. Alexander, and Linda Steffel Olson, "First Grade and Educational Attainment by Age 22: A New Story," *American Journal of Sociology*, Vol. 110, Number 5 (March 2005), pp. 1458–1502.

25. McCloskey, pp. 104–05.

26. Ibid., pp. 41–42.

27. Ibid., pp. 202–03. The second Canada quote is also a McCloskey paraphrase.

28. Ibid., p. 177.

29. This is not the right time or place for a fuller discussion of the relative merits of thinking excessively fondly of oneself as opposed to constructively quaking when it comes to succeeding academically. Suffice it to say, I probably never will be asked to keynote any confab aimed at better esteeming often manufactured notions of esteem.

30. Chester E. Finn, Jr., "Our Schools and Our Future," Center of the American Experiment, November 8, 1991, p. 4. Long one of the nation's most important education scholars and policymakers (and a former boss of mine at the U.S. Department of Education), Finn is president of the Washington-based Thomas B. Fordham Foundation.

31. James S. Coleman et al., *Equality of Educational Opportunity* (Washington, DC: Government Printing Office, 1966).

32. James S. Coleman, *The Adolescent Society: The Social Life of the Teenager and Its Impact on Education* (New York: Free Press, 1961).

33. Laurence Steinberg, with B. Bradford Brown and Sanford Dornbusch, *Beyond the Classroom: Why School Reform Has Failed and What Parents Need to Do* (New York: Simon & Schuster, 1996).

34. See, for example, Harold W. Stevenson and James W. Stigler, *The Learning Gap: Why Our Schools are Failing and What We Can Learn from Japanese and Chinese Education* (New York: Summit Books, 1992). Also, Harold W. Stevenson et al., *Contexts of Achievement: A Study of American, Chinese, and Japanese Children* (Society of Child Development, 1990).

35. Susan E. Mayer, *What Money Can't Buy: Family Income and Children's Life Chances* (Cambridge, MA: Harvard, 1997), p. 2.

36. Ibid., pp. 14–15.

37. Richard Rothstein, Class and Schools: *Using Social, Economic, and Educational Reform to Close the Black-White Achievement Gap* (New York: Teachers College, 2004).

38. The major work in this area is by Betty Hart and Todd R. Risley. For example, see *their Meaningful Differences in the Everyday Experiences of Young American Children* (Baltimore: P. H. Brookes, 1995).

Chapter 4

Fragmentation's Effects on Economic Performance

We've focused so far on the means and degree to which family fragmentation depresses the performance of children and adults educationally and in other ways. Next steps are to consider the ways in which such educational deficits affect the economy. Or, more precisely, we've come to the point of investigating how family breakdown simultaneously weakens the economic competiveness of Americans as individual workers as well as America as a whole. Though, frankly, one would think connections between familial strength—a rather basic component of society—and economic strength are more than obvious enough as to eliminate the need for much argumentation.

Perhaps the most elementary measure—which is far from the most informative—is to calculate how many governmental dollars are allocated to keeping single mothers and their children north of dire poverty as opposed to spending those same funds on what some might view as more productive public and private uses.

A complementary way is to figure how much lower current poverty levels might be if out-of-wedlock birth rates and divorce rates had stayed what they were a generation or two ago.

A third way—working from the self-evident premise that family breakdown has something to do with various achievement gaps—is to calculate how much bigger our economy would be if such gaps didn't exist.

A final and longer-term method of estimating how family fragmentation retards our economy is to review what econometricians have learned about the relationship between a nation's math and science skills on the one hand, and its economic growth on the other. And with that arcane information in hand, factor in and consider—albeit in more self-evident than technical ways—what we've already discussed about how family breakdown constrains those very skills.

All to which skeptics might wonder: It's not as if the United States has been home to huge numbers of fragmented families for only a short economic quarter or two, but rather, for more than a generation now. Yet despite it all, we've somehow continued enjoying the biggest economy in the world throughout the period, with no other country coming particularly close. So how, exactly, have nonmarital births and divorce sapped our GNP in consequential ways? And if nonmarital births and divorce haven't yet damaged us dangerously, why should we be worried they eventually will? These are more than fair questions, with answers of two sorts.

The first is that it would be a mistake to contend, just because family fragmentation has not shredded the economy, that it hasn't caused tears; leakages which have curtailed our productivity and quality of life. Or putting it another way, compared to the rest of the world, the United States continues to do very well economically. But how much better could we be doing?

A second way of thinking about how fragmentation has already caused harm and threatens doing even more has less to do with our nation's overall economic output and more, instead, with how it's shared. Getting to the main point of the chapter, I will argue that the biggest economically rooted danger posed by massive family breakdown is not the way it will continue subtracting from our GNP, but rather, the way it will make it increasingly difficult for millions of young and not-so-young people to make more of themselves, thereby exacerbating class divisions in profoundly un-American ways.

This is not to say that all groups, to one degree or another, won't continue benefiting from America's enormous bounty; our economy is more than vital enough and there's little to suggest it will erode in any perilous way. But even more than is currently the case, some groups—more specifically, those which least frequently sire, bear, and raise their children in the fortifying confines of marriage—will fare less well than others. It's impossible to see how large numbers of people will not be hurt by this and how economic, social, and other cleavages will not grow because of these disparities, as the mass of non-marrying Americans has reached a critical mass and stage.

Or if you will, despite perennial talk of youthful rebellion, more often than not children are encoded to repeat the patterns of their parents rather than break clear of them. For our purposes, this means that various unhelpful and unhealthy behaviors—starting with rampant dismissals of marriage—are more likely to feed on themselves than correct themselves. Increasingly, one reads and hears the word "caste" used in describing the persistent differences associated with marrying and non-marrying parts of the population.[1] Might it be an overstatement? If so, it's by less and less, year by year.

In a 2008 study, economist Benjamin Scafidi and his colleagues calculated that family fragmentation costs U.S. taxpayers $112 billion annually.[2] This obviously is a big number, breaking down as it does to more than $306 million a day. Yet by various measures, it's really not all that large or frightening at all, as far bigger sums have been bandied in recent years particularly in regards to stimulus programs, bailout packages, and treasure consumed by two wars. So if not exactly chump change, what Scafidi talks about doesn't necessarily make for banner headlines either. But before itemizing exactly what expenses he included in his figuring, let's look at the quite substantial ones he purposely left out.

- His study, for instance, looked at female-headed households exclusively, ignoring male-headed households entirely, which represent about one-sixth of all single-parent homes. He acknowledges this division leads "almost certainly" to artificially low cost estimates. It would seem so.
- Scafidi also disregarded a number of major governmental programs, perhaps most notably the Earned Income Tax Credit, insofar as "existing data" didn't allow him and his team to "quantify them with confidence."
- He likewise disregarded the not-tiny amount of money public schools wind up spending on social problems tied in no small way to out-of-wedlock births and divorce.
- Also left out were any Medicare expenses associated with non-married adults and Medicaid expenses associated with the elderly. While single older adults are generally not equated with single younger adults, Scafidi correctly points out that "high rates of divorce and failure to marry mean that many more Americans enter late middle-age (and beyond) without a spouse to help them manage chronic illnesses, or to help care for them if they become disabled." All this inevitably leads to higher Medicare and Medicaid costs. But because they are difficult to quantify (and because most people don't think of such outlays as connected to family breakdown), Scafidi chose to exclude them, too.
- From a different angle, he also paid no attention to how "stably married parents provide human and social capital to their children other than income." The reference here is to benefits described in previous chapters that increase young people's well-being, which in turn, reduce the likelihood of their needing pricey governmental services ranging from repeating grades to further burdening juvenile justice and child protective systems.
- In similar fashion, Scafidi assumed no benign effects of marriage on fathers' earning power. Given that stable marriages tend to increase men's earnings while also decreasing the likelihood of committing crimes and

being incarcerated, he once again conceded that his approach underesti-mated taxpayer costs implicit in unmarried parenthood.

• And finally, Scafidi, for the purposes of his investigation, assumed that married households avail themselves of governmental services for which they are entitled at the same rate as single-mother households. But as he himself acknowledged, lower-income married couples are only about half as likely as single mothers to take advantage of such benefits.

This is some litany of exemptions. What governmental costs somehow managed to make it through his hyper-severe screen?

Scafidi started from the "extremely cautious assumption" that all taxpayer costs of nonmarital childbearing and divorce "stem solely from the negative effects family fragmentation has on poverty in female-headed households." This meant he took account of programs such as Temporary Assistance for Needy Families (TANF); the State Children's Health Insurance Program (SCHIP); Women, Infants, and Children's assistance (WIC); Head Start; certain aspects of Medicaid; school lunch and breakfast programs; food stamps; housing assistance, as well as certain costs associated with the criminal justice system. In terms of unrealized governmental revenues, he factored in categories such as foregone federal income taxes (including FICA taxes) because of nonmartial births and divorce, as well as foregone state and local taxes. All of this, too, is a robust list. Yet given the many and complex ways breakdown diminishes families beyond simply making and keeping them poor, $112 billion annually is clearly but a fraction of its true financial and economic costs. Think of it more as a starting figure than a full accounting.

Like a good academic, Scafidi felt compelled to be extra-cautious method-ologically; overly so, I would contend. But that doesn't mean the rest of us are obliged to hesitate in suggesting that the correct cost is very sizably above $112 billion. Yet whatever that price tag actually is, as economic drains go, it's nearer a whirlpool.

Thinking less in terms of diffuse taxpayer burdens and more in the way fragmentation weighs on affected families themselves, Ron Haskins and Isabel Sawhill, in 2009, wrote that if the "United States had the same pro-portion of children living in single-parent families as in 1970, all else being equal, today's poverty rate would be roughly one-quarter lower than it is."[3] Even more dramatically, Sawhill and another colleague earlier wrote that if family structure had not changed in the 38 years between 1960 and 1998, the poverty rate for black children in the latter year would have been 28.4 percent instead of the 45.6 percent it actually turned out to be.[4] As numbers go, these are immense, drawing in and injuring millions of young and older people.

From yet another interesting angle, researchers at McKinsey & Company, in 2009, calculated the annual economic toll posed by four different achievement gaps: those between the United States and other countries; between black and Latino students on the one hand and white students on the other; between and among students of different income levels; and between similar students in different school systems and regions in the country.[5] For example, if American students, in recent years, had succeeded in matching the achievement levels of "better-performing nations such as Finland and Korea," then our own Gross Domestic Product in 2008 could have been $1.3 trillion to $2.3 trillion higher than it was. That's an extraordinary GDP difference of between nine percent and 16 percent higher.

Referring specifically to the three just-mentioned demographic groups, McKinsey also estimated that if the gap between "black and Latino student performance and white student performance had been similarly narrowed," GDP in 2008 would have been between $310 billion and $525 billion higher than it actually was. Not as big as a trillion or two, but real money still.

Or assuming that achievement gaps between low-income students and other students had tightened in similar ways, U.S. GDP in 2008, McKinsey claimed, would have been $400 billion to $670 billion higher than it actually turned out to be.

This is a fascinating piece of work, and I for one, have no standing to question the number-crunching skills of one of the world's most respected consulting firms. Though I would point out that nowhere in the 26-page study, does it say anything whatsoever about single motherhood, father absence or anything of the sort. Given the routine ways in which many other writers are also mute on these matters, this is not surprising. But also given what we've learned about the ways in which family fragmentation diminishes the collective academic performance of African Americans and Hispanics in particular, as well as the ways in which it depresses household income for all groups, it's no leap whatsoever to attribute a significant portion of such huge economic losses to explosive increases in both out-of-wedlock and divorce rates.

As teased above, a fourth and final way of estimating the degree to which family fragmentation threatens to inflict increasing economic damage is to rely on the work of several econometricians when it comes to connections between economic growth and academic achievement, and then, working backwards, consider what we've come to know about the effects of non-marital births and divorce on the acquisition of math and science skills. This approach warrants a longer discussion.

In several invaluable studies and publications, economist Eric Hanushek, as much as anyone in the field, has demonstrated the vital importance of a nation's competence in mathematics and science in determining its economic

success. Or more specifically, while a country's *quantity* of schooling is critical, even more so is its *quality*—as comparatively measured most accurately
since the 1970s by a series of internationally administered standardized tests
in those two subjects.[6] Or for our purposes, think of them as carefully con-
structed exams similar to those taken by American children all the time, and
on which, boys and growing up in single-parent homes do consistently and
often significantly worse.

"There is now considerable evidence," Hanushek writes, "that cognitive
skills measured by test scores are directly related to individual earnings,
productivity, and economic growth. A variety of researchers document that
the earnings advantages to higher achievement on standardized tests are quite
substantial."[7] But if the relationship between cognitive skills and individual
productivity and incomes is strong, the relationship between "measured labor
force quality" and economic growth is perhaps even stronger, as a "more
skilled society" may lead to higher rates of invention, enable companies
to introduce improved production methods, and lead to faster introduction
of new technologies.[8] And while these patterns, Hanushek writes, hold for
developed and developing nations alike, enhanced cognitive skills have their
"greatest positive economic impact in nations with the most open economies.[9]
Places like the United States, in other words. Arguing similarly, economist
Arnold Kling and his colleague Nick Schulz write that if men and women
with higher cognitive abilities tend to be more productive, "then it stands to
reason that nations with more cognitively gifted individuals will tend to have
higher average productivity." One reason is that such individuals may be
more receptive to innovation.[10]

Hanushek and his colleague Dennis Klimko reached their conclusions in
part by combining, in 2000, all then-available international math and science
test scores into composite measures. They next examined those nation-by-
nation results in light of statistical models aimed at explaining different
economic growth rates over a 30-year span from 1960 to 1990. As expected,
a number of factors proved pivotal, including initial levels of income, population growth, and quantity of schooling. But also "extremely important"
was the "quality of the labor force as measured by math and science scores."
More specifically, Hanushek and Klimko found that a one standard devia-
tion difference in test performance was related to one-percent difference in
GDP growth rates on a per capita basis. This might not sound like much,
they noted, but correctly pointed out how big it really is, given the power of
annual compounding.

Yet begged here again is the question of why the United States continues
to do so well economically, both absolutely and compared to the rest of the
world, when our students—especially the older they get as they work their

way through elementary and secondary school—do so poorly in math and science relative to kids in many other nations. For instance, in Hanushek and Klimko's composite rankings, students in the following 17 countries, out of about 50 tabulated, did better (in rough order) than students here: Taiwan, Korea, Singapore, Japan, Hong Kong, Switzerland, Finland, Netherlands, Austria, Australia, Belgium, Canada, France, Sweden, Ireland, Denmark, China, and the United Kingdom. Hanushek's answer to the paradox is multi-part but to the point.

Yes, a lot of things determine a nation's economic vitality, with aforementioned openness and fluidity of our markets, including our comparative lack of governmental intrusions perhaps overridingly important. But in a 2002 essay, Hanushek went on to explain how days of reckoning even then were approaching.[11]

Education expansion in the United States, he argued, outpaced that of the rest of the world in the 20th century. We opened secondary schools to all our citizens. We enlarged higher education remarkably by further developing land-grant universities, adopting the GI Bill, and funding grants and loans to students. Compared with other nations, the U.S. labor force indeed came to be better educated, even after accounting for the lesser achievement of our high school graduates. In other words, he made the case that "more schooling with less learning each year" had yielded more human capital than found in other nations marked by less schooling but where students learned more in each of those years. But that approach, he summed up, "appears on the verge of reaching its limits."

> Other nations of the world, both developed and developing, have rapidly expanded their schooling systems, and many now surpass the United States. In a comparison of secondary-school completion rates in 1999, the United States trailed a large number of other countries and fell just slightly below the OECD [Organization of Economic Cooperation and Development] average completion rate. The United States gains some by having rates of college attendance above the typical OECD country.[12] Nonetheless, U.S. students are not likely to complete more schooling than those in a significant number of other developed and developing countries. Thus going into the future, the United States appears unlikely to continue dominating others in human capital unless it can improve on the quality dimension.

This is an apt juncture to note that the *Economist*, in 2007, either newly informed or painfully reminded U.S. readers that, "America's high-tech industries are powered by foreign brains." One statistic: Almost a third of all start-ups in Silicon Valley in the previous dozen years had been founded by Indian or Chinese immigrants.[13]

To begin closing a big and important circle, what are some of the things we've already reviewed about the connections between family fragmentation and academic quality and achievement? Returning to the last chapter, for instance, we learned from one study[14] that math and science achievement gaps among third and fourth graders living in single-parent homes versus two-parent homes were largest in the United States (and New Zealand) than in any of the other nine nations examined. This extra large gap, the authors, argued, was tied to their additional finding that such differentials are "greatest in countries where single-parent families are more prevalent."

In a thematically similar study,[15] we learned that the "relative advantage of living in a traditional family for mathematics achievement varies systematically between nations," with the boost being "significantly greater" in nations with higher GDPs—or, if you will, a place like the United States. The authors also found that the educational levels of parents and the mathematical achievement of their middle-school students were positively correlated across the 34 countries examined. Suffice it to say, single parenthood is also correlated with not having excelled in school.

Then there were a couple of studies that didn't deal with nonmarital births and single parenthood head on, but instead, with statuses and conditions enwrapped in them. For example, two scholars concluded that "smaller birth weight is associated with lower math and reading scores at age five," and while such birth-weight-related achievement gaps did not worsen after that, they tended not to ameliorate either.[16] Suffice it to say once more, babies born out of wedlock are more likely to be low weight than babies born within marriage.

I would like to be in position to calculate with some precision just how much the achievement deficits itemized in these and many other studies subtract from our nation's store of math and science competence, and then calculate how such educational shortcomings subtract from our economic growth and GDP. Alas, it's not methodologically in me. Yet I trust the fundamental logic of the dynamic is clear: family breakdown leads to weakened educational performance, which in turn leads to weakened economic performance, suffered by many Americans individually as well as the United States as a whole.

To further recap: We've learned that family fragmentations costs the U.S. economy at least $112 billion annually—really a lot more—in social welfare and foregone tax revenues. A second piece of research noted how much lower poverty rates in the United States would be if current family fragmentation rates more closely resembled those of four decades ago. Another study suggested some exceptionally big numbers in focusing on various domestic and international achievement gaps, all of which are exacerbated, at least to some extent, by family fragmentation. And a fourth study, just discussed, emphasized the importance of math and science skills—both of which are curtailed when children grow up without two parents at home—in determining a nation's GDP and economic growth.

Yet as giant as these numbers are, given that the United States continues to lead economically, one must entertain the possibility that our high family fragmentation rates—thought to be the highest in the industrialized world—may not be especially worrisome in actual fact. After all, how could family breakdown be all that fiscally debilitating (goes the contention) if we remain the most powerful economic engine in the universe? It's a fair caution which is implicitly reinforced by a number of economists who have been just as adept in recent years as various education writers—perhaps even more so—in ignoring the role and ramifications of family fragmentation, this time in terms of our nation's economic prospects.

For example, virtually the only thing Kling and Schulz say directly about the importance of families when it comes to economic success and failure around the world in their 2009 book, *From Poverty to Prosperity*, is this: "Self-reliant families will be able to contribute to civil society. They have the ability to start businesses, participate in charitable organizations, and join clubs. They also will have high expectations for public servants and little use for corruption."[17] Not a word about kids coming of professional and vocational age with missing parents and parts.

Then, again, one might point out that *From Poverty to Prosperity* is a determinedly optimistic book, without great interest in dredging up undersides of American life. Yes, it's a weak excuse but let's accept it. Yet what about another well-received book, with the far less sunny name of *The Coming Generational Storm*?[18] To the not insignificant extent it discusses marriage it focuses on the implications of women delaying getting married, if ever marrying at all, as well as U.S. birth rates dropping precipitously compared to the height of the Baby Boom in the 1950. Yet rather than focusing on what all this might imply for current-day children, authors Laurence J. Kotlikoff and Scott Burns dwell on what they portend for aging adults down the road. What, they ask, do these developments mean for the elderly of the future given that their only non-institutional source of help, whether physical or financial, may be their children—if they have any? "As we've already seen," they write, "the *supply* of children—and the working adults they become—is shrinking [emphasis supplied]."[19]

Perhaps such de-emphasis on the cognitive and emotional well-being of young people, and accentuation instead on their volume, is neither suspect nor surprising given Kotlikoff and Burns' principal interest in something called "generational accounting," not exactly the most child-friendly term ever coined. Nevertheless, their book is about what one blurb writer called "by far the single most important problem in U.S. economic policy." Leading a reader to possibly think that the way American children come into this life and are raised—especially given their future caretaking obligations—might be attended to better. Might their capabilities and not just their sheer numbers have bearing?

For the sake of argument and moving forward, let's split the difference and proceed from the premise that while family fragmentation surely doesn't spur growth, the U.S. economy has enough going for it so that high out-of-wedlock and divorce rates (as well as generally short-term cohabiting relationships) are not drastically damaging. Yet where might that leave us economically? I would argue that the most acute answer, at least as gauged by mega-measures such as GDP, is in comparatively better shape as a national whole than as specific individuals in many millions of cases. Fragmentation's major fallout likely will be the way in which large numbers of men and women, following disproportionately poor performances as students, simply won't have the tools to succeed in an economy that will continue demanding strong cognitive and other skills—with similarly constrained fates often waiting disproportionate numbers of their children and grandchildren. What, in turn, might this suggest, not necessarily for our economic health overall (which may well remain superior), but for our social and political fabric? Clearly not good things, as it's impossible to see how family breakdown will not deepen demarcations and cleavages in very un-American ways.

Faith in American exceptionalism has never required any leap on my part, as I've always been one with Lincoln, who believed the United States (at a far rougher moment) was the earth's last best hope. Nevertheless, if forced to offer a more practical-sounding explanation for American economic leadership, as already partly teased, I would talk about our allegiance to freedom, free markets, and the rule of law. I would salute our innovative spirit and entrepreneurism, as well as our superior research and graduate programs. And I would argue how all of it is made more potent—keeping us in generally good stead—by an uncommon faith in the future, in each other, and in belief itself.

But a "generally" good stead can hide tons of trouble, very much including growing numbers of pained men and women, not just data points, floundering because they are under-prepared for the occupational demands ascending all around them. Or, if you will, an exceedingly elite few Americans may well continue winning far more than their share of Nobel and other prizes. But their successes will grow even more vastly great than those of other Americans who increasingly will find themselves in competition with legions of better trained and more proficient people in other parts of the world. Paradoxically, this will make it extra difficult for many ill-prepared stateside workers to build and enrich their careers by taking occupational advantage of their countrymen's scientific and technological breakthroughs, thereby leading to more outsourcing, and not just of menial tasks. (George Will has quoted an Intel official as saying, "Now our business operations are two-thirds in the United States and one-third overseas. But that ratio will flip over [in] the next ten years."[20] The column's context suggests the reversal was being provoked by educational deficits here rather than cheaper labor elsewhere.)

So as not to get bogged down over whether the United States has already turned into an overly skewed nation economically, let's simply stipulate that current matters of income inequality and mobility might be viewed simultaneously as glasses both half full and half empty. On the one hand, it's hard to ignore the fact that from 1980 to 2005, according to one calculation, more than 80 percent of the total increase in Americans' income was enjoyed by the top one percent of earners.[21] And given what we've long believed about ourselves nearly genetically, it can be disconcerting to learn that upward income mobility is less fluid in the United States than in various other countries.[22]

Nevertheless, American mobility is far from stuck, particularly for those with good educations. More specifically, while increasing proportions of income indeed have been gravitating (some might say *anti*-gravitating) to top quintiles and deciles, regularly lost in discussion is the fact that actual earners move from one category to another all the time. According to another study, about half of taxpayers in the bottom quintile in 1996 (56 percent by one estimate and 42 percent by another) moved to a higher quintile by 2005.[23]

My preferred authority for all things pertaining to income mobility has long been economist Isabel Sawhill, long of the Brookings Institution and late of the Clinton administration. Based on quite recent data, she has come to make three core points (among not a few others): (1) income in the United States is less equally distributed than it was several decades ago; (2) income is more correlated with education than it had been; and (3) it's also more correlated with family structure than it had been. Even if parental income were not tied to children's success (she acknowledges that it is, of course), Sawhill writes, we would still have "good reasons to believe that the particular form of income inequality we have experienced in the U.S. has set the stage for the greater persistence of class in the future." To be sure, she adds, class structure here is largely grounded on "meritocratic principles and on stable family ties" rather than on the inheritance of wealth or exploitation of connections. But all of the above, Sawhill writes, very much suggests the importance of dealing not just with income as such, but also with the "distribution of educational opportunities and with differences in family structure."[24]

Writing at least halfway similarly in the *National Tax Journal* in 2009, Gerald Auten and Geoffrey Gee argued that mobility, both up and down, is the result of many factors, with two of most important being "initial position in the income distribution and changes in marital status."[25]

Marital status, it needs to be added, is an overwhelmingly important factor when the unit of measurement in comparing incomes is households rather than individual taxpayers. This is a statistical fact of life far more often missed than taken into account in the media and elsewhere. In the Twin Cities, for example, much has been made in recent years of large income differences between white and black households, among others. Without question, these are consequential and disturbing disparities. But virtually never is it pointed out that white households in the Minneapolis and St. Paul area, because of higher proportions of two-parent families, presumably contain more employable adults in their prime working years—which is to say, more available income earners on average—than do black families.[26]

Or consider the use of the word "household" by columnist Paul Krugman in his analysis of the "The Great Divergence," a term meant to denote growing income inequality in the United States since the early 1970s. If the goal is to figure out whether typical Americans (as opposed to very rich ones) have benefited from the nation's growing riches, he correctly notes that "we can't just line up all 300 million people in America in order of income and calculate the income of American number 150,000,000." This is the case, he recognizes, because children should not be included in the math, as "they only have income to the extent that the households they live in do." Meaning, he concluded, maybe "we should be looking at households rather than individuals."[27]

That would be a fine approach, but only if he also dealt with the fact that any method used to gauge income inequality is lacking if it doesn't also recognize divergence in the number of adult men and women in various households (excluding adult children and extended family members who may or may not be working), as such living arrangements are often starkly distinguishable by class and race. By definition again, a nation in which households routinely contain two potentially working married adults (as is disproportionately the case with upper-income households) likely will be home to less income skewing than one containing a high number of households with only one potential working adult (as is disproportionately the case with lower-income households). As a Nobel Laureate in economics, I would like to think Krugman doesn't need any instruction on the subject from me. So what explains the obfuscation? Might it once more be an example of a scholar not terribly eager to address matters of family breakdown head-on?

Yet whatever one thinks about the distribution of income and the dynamism of its mobility in recent times, it's not debatable that as long as fragmentation-related educational deficiencies persist, those who are particularly worried about the rich growing richer and the poor growing poorer in the United States are unlikely to find their spirits lifted anytime soon. Columnist Thomas L. Friedman implicitly reinforced this point in a 2009 piece in which he quoted Todd Martin, a "former global executive," who said that our "education failure is the largest contributing factor to the decline of the American worker's global competitiveness, particularly at the middle and bottom ranges." He also quoted Martin as contending that such a decline has diminished the ability of many American workers to create wealth "precisely when technology brought global competition much closer to home." Friedman concludes the point by arguing there's "no telling how 'jobless' this recovery will be" unless and until "we create enough new jobs and educated workers that are worth, say, $40-an-hour compared with the global alternatives."[28] (For those keeping score, Friedman and Martin use the word "global" four times in a tight space.)

Lest one assume, by the way, that the sole or even primary skills referred to here are technical ones, Friedman cites a labor economist talking about men and women "at the high end of the bottom half" who are doing reasonably well because of strong interpersonal skills, such as those of salespeople capable of dealing effectively with customers face to face. Yet such softer skills, including adroitness in Standard English, as William Julius Wilson has pointed out, also can be very much related to family background. Also recall Susan Mayer last chapter writing of the importance of enthusiasm, dependability, hard work, and "social adjustment" on the part of low-income parents in shaping how well their children do when it comes to their own educational attainment and labor-market success.

This is as good a spot as any to cite a letter from the president of a manufacturing business who read a newspaper column I had written about a related subject. His company, which has seven plants across the United States and employs about 650 people, focuses on machining and fabricating metal components for the aerospace, defense, industrial, and medical markets. As opposed to regularly cutting employees, they regularly seek to add new ones, but the biggest inhibitor to growth both for his firm and broader field, he reported, is finding qualified people, particularly machinists. "Because we often work with exotic materials and very high tolerance components," he wrote, "we require machinists that are at the upper end of the pyramid of skills."

> We compensate at a level we think provides a good employee with an income that support themselves and a family. An entry-level machinist will typically make roughly $40,000 per year with overtime. A middle-of-the-road machinist with good experience will typically be at a compensation range of

$60,000–$80,000, and our high-end machinists will be at an even higher rate. We also offer very lucrative benefit packages.

Nevertheless, my correspondent wrote of his concern, and that of his colleagues, about the future of their industry, as they just don't see enough new machinists entering the workforce. "What is even more troubling," he went on, "is that when we find a young machinist that has the right intellect we often lose them because of attendance issues." Even more perversely under the circumstance, he wrote of how the type of manufacturing they do does not lend itself to doing it overseas. "As you can imagine, it is frustrating to continually hear about high unemployment, skyrocketing college costs, and chronic unemployment, while we sit here with well-paid vacant positions just waiting for qualified people to show up."[29]

Americans—especially conservatives—generally don't like talking about individual citizens or cohorts or generations getting locked into social or economic place. But the way in which extensive family fragmentation is already making it unduly hard for many citizens to hit many of the higher educational notes demanded by unstoppable worldwide changes, it would seem that conversations and debates about class and perhaps even lower-case caste will be increasingly difficult to evade.

Among the relative few who have not shied away is writer Kay Hymowitz, who put matters succinctly in her aptly named *Marriage and Caste in America: Separate and Unequal Families in a Post-Marital Age*, a book in which she describes the "most vulnerable" as "poor or working-class single mothers with little education having children who will grow up to be low-income single mothers and fathers with little education who will have children who will become low-income single parents—and so forth." Paralleling this perverse cycle, she continues, is a radically more benign one in which college-educated and middle-class married mothers raise boys and girls who go to college, get married, and only then have children—and who then themselves grow up, go to college, get married, have children, and on. "A self-perpetuating single-mother proletariat," is what Hymowitz calls it. "Not exactly what America should look like, is it?"[30]

Friedman above is again implicitly on target with his $40-an-hour example, as a useful definition of "competitiveness" is that jointly used by the National Academy of Sciences, National Academy of Engineering, and the Institute of Medicine in a 2010 report with the cyclonic name, *Rising Above the Gathering Storm Revisited: Rapidly Approaching Category 5*.[31] "Competitiveness," the presidents of the three organizations wrote, pertains to the ability of Americans to compete for quality jobs in an employment market that increasingly knows no geographic boundaries.

But what if the biggest problem threatening many American workers—especially those without compelling skills—is not just the way competition in getting hired is getting even stiffer, but the way in which many jobs for which they are equipped are growing scarcer or simply fading away entirely? A useful way of framing this profound worry for many is to consider the relative numbers of workers that major businesses, including start-ups have needed, then versus now.[32]

Industrial-age entrepreneurship required great numbers of people, tens of thousands in many cases. To make cars and steel, Henry Ford and Andrew Carnegie had to build immense factories as well as other fixed assets. Much of the labor was just that; semi-skilled and unskilled men whose muscle power was the first Job One. As for women, paperwork was everywhere, meaning secretaries and clerks were, too. In some ways not a great deal changed by the early days of giant electronic firms, as IBM and Hewlett-Packard were obliged to once again build large factories, people them plentifully, hire large sales forces, and the like.

In sum, it was cheaper to do nearly everything that needed to be done on site and at home rather than via outsourcing in any serious way. But all this changed, of course, with the advent of modern communications; miracles wrought by IBM, HP and other remarkable enterprises with equally remarkable speed. Seemingly more mundane advances, such as improved air freight with its cheaper and more frequent deliveries, also moved the ball forward, which is to say in many instances, overseas.

As for newer mega-start-ups like Facebook and Google, they employ even fewer non-knowledge workers as their virtual products have no physical components beyond software codes running in server farms tied to high-capacity fiber optic pipes. And even much of what legitimately can be viewed as intellectual work can be done remotely from lowest-cost locations. All of which is to say, big start-ups still make big bangs, but in terms of problems addressed here, they don't necessarily spend big bucks hiring men and women trying to make it without reasonably robust skills and latter-day talents.

Increasingly by the day and work week, we live in an occupational world in which people with good educations tend to get rewarded and people without tend to get penalized. Or to colloquially and perhaps rudely repeat the most bottom of lines: To succeed economically, Americans increasingly have to bring something to table. But from everything we know, men and women who grow up in single-parent and no-parent homes—always on average—have less to bring.

This is a good point to reinforce the fact that high nonmarital birth rates and high divorce rates are far from exclusively or decisively a low-income phenomenon, but increasingly one characterizing and shaping the great American middle. Returning to a new-trail 2010 report,[33] Brad Wilcox and Elizabeth Marquardt wrote about how family fragmentation has come to be a powerful force also among Americans they describe as comprising the "moderately educated" middle; a full 58 percent of the adult population who have graduated high school but who don't have four-year college degrees. Or if you will, they looked closely at a swath of men and women big enough to cover the bulk of the nation, very much including those cited by Tom Friedman above. Wilcox and Marquardt's numbers and other data include amazements like these:

- In the 1970s, moderately educated and highly educated Americans were equally likely to be married. Current odds, however, of a moderately educated man or women now being married more closely resemble those of the least educated.
- Going back to the early 1980s, only 2 percent of babies born to *highly* educated mothers (those with at least four-year college degrees), as opposed to 13 percent of those born to *moderately* educated mothers (as defined by having a high school diploma but not a four-year collegiate degree), as opposed to 33 percent of those born to *least* educated mothers (girls and women without high school degrees) came into this life outside of marriage. By the late 2000s, the corresponding proportions were 6 percent, 44 percent, and 54 percent, respectively. Meaning, members of the moderately educated middle are now significantly more likely—not just modestly more likely—than highly educated Americans to have children without first getting married.
- Between the 1970s and 2000s, the percentage of 14-year-old girls with highly educated mothers who lived with both parents actually increased, albeit barely, from 80 to 81 percent. The percentage of 14-year-old girls, however, with moderately educated mothers who also lived with both parents fell markedly from 74 to 58 percent, while the corresponding numbers for 14-year-old girls with least educated mothers fell from 65 to 52 percent.

In other words, not only was the just-cited decrease steepest for girls with moderately educated mothers, but as described by Wilcox and Marquardt in one of their summations, "[T]he family lives of today's moderately educated Americans increasingly resemble those of high-school dropouts, too often burdened by financial stress, partner conflict, single parenting, and troubled children." As for what all this implies more specifically for economic growth, the focus of this chapter, their argument is again persuasive. Moderately educated Americans, as opposed to their better educated fellow citizens, are now less likely to embrace "bourgeois values and virtues" such as delayed gratification, temperance, and an emphasis on education; which is to say, the "*sine qua nons* of personal and marital success in the contemporary United States." This is the case, in contrast again to highly educated Americans, as well as their children, who are more likely to "adhere devoutly" to putting education, work, marriage, and childbearing in that four-part ordering, thereby maximizing their chances of "making good on the American dream and obtaining a successful family life."

Perfectly aligned here is further evidence that divorced and separated parents contribute "significantly" less than do married parents to their children's college education. This is the case in terms of absolute dollars, as well as a proportion of their income, as well as a proportion of their children's financial need. More specifically, two sociologists from Rice and Harvard universities, in a study of 2,400 dependent undergraduates, discovered that children of mothers and fathers who were married to each other took care of about 23 percent of their own college expenses. The corresponding figure for students whose parents divorced was more than twice as high, at 58 percent. As for students whose parents divorced but then remarried, the figure was much closer to the higher than lower ratio at 47 percent—a fact which shouldn't be surprising insofar as the research literature, as we've seen, is thick with evidence of children in stepfamilies more closely resembling children living with a single-parent rather than children living with two birth parents on a wide range of measures. Based on their statistical models, in fact, the two scholars, Ruth N. Lopez Turley and Mathew Desmond, predicted that divorced or remarried parents earning $70,000 a year are likely to contribute less to their children's collegiate expenses than married parents making only $40,000 annually.[34]

Given the high marks for success attributed to learning, let's have one more go at contrarian notions about how important education truly is when it comes to our overall economic performance. Former Gov. Tim Pawlenty, for example, has been known to say that Minnesota will never do sufficiently well with "half the team on the bench." Yet as egalitarian and enlightened as that sounds, and notwithstanding what scholars like Eric Hanushek have discovered about the importance of a nation's math and science skills, might Pawlenty's comment be more rhetorically than substantively compelling in the sense (making the case again) that the greatest economic threat faced by the United States is not that other countries may surpass our GNP, but rather, how growing inequalities in personal income and wealth will cause us to fracture jaggedly?

The aforementioned National Academy of Sciences, the National Academy of Engineering, and the Institute for Medicine—a pretty elite group—have been thinking hard about everyman education and economic vitality. It's fair to say they're concerned that average Americans don't know nearly enough, and unless American schools get a great deal better very soon, the nation will suffer for it. At the very same time, though, they cite an economist named Jonathan Hughes, who has argued that the welfare of society, tied as it is to innovation and entrepreneurship, hangs on but a small number of fellow citizens.[35] Another economist, William Baumol, spoke in similar spirit, when in an interview, he talked about how in the "international map of physics competition," the United States routinely comes in "number 27 or 19 or something unworthy like that." Nevertheless, year after year, Americans win loads of Nobel Prizes in the field.[36]

So what is it? Do American kids have to start challenging kids from Singapore, Seoul, and Shanghai in math and science for the United States to economically prosper, never mind continuing to lead the world? Or, at the end of days and fiscal years, does it really matter all that much? (China—or more specifically, boys and girls in Shanghai—participated in 2009 for the first time in the OECD's Programme for International Student Assessment. Sixty-five nations in all were involved, with samples of 15-year-olds in each tested in math, science, and reading. Students in Shanghai finished first in all three categories, and not by a little.[37])

So as not to be too iconoclastic (which is to say, simply wrong), let's read-ily agree that Americans' academic performance as a *people* is a big and con-sequential deal. But maybe, just maybe it's not as big and as consequential a deal as various boilerplates have it, as we've been getting by quite nicely as a nation with our teenagers nevertheless performing less well in key subjects than teenagers in countries like Iceland, Hungary, and Spain, never mind predictable places in East Asia. Yet as worrisome conclusions go, there is precious tiny doubt that as long as large-scale family fragmentation is implicit in very large numbers of citizens doing less well in school than they other-wise might . . . which in turn leads their doing economically less well than they otherwise might . . . with everything compounded by our best-educated citizens reaping bigger and bigger financial rewards all the time, cleavages and gaps grounded in class and race cannot help but grow.

Except for sociologists, most Americans try hard not to dwell on social class, viewing such preoccupations as at least mildly alien to American Dreams and Experiments. Yet that is not to say that a growing number of observers in various lines of work haven't been saying an increasing amount about income inequality in recent years. Pungently from the left, for example, journalist Timothy Noah has written about how he had always viewed Latin

America as a collection of failed societies because of their "grotesque maldistribution of wealth." But now he has come to learn (via the CIA, he's quick to note) that "income distribution in the United States is more unequal than in Guyana, Nicaragua, and Venezuela, and roughly on par with Uruguay, Argentina, and Ecuador. . . . Economically speaking, the richest nation on earth is starting to resemble a banana republic."[38]

To which cagey scholars on the right like William Voegeli cite unconventional scholars on the left like Dalton Conley, who has argued that economic inequality is a "luxury" that people worry about in lieu of more pressing problems. And while inequality really does make Europeans less happy, in this country (according to Conley) "only the moods of rich leftists are adversely affected." The biggest issue, Voegeli quotes Conley as suggesting, is not inequality "in and of itself," but instead, the need to maximize opportunity across the board.[39]

No argument herein rises or falls based on how Hugo Chavez divvies up paychecks in Caracas. Just suffice it to say, as a child of the lower-middle class who grew up in Queens, I'm eternally grateful I was born in North America rather than South. Also suffice it to say, it's conceivable that critical masses of Americans someday may not be as accepting as they currently are of CEOs making hundreds of times more money than employees on the line. This, I would suggest, is a possibility, even though the unusually astute political analyst Michael Barone was firmly on Voegeli and Conley's page when he wrote shortly after the 2010 elections that "American voters are not seething with envy over income inequality and not convinced that we'll all do better if the government takes away more of Bill Gates' money."[40]

But for the sake of argument, let's accept that both Noah and Voegeli, clever combatants as they are, draw equal blood, even bloody laughs. Also for the sake of argument, let's keep in mind the United States is not the only country in the world with painfully serious problems, whatever and wherever they may be, including China's one-child-per-family demographic time bomb[41] as well as India's still widespread illiteracy. And let's certainly take comfort in the strong unlikelihood of the United States exploding or imploding economically anytime soon or much longer term. Which leaves us where? Hardly a whit less threatened by an experiment in child bearing and rearing heretofore unknown by any great power.

Which, in turn, leaves and begs a not-so-modest question for the next chapter: Based on what we know about millions of children growing up in far-less-than-ideal family situations, what different kinds of education might work best for them?

Notes

1. For an excellent example, see *Marriage and Caste* in *America: Separate and Unequal Families in a Post-Marital Age*, by Kay S. Hymowitz (Chicago: Ivan Dee, 2006).

2. Benjamin Scafidi, *The Taxpayer Costs of Divorce and Unwed Childbearing: First-Ever Estimates for the Nation and All Fifty States*, Institute for American Values, et al., 2008. For a thematically and bottom-line similar study, see *The One Hundred Billion Dollar Man: The Annual Public Costs of Father Absence*, by Steven L. Nock and Christopher J. Einoff, The National Fatherhood Initiative, 2008.

3. Ron Haskins and Isabel Sawhill, *Creating an Opportunity Society* (Washington, DC: Brookings Institution, 2009), p. 42.

4. Adam Thomas and Isabel Sawhill, "For Richer or For Poorer: Marriage as an Antipoverty Strategy," *Journal of Policy Analysis and Management* 21 (2002), pp. 587–99.

5. *The Economic Impact of the Achievement Gap in American's* [sic] *Schools*, McKinsey & Company, April 2009.

6. The Programme for International Student Assessment (PISA) has been conducted since 2000; Trends in International Mathematics and Science Study (TIMSS) is a continuation (according to Eric Hanushek) of an international testing series that started in 1960.

7. Eric A. Hanushek, "The Economic Value of Education and Cognitive Skills," in *Handbook of Education Policy Research*, Gary Sykes, Barbara Scheider, and David N. Plank, editors (New York: Routledge, 2009), p. 42.

8. Ibid., p. 43–44 .

9. Ibid., p. 46.

10. Arnold Kling and Nick Schulz, *From Poverty to Prosperity: Intangible Assets, Hidden Liabilities and the Lasting Triumph Over Scarcity* (New York: Encounter, 2009), p. 144.

11. Eric A. Hanushek, "The Seeds of Growth," *Education Next*, Fall 2002, pp. 10–17.

12. A year after Hanushek wrote in 2002 about the United States having a higher college attendance rate than the average OECD country, we fell below that organization's mean in "Expected Total Years of School Completion, Including Higher Education." Eric Hanushek and Alfred A. Lindseth, *Schoolhouses, Courthouses, and Statehouses* (Princeton: Princeton University Press, 2009), p. 28.

13. *The Economist*, March 24–30, 207, p. 40.

14. Suet-Ling Pong, Jaap Dronkers, and Gillian Hampden-Thompson, "Family Policies and Children's School Achievement in Single- Versus Two-Parent Families," *Journal of Marriage and Family*, 65 (August 2003), p. 681.

15. Kathryn S. Schiller, Vladimir T. Khmelkov, and Xiao-Qing Wang, "Economic Development and the Effects of Family Characteristics on Mathematics Achievement," *Journal of Marriage and Family*, 64 (August 2002), pp. 730–742.

16. Bridget J. Goosby and Jacob E. Cheadle, "Birth Weight, Math and Reading Achievement Growth: A Multilevel Between-Sibling, Between-Families Approach," *Social Forces* (87)3, March 2009, pp. 1291–1320.

17. Kling and Schulz, p. 145.

18. Laurence J. Kotlikoff and Scott Burns, *The Coming Generational Storm: What You Need to Know about America's Economic Future* (Cambridge: MIT Press, 2005).

19. Ibid., p. 30.

20. George Will, "Let the States Mix It Up on Education," (Minneapolis) *Star Tribune*, January 27, 2011, p. A11.

21. Timothy Noah, "Introducing the Great Divergence," *Slate*, posted September 3, 2010.

22. Ibid. Also see, for example, Gary Solon, "Cross-Country Differences in Intergenerational Earnings Mobility," *Journal of Economic Perspectives* 16, No. 3 (Summer 2002), pp. 59–66.

23. Gerald Auten and Geoffrey Gee, "Income Mobility in the United States: New Evidence from Income Tax Data," *National Tax Journal*, June 2009.

24. Isabel Sawhill, "Do We Face a Permanently Divided Society?" Paper for Tobin Project conference on *Democracy & Markets: Understanding the Effects of America's Economic Stratification*, April 1, 2010.

25. Auten and Gee.

26. Mitch Pearlstein, "'Gap' Package Left Out Some Key Factors," (Minneapolis) *Star Tribune*, December 25, 2005.

27. Paul Krugman, *The Conscience of a Liberal* (New York: W.W. Norton, 2009), p. 126.

28. Thomas L. Friedman, "The New Untouchables," *The New York Times*, October 20, 2009. Friedman, by the way, uses the word "untouchables" not to refer to people at the very bottom, but rather men and women (specifically lawyers in this instance) "who have the ability to imagine new services, new opportunities and new ways to recruit work. . . ." Most likely to keep their jobs, in other words, are the most skilled.

29. Personal letter from Jim Merritt, president of Premier Precision Group, January 7, 2011.

30. Hymowitz, p. 4–5.

31. *Rising Above the Gathering Storm, Revisited: Rapidly Approaching Category 5*, The National Academy of Sciences, 2010, p. xiii.

32. I'm indebted to Keith Kostuch for several of the insights which follow. Personal e-mail correspondence, November 30, 2010.

33. W. Bradford Wilcox and Elizabeth Marquardt, *When Marriage Disappears: The New Middle America*, The National Marriage Project, December 2010.

34. Ruth N. Lopez Turley and Matthew Desmond, "Contributions to College Costs by Married, Divorced, and Remarried Parents," *Journal of Family Issues*, as reported by *Inside Higher Education*, December 10, 2010. While Turley and Desmond conducted more recent interviews with parents, it should be noted that the survey portion of their work drew on less-recent data from the National Postsecondary Student Aid Study of 1995–96.

35. *Rising Above the Gathering Storm*.

36. Arnold Kling and Nick Schulz, p. 290.

37. Chester E. Finn, Jr., "A Sputnik Moment for U.S. Education," *The Education Gadfly*, Thomas B. Fordham Institute, December 9, 2010.

38. Timothy Noah, "The United States of Inequality: Introducing the Great Divergence," *Slate*, September 3, 2010.

39. William Voegeli, "Why Isn't Populism More Popular?" *StarTribune.com*, December 1, 2010.

40. Michael Barone, "Even After the Shellacking, 2012 Looks OK for Obama," *Washington Examiner*, December 26, 2010.

41. "In 2005, China's median age was 32. By 2050, it will be 45 and a quarter of the Chinese population will be over the age of 65. The government's pension system is almost nonexistent, and One-Child has eliminated the traditional support system of the extended family. . . . China will have 330 million senior citizens with no one to care for them and no way to pay for their upkeep." Jonathan V. Last, "America's One-Child Policy: What China Imposed on Its Population, We're Adopting Voluntarily," *The Weekly Standard*, September 27, 2010.

Chapter 5

Strengthening Learning

Lest there be any confusion in what follows, and at the risk of leaving the impression of both protesting and praising too much, I have the greatest respect for educators who devote themselves to the often hard-to-teach children talked about in these pages. Their jobs are the definition of tough, and whatever talents I may have, I certainly don't have theirs, at least not in sufficient quantity to enrich and turnaround newly lucky lives in the ways they do every day. How can one not be impressed to the point of grateful awe by people like Geoffrey Canada of the Harlem Children's Zone, the late Orlando Gober of Rice High School, also in Harlem, and the talented and sacrificing teachers, among many others across the country, they have led? Yet no matter the tenacity of their commitments and ministries—here are the depressing points—their often remarkable victories are usually not remarkable enough. Yet when they do occur, they don't necessarily portend adequate educational progress other places in our country, especially in our great cities.

Do we need to ceaselessly plug and pursue as if the prospects of millions of boys and girls are at stake, as they are? The only acceptable answer is yes. Yet can we realistically expect as much progress as we require as long as American families are fragmenting so? The inescapable answer this time is no.

In such mixed light, the analysis which follows might be read as wrestling with itself, as I will argue that we do, in fact, have a decent sense of the kinds of instruction mostly like to work best for children suffering father wounds and similar problems. But just because it's easy to identify truly exceptional programs in many places throughout the United States, that's far from likewise saying they can be successfully replicated and brought to scale nearly often enough. But first things first, as we need a firm sense of how difficult educational reform really is even when it comes to the most fortunate students and families. We also need to recognize (this should go without saying, but it often requires repeating) how the word "reform" doesn't merely mean "change," but actual improvement. A good but again sobering way of doing these things is to quickly review an incomplete but still long list of major educational movements and strategies pursued over the last nearly half-a-century.

What specifically has been tried going back to the first iteration of the Elementary and Secondary School Education Act, passed in 1965 as part of the War on Poverty? Just about everything educators, politicians, foundation officials and others could think of may sound glib, but it's no less accurate.[1]

- The three-legged stool of standards, assessments, and accountability. No change in K–12 over the last two decades-plus has been wider and deeper than the drive to strengthen academic standards, then testing whether students meet them, and subsequently and somehow holding schools and other players accountable if boys and girls fail to do well.
- Increased spending. While growth in K–12 spending has slowed in recent years along with the rest of the economy, it still has grown on an inflation-adjusted, per-pupil basis going back to mid-century by factors of two, three, and more.
- Smaller classes. As spending has gone up dramatically, class sizes have gone down, albeit not as dramatically. By one calculation cited in 2005,[2] while K–12 enrollments grew by about 50 percent over the previous approximately 50 years, the number of teachers *nearly tripled* over the same period. One of the great mysteries of modern education (or not so great, given the substantial rise in administrators and other non-classroom personnel) is why class sizes haven't grown *as* small as the increase in dollars suggests.
- Smaller schools. Admiration for smaller schools—"where everyone knows your name"—has been rediscovered in recent years. Sometimes this is implicitly framed as a matter of small schools being more educationally helpful than small classes. It's also an implicit or explicit acknowledgment that for all their frequent benefits, school mergers and district consolidations have come with costs.
- Teacher-run schools. Perhaps the best known example is Minnesota New Country School in rural Henderson, a charter covering sixth through twelfth grades.
- Privately managed public schools and districts. Perhaps the best known private contractor nationally (or "partner" as it prefers) is Edison Schools.
- Public school choice. This category also can be divided into several components, particularly when it comes to pivotally important charter schools, first adopted in Minnesota in 1991. In the half-dozen years beforehand

Minnesota also led the way in adopting open enrollment across district lines, formerly understood as the Berlin Walls of public education, as well as "Post-Secondary Educational Options," a program enabling high school juniors and seniors to take college courses.

- Private school choice. This category once again can be divided, principally into publicly funded and privately funded programs enabling low-income children to attend private, including religiously animated schools. While these ventures have been energetically pursued by eclectic coalitions across the country, relatively very few have been instituted, as opposition from the educational establishment and other sources, but especially the National Education Association and the American Federation of Teachers, continues to be ceaseless and powerful.
- Extra courses. The 1993 National Commission on Excellence in Education (the "rising tide of mediocrity" report) urged that all students take four years of English, three years of math, three years of science, three years of social studies, and a half-a-year of computer science. College-bound students were said to also need two years of a foreign language.
- Extra-intensive new schools. The best known example here is KIPP (Knowledge Is Power Program). Among other key differences, these are institutions, located invariably in lower-income communities, in which school days and school years are much longer than those found almost anyplace else, at least in the United States. Not unrelated here are charter and other schools inspired by literature scholar E. D. Hirsch, starting with his seminal book, *Cultural Literacy*.
- Early childhood education. Increasingly seen as the educational endeavor for which expansion is most essential if low-income children are to catch up academically and otherwise make it, advocates routinely reinforce their view by citing a small number of well-studied programs mainly in Michigan, Illinois, and North Carolina.
- Compensatory education. Nothing like federally funded Title I programs existed before 1965 aimed at helping low-income students behind in their work. They now constitute a significant source of income for many schools and districts.
- Special education. Although originally intended, by definition, to help but a small minority of children, special education programs (and funding for them) have grown markedly as definitions of handicapping conditions have grown, especially in terms of *learning* as opposed to *physical* disabilities.
- Multicultural education. Perhaps no word in American education has had a more meteoric and consequential rise in the last generation than "diversity." No desideratum has been more ubiquitous than "celebrating" it, and barely a textbook or curriculum has escaped being rewritten by it.

- Bilingual education. Propelled by friendly legislation, friendly court rulings, friendly colleges of education, and not-always-smiling proponents, many boys and girls for whom English is not their first language have been assigned to classes in which English has been spoken hardly at all.
- Different ways of teaching reading. "Whole Word" replaced phonics in many instances. Stellar results did not follow.
- Different ways of teaching math. "New Math" often replaced what was dismissed as "Old Math." Stellar results did not follow.
- Different ways of teaching teachers. Various commissions, foundations, and professional associations have conducted major studies and projects aimed at improving the preparation of new and veteran teachers as well as strengthening the rigor of colleges of education more broadly.
- Different ways of compensating teachers. Many merit-pay plans aimed at improving student performance have been proposed, with far fewer adopted.
- Different ways of hiring teachers. Under the nomenclature of "alternative teacher certification," states either aggressively or not-so-aggressively have made it feasible for mid-career men and women, as well as other non-education majors, to enter teaching without spending years earning traditional teaching degrees.
- Desegregation. Attempts have included the creation of magnet schools and the busing (both voluntarily and involuntarily) of millions of boys and girls. Increasingly, efforts to integrate focus on class rather than race.
- Neighborhood schools. Once desegregation efforts mostly failed, the virtues of neighborhood schools (both real and imagined) often were rediscovered, not least by parents and political leaders of color.
- High tech. Rarely have schools taken more than minuscule advantage of what technology has had to offer instructionally. Nevertheless, not only is virtual education or digital learning growing in sophistication and acceptance, but as opposed to conventional *reforms* which can be politically blocked, they are best understood as a *force* susceptible to slowing, but immune to being stopped entirely or for long, no matter the political opposition.
- Improved ties between schools and parents. Many have sought to strengthen communication and collaboration between teachers and administrators on the one hand, and low-income parents on the other.
- Improved ties between schools and businesses. In addition to collaborations often involving gifts of computers and employee mentoring of students, business groups also are routinely key players in blue-ribbon commissions reviewing the state of American education in various cities and states as well as the nation as a whole and proposing recommendations for improvement.

- Decentralization. Many school districts, especially in big cities, have sought to improve academic performance by decentralizing governance in various ways. Sometimes this has taken the form of parent-rich school and community councils. Other times, principals have been given greater authority in site-based management reorganizations.
- Centralization. Many school districts, especially in big cities, have sought to improve academic performance by centralizing governance in various ways. Sometimes they have done so by hiring retired military officers to spiff things up. Occasionally, these have been the very same districts that first tried decentralizing.

In no way am I suggesting that this list is composed of mostly bad or inferior ideas, as many of the entries remain imperative, starting with the need to more than marginally raise academic standards, accurately determine what kids really know, and based on those results, take necessary and sometimes painful actions to rectify shortcomings. Likewise, KIPP and similarly demanding programs have demonstrated their value, and I would argue that expanded educational freedom is essential, as is assuring that progress in virtual education not be retarded by interest group opposition or all-purpose stasis. The litany's main point, rather, is that we have tried a lot of good things and spent a lot of good money, for decades now, without anything approaching commensurate progress, as witness barely budging NAEP scores and barely budging graduation rates, not to mention falling international rankings. In sum, pulling off real education reform—the kind where academic performance improves as much as we deem it must—is real rugged. Yet if this is the case even when students are from advantaged families, how much tougher is it when students are far less lucky?

Beyond repeating what we've already discussed about extra-high hurdles often confronting students in fragmented families, as well as beyond bromides about how changing direction can be hard under the best of circumstances, what else might be blocking progress for kids who need it most?

Big social programs and projects generally do not work as well as advocates predict. This is less a right-of-center politicized stricture, but more a lesson derived from sociologist Peter Rossi's well-known "iron law of evaluation," which holds that "the expected value of any net impact assessment of any large-scale social program is zero." Writing a few years into the new millennium, Timothy M. Smeeding and the late Daniel Patrick Moynihan drew on the axiom in discussing how no interventions had "seemed to reverse" the rising trend of single-parenthood and out-of-wedlock births since the 1960s, particularly in the African American community. A sentence earlier, they cited Eleanor Holmes Norton, who served as chair of the Equal Employment Opportunity Commission, whom they paraphrased as saying that "repair of the black family was central to any serious strategy to improve the black condition." With such failures, Smeeding and Moynihan wrote, the optimism of the '60s "gave way to an almost painful silence" on the subject.[3]

Rossi's iron law may not be ironclad literally, but it's accepted in academic circles as containing more than kernels of truth. Grover J. Whitehurst, for example, a former director of the Institute of Education Sciences in the U.S. Department of Education, has written that it's "more or less right," which is not to say that programs with "substantial positive impact" don't exist. Only that they are rare.[4] Less-well known, I should add, but supremely important for our purposes is Rossi's *"brass* law of evaluation" which states that "the more social programs are designed to change *individuals*, the more likely the net impact of the program will be zero [emphasis supplied]."[5]

All this is congruent with what the aforementioned Susan Mayer has argued about the limitations of money—which in many ways is to say *programs*—in improving the educational and other fortunes of children. Every generation of reformers, she has written, has believed it could solve the problems of poor boys and girls "by devising new and improved policies," but none of these have made more than small dents. In fact, she adds, "the sequence of policies implemented over the last hundred years strongly resembles the sequence of policies implemented over the previous hundred years."[6]

In this light, what makes anyone think it's anything less than extraordinarily hard and improbable to successfully bring exceptional educational programs to national scale? What makes anyone think, more specifically, that great numbers of educators are sufficiently eager to adopt various policies developed by "others," no matter how intrinsically terrific such approaches may be? For that matter, what makes anyone think that adequate numbers of powerful state and local players over and beyond teachers and administrators might be so inclined? Or, that there is enough money in state and local tills to the extent more dollars are required? Or on the chance that breakthrough practices are, in fact, adopted by large numbers of practitioners, what makes anyone think they will be replicated faithfully and accurately enough so as to succeed as originally celebrated?

All the evidence needed, it would seem, showing that bringing game-changing educational ideas to mass scale is beyond difficult has been demonstrated every school day since results of the "effective schools" research started emerging in the 1970s. If, after all, enormous numbers of superintendents, teachers, and others somehow have found it too taxing to assure that children are actually learning their lessons; that principals are strong instructional leaders; that all adults involved with a school are more or less on the same page; and that classrooms and hallways are orderly among other quite uncomplicated insights and rules, what makes anyone confident that more demanding aspirations stand a chance?

What about KIPP, you say? Given how its second generations of schools appear to have maintained the spirit and rigor of its original schools in Houston and the Bronx, it's a fair question. But as of this writing the grand total of up-and-running KIPP schools in the country is 99. Brilliant though they may be, prodigious in a coast-to-coast way they are not—nor are they ever likely to be precisely because of their uncommon spirit and unusual rigor.

All to which a distinguished educator like Thomas Payzant might mildly agree when he writes that, with 95,000 public schools in the United States, preparing all students to eventually graduate from high school and then be ready for postsecondary education without remediation, and doing so by effectively embracing standards-based reforms, might well be an "unreasonable, if not impossible" assignment to take to scale. Nevertheless, he does in fact believe there are compelling reasons to "invest and be hopeful about raising student achievement in urban education." One reason for his seemingly mild confidence—or, more exactly, five reasons—are five award-winning urban districts about which Heather Zavadsky writes; a book for which Payzant provides a sober but anticipative foreword.[7]

As for Zavadsky, a University of Texas official, she acknowledges that "some education commentators voice skepticism about the ability of educational reforms to actually affect student achievement on a scalable level, as few large-scale reforms have had significant measurable effect on student learning." She goes on to outline one such scholar's doubts and agrees that districts will continue to find such improvements to be "difficult." Yet she's very much of the mind that "intentional, sustained, patient focus on improving teaching and learning" by means of aligning instructional practices throughout a school system is something that "can be done in any district given the *right knowledge and tools* [emphasis supplied]."

All to which a skeptic might ask: What disaster or conspiracy has been preventing more districts from already taking advantage of these "right knowledge and tools"? Haven't they—just like the half-dozen or so key effective schools principles—been far from secrets for quite a spell now? There must be something menacing standing in the way. Might it be politics (broadly and not necessarily pejoratively defined)? Might it be bureaucracy (hard to control by its very nature)? Might there be too few leaders willing to get almost everybody in town mad at them (not unique to educational institutions)? Might creators of successful programs better grasp and more readily fight and die for them than second and third rounds of adopters (how could this not be the case)? Might we live in a very big country (yes)? Or might the everyday and handicapping complexities and stuff of urban—and suburban and not infrequently rural—education simply muck things up? Yes, one more time.

Zavadsky tells the story of obviously impressive districts in Connecticut, Florida, New Jersey, and two in California. Her reasoned faith threatens to make views like mine, in contrast, sound coldly disbelieving about a core American institution and the men and women, boys and girls in it. Not an attractive personal picture. But I'm compelled to ask two questions. Yes, children in the districts she writes about are doing better than they otherwise might, but are they and students in other saluted districts doing *well* by any reasonable 21st-century standard? And what about the kids from fragmented families: How are they doing compared to kids growing up with their two parents, all under the same roof? To the first question, based on reams of test results and comparative international data, the only answer is "no'; they're not doing nearly well enough, not that nearly enough American kids, regardless of their backgrounds, doing so. And to the second question, based on everything we've learned, it's impossible to imagine students growing up in single-parents homes, in the main, are doing as well as their classmates whose family stories are more traditional.

New York City public schools, especially under the leadership of superintendent Joel Klein, has received many salutes in recent years, including the highly regarded Broad Prize honoring urban districts in which student achievement has improved in attention-getting ways. Presented to the city in 2007, it's a serious award for significant accomplishment. Yet without suggesting that anything other than impressive work in the five boroughs led to it, consider the following 2010 controversy involving an oddly coupled Harlem Children's Zone and the Washington-based Brookings Institution.

In July of that year, the above-mentioned Grover "Russ" Whitehurst, by this time a senior fellow at Brookings, led a study in which he concluded that while students in the HCZ's Promise Academy charter school were in fact doing better than students in other regular NYC public schools, they were not doing better, on average, than students attending nearby charter schools in Manhattan and the Bronx. (Promise Academy, which enrolls students from elementary through high school, is the more established of the initiative's two charter schools.) More specifically, the HCZ kids were found to be scoring higher than about half the non-HCZ charter kids but lower than the better per-forming half. This was the case even though Promise Academy participated in the HCZ's celebrated comprehensive range of social and other services such as early childhood programs with parenting classes, fitness and nutrition programs, foster care prevention programs, community centers, and more, while the other schools featured none of these. "The inescapable conclusion,"

Whitehurst (along with his colleague Michelle Croft) wrote, "is that the HCZ Promise Academy is a middling New York City charter school."[8]

None of this is to suggest that Geoffrey Canada's Harlem Children's Zone is not an admirable program, as it very much is, and Whitehurst readily acknowledged it as such. His disagreement, rather, had to do with whether expensive wraparound services, the kinds which veritably define the HCZ, actually improve academic achievement and whether, thereby, they constitute a wise use of limited public dollars. In each instance his answer was a persuasive "no," although as one might expect, Canada disagreed vigorously on several scores.[9]

Here's a thought (not-unrelated to the spirit of Canada's response): Disagreements over test scores and their meaning notwithstanding, what if the full value of a program like the Harlem Children's Zone can't be adequately captured by a series of standardized tests? What if other possible virtues need to considered, such as stronger school safety, greater parental satisfaction, higher high school graduation rates, and who knows what other measures which, by definition, are impossible to gauge immediately, starting with college graduation rates and professional success? Without suggesting that reading, writing, and higher order arithmetic, along with science and other subjects, are anything but centrally important, this is a fundamentally fair and important point, and one we'll return to when discussing expanded educational choice below, especially the kind including religiously animated schools.

I recall the HCZ-Brookings episode to make three germane points. The first is to wonder how well boys and girls in New York City's prize-winning district schools really are doing if their counterparts in charter schools are doing measurably better. The second pertains to just how worthy of high-dollar emulation the Harlem Children's Zone truly is if its signature social programs have little if any bearing on academic achievement. As for a third point, is this not additional evidence, putting matters simply, that figuring out and then effectively replicating what works is awfully complicated?

But what about Florida, you ask? Isn't that a state, as teased in Chapter Three when I cited Governor Jeb Bush's great work, in which both white and minority students have made remarkable progress? Yes, it is, and "remarkable" is very much an apt word in regards to this blog post by Jay Greene about 2009 NAEP reading scores for Hispanic and African American fourth graders in the state. Bush served two terms as governor of Florida, from 1999 to 2007.

The NAEP released scores for the 2009 Reading exams for both 4th and 8th grade. Florida once again crushed the ball in improving student performance. While the nation's 4th grade reading scores remained flat, Florida's surged ahead.

In 2007, Florida's Hispanic students outscored 15 statewide averages for all students on 4th grade reading. Two years later, Florida Hispanics tied or outscored *31 statewide averages* . . . Florida's African American students *outscored or tied the statewide scores for eight states* [emphases in the original].[10]

Yet at the risk once more of snatching sour news from the jaws of sweet, and keeping in mind that examples of exceptional schools are much more likely to be found in lower grades, consider the following mixed evaluation of Florida's reform efforts by the Fordham Foundation in 2006. On the one hand, "Florida is one of just three states whose African American and Hispanic children made statistically significant progress in math and reading in the National Assessment of Educational Progress over the past decade." On the other hand, however, "Improved test scores in the elementary grades haven't been followed by better performance at the high school level and the state's graduation rate remains low, as does student performance on the SAT."[11] Four years later in 2010, the Florida Department of Education reported that dropout rates for blacks were almost exactly twice as high as for whites.[12]

There is decent reason to hope the substantially improving performance of Florida's younger students will continue as they grow up, but it's essential to recognize just how much progress still needs to be made, as it is enormous. We'll continue expanding on this broader national point in the next chapter.

Before completing these thoughts about obstacles to substantial improvement in K–12 education, we need to spend a few abridged moments on matters of culture and then politics. From there, it's on to a discussion about the kinds of programs and approaches which might work best—which is not to say routinely work *great*—for students growing up in a world of widespread and generationally deepening family fragmentation. As shorthand for school-related culture, think of school-related effort; or more specifically to begin, what has come of Far Rockaway H.S. in Queens, from which I graduated in 1966.

A year earlier in 1965, Richard Feynman, an alumnus from several decades prior, won the Nobel Prize for physics. Eleven years later, in 1976, two more Rockaway alumni won Nobel Prizes: Burton Richter, once again in physics, and Baruch Samuel Blumberg in medicine. That was also the year that another FRHS alumnus, Alan M Kriegsman, won a Pulitzer Prize for criticism. Not a bad stretch, and really not a bad American bicentennial year for an all-purpose high school in New York City that took all-comers, as opposed to better known albeit selective high schools like Stuyvesant and the Bronx High School of Science.

Yet all that was then, as Far Rockaway H.S. stopped accepting students a few years ago (in the understated words of Wikipedia) because of "bad grades." What in the world happened? I presume that some of the policies and practices that encouraged rigor when Feynman, et al., attended eroded over time (not that those policies and practices successfully sculpted me at the time). I absolutely know for a fact that too-small budgets weren't the culprit, as New York City public schools have been top-of-the-line in spending money on a per student basis forever. Which leaves what for an explanation?

It's impossible not to conclude that much of the responsibility rested with the kids themselves—not entirely surprisingly given the radically trickier family hands many of them were dealt compared to what my friends and I had to contend with. (Then again, in the case of Feynman and others, the Depression wasn't conducive to easy or giddy times either.) It's no leap, in other words, to assume (in the muted language of sociologist Lawrence Steinberg) that more recent generations of FRHS students had come to be less "strongly engaged in school emotionally" than generations of their predecessors had been.

Forgetting about family structure for a moment (or at least mostly fragmented types), journalist Malcolm Gladwell took an original tack in writing about impossible-to-deny connections between effort and academic performance on the part of Asian boys and girls.[13] It's not exactly novel for observers to note that both Asian and Asian-American students have been known to worker harder than their counterparts in the United States. It's also not rare to credit genetics, as in the commonplace assumption that Asians are simply and inherently better at certain subjects, especially math, than other groups. Gladwell, however, suggests that Asian children (and adults) are culturally primed to do better at math in part because their forebears spent a lot of time working very hard and long hours in exceptionally demanding rice paddies, all the while repeating effort-affirming aphorisms to each other over and over. A reach? Maybe. But who can say definitely no? Citing anthropologist Francesca Bray, Gladwell writes about Japanese, Chinese, and other farmers and how, if they were willing to "weed a bit more diligently, *and* become more adept at fertilizing, *and* spend a bit more time monitoring water levels, *and* do a better job keeping the clay pan absolutely level, *and* make use of every square inch" of their rice paddy, they'd harvest a bigger crop. Throughout history and unsurprisingly, he contends, people who have grown rice "have always worked harder than most almost any kind of farmer."

As for the aphorisms, peasants working 3,000 hours a year in the "baking heat and humidity" of leech-filled Chinese rice paddies, would say things to each other like: "No food without blood and sweat." Or sometimes, "Don't depend on heaven for food, but on your own two hands carrying the load." And most telling of all, according to Gladwell: "No one who can rise before dawn three hundred and sixty days a year fails to make his family rich."

How does this translate to young people hitting the books now? One mani-festation as well as proxy is the willingness of students in different countries to fill out long questionnaires at the start of international tests in math and science. As it turns out, the nations in which students tenaciously complete the most questions are the very same nations which score best on the actual math exams themselves. Actually, the correlation has been known to be per-fect, with the two rankings lining up identically with each other. So which countries, Gladwell asks, lead both lists? The answer, he says, shouldn't sur-prise: Singapore, South Korea, Taiwan, Hong Kong, and Japan. And what do those five have in common? "[T]hey are all cultures shaped by the tradition of wet-rice agriculture and meaningful work."

But as exquisitely congruent as certain cultures and superior academic performance can be, other cultures—or for our more precise purposes, subcultures—can be equally and destructively incongruent with learning, as seen in what presumably crippled my alma mater before its fall. And no such sets of norms, beliefs, and behaviors are more toxic when it comes to the academic fortunes of many children of color—which is to say, disproportion-ately boys and girls growing up in single-parent and no-parent homes—than the notion that endeavoring hard and succeeding in school is tantamount to "acting white."

Again, no lengthy dissertation is needed here, as the pathology (and that's what it is) has come to be well known, if not always acknowledged or dealt with sufficiently seriously. Linguist John McWhorter, for instance, in review-ing and praising Stuart Buck's very good recent book on the subject,[14] recalled the not always rational and collegial reactions to a book of his own a decade earlier. "I was hardly the first to bring up the 'acting white' problem," he wrote. "An early description of the phenomenon [came] from a paper by John Ogbu and Signithia Fordham in 1986, and their work was less a revelation of the counterintuitive than an airing of dirty laundry. You cannot grow up black in America and avoid the 'acting white' notion, unless you by chance grow up around only white kids." To substantiate his point, McWhorter cites Roland Fryer, the Harvard economist we met earlier in conversation with Geoffrey Canada, who has statistically shown, based on a very large sample, how high-achieving African American students have many fewer friends, on average, than do high-achieving students of other backgrounds.

Suffice it to say, the academic penalties suffered by black students because of the profligate tossing of "acting white" as an epithet can be dispiriting and large. Also suffice it to say, they are exacerbated by the kinds of added bur-dens more common to fragmented rather than intact families.

In regards to politics, my basic conception of it is anything but pejora-tive, as I begin from the self-evident position that democracy is not possible without politics, and politics is not possible without politicians. But I also work from the premise as famously elucidated by John Chubb and Terry Moe that public schools often suffer too much democracy, disruptive and complicating as it can be. "It is one of the prices Americans pay for choosing to exercise direct democratic control over their schools."[15]

Returning once again to my home in Minneapolis, as I write, Superintendent Bernadeia Johnson continues to deal with controversies surrounding her decision to close several schools because of depleting enrollments and poor test scores, including an often venerated high school in a mostly African American neighborhood. True, if North High School was truly and adequately venerated, parents wouldn't have chosen to send their children to charter and other schools in the area in great numbers, causing enrollment to collapse to about 300. But that's not to say opposition to closing the institution hasn't been intense.

Also at play (although that's not exactly the right word) is the recent creation of a group called the "Public Education Justice Alliance of Minnesota," which opposes the closings, equating the very idea of charter schools with the "privatization of public education." According to a newspaper story, PEJAM leaders include two officials with the Minneapolis Branch of something called the Socialist Alternative, with a third leader, a Minneapolis teacher, quoted as saying approvingly that "public education is socialism by my definition." The story also noted how any attempt by the district to close additional schools will provide PEJAM an opportunity to "dust off its bullhorns and begin protests and e-mail blasts anew."[16] All of which is the group's absolute constitutional right, though it's hard to see how their less-than-consensual views and sharp-elbowed activism will not further complicate the system's management, thereby making the coherence of its mission and practice more problematic.

Then, in another flap but two weeks after that story broke, it was reported that four (of five) recently elected Minneapolis school board members had signed and sent stern letters to other members of the board demanding they quit their supposed recalcitrance and conclude long-prolonged contract negotiations with the local teachers union, the Minneapolis Federation of Teachers. Particularly intriguing and unpromising was not just that the four letters were word-for-word identical, with all arriving in the same envelope, but they also were all on MFT letterhead.[17] So much for independent-minded governing board members representing the entire community and holding all parties to comparable task.

A simple question, especially in light of the fact that achievement gaps in Minneapolis public schools between white and minority children are among the highest in the nation: Is there anything about this barely sketched political lay of the land that's the least bit conducive or encouraging if a main goal is significantly narrowing those gaps anytime soon, much less significantly improving the performance of all children in the system? I would fear not.

As a postscript to this section, I should add that the above should not be read as a veiled rant against teacher unions, as my starting premise is that the principal fiduciary obligation of any union is safeguarding and advancing the well-being of its members and not that of anyone else. For a union to behave differently is to expect the unreasonable. Meaning, *of course* the National Education Association and the American Federation of Teachers are opposed and will remain opposed to any number of ideas discussed immediately below which I believe would be helpful, even essential if we are to adequately serve millions of girls and boys growing up in ways largely foreign to the ways most men and women beyond a certain age did. Would I prefer this fact of political and educational life not to be immutable, and do I contend that the NEA and AFT routinely need to be overcome and/ or bypassed if many more kids are to do much better? Needless to say yes is once again the answer in both instances. But frankly, as roadblocks go, teacher union heavy-treading needs to be understood as an unremarkable given and unflappably countered as such.

Much of the above, going back to the roster of unsuccessful and only partially successful reforms over the last several decades should be read as counterweights to overconfidence about what we think we know and are within reach of accomplishing. Or to the extent that we really do know what works quite well in some settings, that doesn't begin to mean we know how to replicate and bring highly effective programs to anything approaching decent scale. Likewise and nationwide in scope, the above is meant to reinforce the more modest view that "No Excuses" is more of noble rallying cry than feasible mission.

Gerald Grant, from whom we will hear more later captured many of these caveats when he wrote of unusually successful schools in poverty-stricken neighborhoods. "I have visited more than a dozen of them," he wrote in 2004, "including some Catholic schools, in New York, Chicago, Los Angeles, and other cities. They are almost always anomalies in that they have charismatic leaders and a strong, positive ethos that act as magnets to draw together the most stable, healthy, and highly motivated inner-city parents." But such parents, he contended, comprise only a small percentage of impoverished families in urban areas. Grant concluded that it is inaccurate to believe that "lighthouse" schools can be "broadly replicated within existing urban systems while maintaining the imbalances of financial and social capital characterizing today's urban and suburban schools."[18] In regards to taking terrific programs to scale, he also wrote elsewhere of the tendency of bureaucracies to reproduce themselves by "replacing leaders who exercise discretion with specialists who interpret rules."[19]

I might disagree with Grant regarding "financial capital" insofar as it's far from uncommon for big-city districts to spend more money per child than other districts, and at any rate, truly exceptional schools sometimes spend *less* per child than far less successful ones right in the neighborhood. But I concur totally in regards to his take on social capital.

With dour but necessary qualifiers out of the way, what might work at least reasonably well for the children we've been focusing on? Boys and girls contending not only with "father wounds," but not infrequently "mother wounds"? While single mothers outnumber single fathers, it's not as if men never raise children on their own, as a couple of million do.[20]

Any recitation of potentially worthwhile programs is no less lengthy than lists of roadblocks, as it is cramped not to believe that different educational strokes for different folks are essential routes for a nation of more than 300 million eclectic people. In much the same way the land-grant tradition has demonstrated that a surprisingly wide variety of things can be taught well and studied with profit in universities, there are more than just a few favored ways of educating and inspiring younger students as long as such methods are rigorously grounded and pursued. Yet at the same time, I would argue that when it comes to kids short a parent in their lives—and, therefore, often structure as well—most worthy of consideration are not necessarily any particular program or curricular preference as such, but what might be viewed as rigorous *approaches* and *expectations*: Themes brought to daily school life in notions such as intensity, nurturing, and paternalism, as well as Gerald Grant's vital conception of intellectual and moral authority. Such a starting point might further suggest the kinds of schools profiled in David Whitman's *Sweating the Small Stuff: Inner-City Schools and the New Paternalism.*[21] This is the case even though Whitman disagrees with Grant on some points, most notably in regards to the importance of money and the role of parental motivation.

Accompanied by strong discussions about how such schools have come to be—what ideas drive them, why they work so well, why some people probably never will be fans, and how they might be replicated across urban America—Whitman writes with detail about six secondary schools[22] in which achievement gaps between white and minority children have narrowed significantly, sometimes closing completely. Three of the schools are charter middle schools, one is a traditional neighborhood public school, one is a parochial high school, and one is the nation's lone urban boarding school for low-income students.

According to Whitman, tying the schools together (despite a variety of age mixes) are "deeply committed teachers" and "dedicated, forceful principals." Academic standards are high and students are tested frequently in order to monitor their performance and assess where they might need help. Rather than a dirty word, "accountability" is a "lodestar." All students pursue college-prep curricula, with none of the schools countenancing social promotions. Most of the schools have dress codes or require uniforms, extended days, and three weeks of mandatory summer school. Above all, Whitman, a journalist, writes of how the schools "share a paternalistic ethos supporting a common school culture that prizes academic achievement."

> By paternalistic I mean that each of the six schools is a highly prescriptive institution that teaches students not just how to think but how to act according to what are commonly termed traditional, middle-class values. Much in the manner of a responsible parent, these schools tell students that they need an "attitude adjustment." Like secondary schools elsewhere, paternalistic schools can value freedom, curiosity, and self-expression, too—but not at the expense of inculcating diligence, thrift, politeness, and a strong work ethic.

Beyond focusing on such virtues as abstractions, the schools make it clear to students precisely how they are expected to act. Boys and girls, Whitman continues, are required to "talk a certain way, sit a certain way, and dress a certain way," with even minor transgressions unacceptable. "These schools thus require and teach students to meet high expectations for behavior and academic achievement—rather than just encouraging them to aim high." As for what's wrought, Whitman persuasively concludes that the "new breed of paternalistic schools" looks to be the "single most effective way of closing the achievement gap," as no other model or method "seems to come close to having such a dramatic impact on the performance of inner-city students."[23]

Looking at some of the numbers, it would seem impossible to disagree and I have no interest in even trying, as I'm no less impressed and amazed than many others. For example, while only 31 percent of low-income 18–24 year olds across the country ever enroll in college, the three featured high schools send 85 percent of their graduates and more. As for the three middle schools, students regularly score in the 80th and 90th percentiles on nationally normed tests.[24] This is an apt spot to note again that twelfth-grade black students nationally score no higher than eighth-grade white students on various NAEP exams, with Hispanic students not doing much better. Some critics, including Richard Rothstein, whom we discussed in the Introduction, have claimed that the creaming of comparatively strong students from comparatively strong families has had a fair amount to do with the claimed success of KIPP and similar programs, though Whitman's rebuttal to this and similar charges is once again convincing—while also acknowledging some of the schools' flaws, including sometimes high attrition rates and an inability to serve significant numbers of children with disabilities.

As political scientist Larry Mead has explained more fully than perhaps any other current scholar, "paternalism" is not a readily revered precept in a nation defined more by freedom and liberty than any other two words. His work has focused mainly on matters of welfare reform over the last few decades, but Whitman applies it judiciously to education, as in his observation that "the new paternalistic schools . . . are founded on the premise that minority parents want to do the right thing but often don't have the time or resources to keep their children from being dragged down by an unhealthy street culture."[25] A crippling ethos of the street—returning to the notion of "father wounds," with Whitman this time citing Bill Cosby and psychiatrist Alvin Poussaint—in which city blocks can stretch on with "scarcely a married couple" as well as without "responsible males to watch out for wayward boys."[26]

In other words, think of Whitman's conception of paternalism not just as directive, but as in loco parentis epitomized. All of which, as one might imagine, is far from what many educational progressives take to be progress. This is the case even though another journalist has described "no excuses" schools as a "counterintuitive combination of touchy-feely idealism and intense discipline."[27] It's also the case despite the fact, as Whitman makes clear, that most of the brilliant founders of KIPP and similar schools view themselves as men and women of the left; a worldview on their part which nevertheless has not led to large numbers of other philosophically likeminded educators flocking to their pedagogical side. The result is just one more obstacle stunting replication.

My only serious problem with Whitman's arguments, and as already understood, is that I'm just not as confident about bringing such promising schools to scale. It's not entirely comfortable arguing as I do about the hard-to-escape academic costs of family fragmentation when Whitman writes as persuasively as he does about how many children in single-parent homes do superbly well in the schools he has studied. It's even more uncomfortable when Chester E. Finn, Jr.—a prolific education scholar whom I deeply respect and worked with (and for) for more than 30 years—reinforces Whitman's main points in the Foreword of *Sweating the Small Stuff*. But then, as to inadvertently allay concerns that I may have grown cynical, Whitman, lists twenty "habits of highly effective urban schools," with Number Thirteen reading: "Eliminate (or at least disempower) local teacher unions." It's a desideratum reminiscent of the proverbial economist who, upon facing financial demise, urges: "Imagine a million dollars." Or one of those guys trapped in a deep pit who advises: "Imagine a ladder."

Can determined educators sometimes find ways of bypassing the not-rare obstructionism of teacher unions? Of course they can, as witness the very men and women who lead the five public schools celebrated by Whitman. But note how four of the five are charter schools, with only one a district school (and for a host of reasons, decidedly not a "regular" one). So unless prospects are a lot better than I think they really are for turning the bulk of public elementary and secondary schools in big and smaller cities into charter schools anytime soon, highly effective habit Number Thirteen needs to be seen as other than lucky or likely. (Number Sixteen is also a good one: "Escape the constraints hobbling traditional district schools.")

Which is not to say—and I stress the point—that Whitman fails to point a way for potentially improving urban education significantly, as he very much does. Yet as with virtually all reform efforts, and at the risk of belaboring the point, rarely is the difficulty of successfully copying programs adequately credited. In the particular matter of the schools considered here, I find it hard to believe that adequate numbers of teachers and principals are temperamentally suited to so ceaselessly hold to such high and exacting standards. Matters of temperament aside, colleges of education are simply not thick with professors who subscribe to what Whitman and innovators like David Levin and Michael Feinberg of KIPP hold intellectually sacred, leading in turn to a teacher and administrator corps thin on paternalistic skills and devotions. Think Rousseau more than regimen.

Whitman does argue that "Socrates or Jaime Escalante don't need to take roll" in order for an inner-city school to succeed. It's a good line, grounded in his belief that early efforts to copy great schools have been encouraging. But I find him more convincing when he writes that "replicating successful paternalistic schools is a demanding task," and that while it probably can be done in "hundreds of schools with tens of thousands of students," getting to a half-million may take longer than supporters prefer. "Building the organizational capacity to support reform is painstaking work," he concludes. "Rushing the launch of new schools or opening copycat schools without ensuring that the crucial elements of the school model are present, could prove disappointing."[28] He's correct, of course, although I would put the caution even stronger. Yet be as all that may, the larger takeaway point here is that the type of education Whitman writes so enthusiastically about is one of the kinds the children we've been reading about crucially need.

This is an apt spot to note that the views of KIPP leaders, when it comes to the capacity of many single mothers in poor neighborhoods to spur and reinforce their children's educational lives, seem more optimistic than those of the aforementioned Gerald Grant. "The parents of students at KIPP Academy," the principal of the KIPP school in the Bronx has said, "are very similar to the parents I worked with when I taught in Newark, New Jersey. We look here for ways to encourage parents to read with their kids because that is not an expectation in many homes."[29]

As for Dr. Grant, I read his *The World We Created at Hamilton High* shortly after it was released in 1988. A study of how a high school in Syracuse, New York (not really named "Hamilton") swirled from a stable and almost all-white institution in the 1950s, through painful racial and other revolutions of the '60s and '70s, and then into a newly won albeit different stability in the '80s, I thought it was an exceptional book then and thought so once again when I reread portions more than two decades later. Somehow, however, it looks like I spent the entire interim mildly misquoting him, as I had distinctly remembered him spotlighting and building on the term "adult moral authority," which I very much resonated to. Yet the more recent review of the book suggests that the exact phrase in question—used to capture what teachers and administrators crucially need if schools and children are to flourish—was "moral and cognitive authority." No grand difference, obviously, and maybe he did use the one about grown-ups some place. Still, I would respectfully contend the addition of the word "adult" would have even better embodied what I continue to find compelling in Grant's conception of effective elementary and secondary education as well as what I would argue is essential if we are to best serve many of the children we've been talking about.

Early in a discussion about "authority" as a concept, Grant, now an emeritus professor of education at Syracuse University, quotes political theorist Hannah Arendt, who had died thirteen years earlier, in 1975.

"[T]he necessity for 'authority,'" she had argued, "is more plausible and evident in child-rearing and education than anywhere else," but that the cultural upheavals of the late 1960 had persuaded many to "want to eradicate even this . . . extremely limited form of authority." A few sentences later he quotes Arendt as saying: "Authority implies an obedience in which men retain their freedom." In between, Grant refers to the need of every organization, very much including elementary and secondary schools, to strike a right balance between authority and liberty.[30]

Further along, and referring specifically to private schools this time, he writes forcefully about the indivisibility of intellectual and moral virtue. Permit me to quote here at some length for reasons vital to arguments soon to be made. The several passages—growing out of visits Grant and his team made to a number of schools—also provide a much richer view of education than that gauged by test scores alone, which up until now have been our unavoidable preoccupation, as incomplete a measure of learning as deciles, quintiles, and quartiles inescapably are.

"Intellectual and moral virtue," Grant writes, "are seen as inseparable."

The aim is harmony. A good school is not one that is merely 'effective' in raising test scores. While intellect is important, maximizing test scores cannot to be the highest aim; rather, harmonious development of character must be the goal. There needs to be concern for rigorous academic education but also for qualities of endurance, resilience, responsibility, resourcefulness, and social responsibility. Teachers must have equal concern for mind and for character. . . . Like a good parent, the school does not want to squeeze a student too hard to raise his or her grade average at the expense of other aspects of development.

References to the spirit of the place were made frequently in both of the private schools we studied. Teachers expressed belief in the saving power of the community and exhibited great reluctance to expel or give up on a difficult student. As one teacher noted, "I can't let go of our rescue fantasy."

Adults make plain that they are responsible for shaping and maintaining [such an] ethos, and that how they do so makes a difference in the lives of all in the community. That sense of responsibility is fostered by detachment from bureaucracy. Teachers are not waiting for curriculum guides, nor are principals reading "directives." They are mutually creating and sustaining a world.

Or in sum for our purposes: "In these schools the adults stand unambivalently in loco parentis, and, like good parents, the teachers and staff exercise a caring watchfulness, concerned with all aspects of a child's development."[31]

Now, it's very much understood that not all private schools, religious or otherwise, are nearly so stellar. Actually, a good case can be made that given their autonomy and greater latitude, private schools should be considerably better than they frequently are. It likewise must be understood that Gerald Grant is very much a believer in public schools, who does indeed believe that "strong ties" need not be the exclusively sole province of sectarian and other private schools. Put more colloquially and less divinely, secular soul is not necessarily a contradiction in terms. Yet he also recognized back in the late '80s, when writing about Hamilton High, that American public schools were most likely to be characterized by "passive consent," which he described as "benign skepticism combined with intelligent consumerism" on the part of families.[32] Twenty-plus years later, I trust the comparison hasn't changed much.

Or, if you will, is it possible for public schools to create and maintain a "strong positive ethos" characterized by "moral and intellectual authority"? Yes, as Grant made clear. Is doing so, however, generally much harder in public compared to private schools? Clearly, again, he explained.

Returning to the boys and girls we've thinking most about, what might all this suggest so they might have better fighting chances? Without any leap, I would argue that the nation has an obligation—no less moral than pedagogical—to make it more feasible for them to attend schools in which loco parentis is more than unused Latin. Which brings us to vouchers and variations on that access-expanding theme; a pleasing thought to many, but far from all.

Anecdotal as the comparison is, it occurred to me while reading about the paternalistic *public* schools David Whitman writes about in *Sweating the Small Stuff*, that students attending them are doing significantly better academically than students at the paternalistic and *private* as well as *religious* Rice High School, as described by Patrick McCloskey in *The Street Stops Here*. One of the points being, that while I have long been involved in efforts to make vouchers much more widely available, it's easy to overestimate what they can realistically accomplish—exactly as is the case with every other educational idea or strategy on current or future agendas. A careful reading of the best empirical research on the topic suggests that the low-income and overwhelmingly African American and Hispanic students in the still-small number of publicly and privately funded voucher programs across the country often do better than they otherwise might in their former public schools, but by no means stunningly so.

Jay Greene, for example, in summing up the state of knowledge in the field, as understood in the middle of the last decade, noted there had been eight random assignment studies (the "Gold Standard" of social science research) to that point, with all eight having found "at least some" positive academic effects, with benefits in all but one of the eight investigations rising to statistical significance. It was indeed true, he acknowledged, that the studies differed on whether all students do better or only African American boys and girls; whether voucher students do better in both reading and math or only math; and whether improvements are small or large. But the basic lesson to be learned, he wrote, is that the "highest quality research consistently shows that vouchers have positive effects [academic and/or other kinds] for students who receive them." And that the evidence for these improvements justifies substantial confidence "especially when compared to much weaker evidence supporting most other education policies." The last reference is to proposed reforms such as spending more money and reducing class sizes.[33]

About the same time Greene wrote in 2005, William G. Howell and Paul E. Peterson reviewed studies of programs around the country in which low-income students received very modest vouchers ($1,030 on average) from the privately funded Children's Scholarship Fund. "Especially noteworthy," they wrote, was the "positive impact" on African American test scores, while also acknowledging that test scores of "students of other ethnic backgrounds were not affected by the voucher intervention." While far from boundless good news, Howell and Peterson did point out that the results were consistent with other findings showing that African American students tend to do better in private rather than public schools, not just in terms of test scores, but also "educational attainment, likelihood of pursuing an advanced degree, and future earnings." Even studies, they added, that find little comparable benefits for white students generally find that private schools help African American boys and girls.[34]

More recent research has focused much more on charter rather than voucher programs, but of the work that has been conducted on the latter, the pattern persists. Some studies show positive albeit statistically insignificant effects on test scores, with others showing no real difference. Yet in keeping with Howell and Peterson's comments about attainment, a study of the federally funded voucher program in Washington, DC, showed (in the words of political scientist Martin West), "big positive effects on graduation rates."[35] Surrounded by lukewarm and colder results, this is no small accomplishment. Paul Peterson reported similarly about Milwaukee in recent years ago, noting that the high school graduation rate for students there who were in voucher schools in ninth grade has been estimated as high as 87 percent (in 2007). In comparison, while graduation rates in Milwaukee Public Schools have in fact improved markedly, they haven't been higher than 70 percent (in 2009).[36] Results like these have led Peterson to conclude that the "biggest impact of creating a private educational experience for minorities comes in later years, and it has to do with keeping those kids in an educational environment that sustains them through graduation."[37]

Without getting too metaphoric, let's stick for a moment with the idea of "sustaining."

Minor wounds usually heal fast. Serious ones usually take a lot longer. In the lives of many children, it's hard to conceive of hurts much deeper than father wounds and other family absences and disruptions, very much including missing mothers, and not just rarely so. For many boys and girls in such situations, I would argue the most sustaining type of education—providing *sustenance* of the most personal and vital kind—is best found in the sort of school led by a nun I once met. The principal of a Catholic elementary school, I asked her what its mission was. "To manifest God's love in every child," she said, or words close to that. As educational mission statements go, this was simultaneously one of the briefest yet meatiest every devised. One can easily envision intellectually, as well as viscerally *feel*, how such a command might powerfully and uncommonly nourish, not all children by any stretch, but certainly many, including those most in need of feeding.

On more than one occasion, the late economist John Brandl wrote and spoke about how sectarian schools may well "provide some disadvantaged children with a substitute for the care they are not receiving from family and neighborhood—something possible but very rare in public schools."[38]

Actually, it's impossible to imagine this benevolent dynamic not at work in the lives of many children in private schools, helping them do better than some people might presume. It's also impossible not to recall James Coleman's argument that many at-risk children do better in private, especially Catholic schools precisely because of their greater sense of community.[39] Readily granting that men and women need not teach in a religious school in order to view their profession as a ministry, might it be possible that little in life is more powerful, educationally and in other ways, than what people of faith see as their obligations to God?

Let's begin to finish this chapter with a quick note about digital learning, an intriguingly promising teaching and learning method that might appear to be the antithesis of structured. And also early childhood education, a link in the academic chain that few observers don't believe is essential to the success of many low-income students and, thereby, in serious need of strengthening and expansion.

Unsophisticated as I may be about things high tech, I take it for granted that increasing numbers of young people, regardless of background, are equipped to take increasingly large advantage of digital learning. Actually, it may very well be my own age-related lack of competence that most prompts my confidence. But given how so many young people are expertly attracted, as if genetically endowed, to computers and other remarkable devices, my trust in their talent is likely not misplaced.

I'm struck, for example, by a comment by Curt Johnson, an old friend, about how digital learning (a term I used interchangeably with "virtual education") has the potential of "opening up the world" to low-income children. If navigated well, this can be an immense gift to boys and girls who, not infrequently, are familiar with little beyond their tough neighborhoods' nearby boundaries and hard demarcations. Johnson, not at all incidentally, is coauthor, along with Clayton Christensen and Michael Horn, of *Disrupting Class*,[40] one of the two most influential recent books dissecting and highlighting breakthrough connections between technology and learning. The second is Terry Moe and John Chubb's *Liberating Learning*,[41] with both books persuasively making the case that, as opposed to other educational *reforms* which can be stymied by numerous interests at multiple chokepoints, technology is a *force*; one which opponents may well slow down if they're determined, but never halt no matter how they might try. This is a distinguishing feature, however, for another discussion, as the pertinent virtue to be emphasized here is the way technology can "differentiate instruction" (in Moe and Chubb's words), better enabling students at "vastly different achievement levels to master broad and demanding curricula." Christensen and his colleagues write correspondingly of how education can be customized as never before because of ongoing technological breakthroughs. This is very big deal given how "students have different types of intelligence, learning styles, varying paces, and starting points."

Take reading, for example. Moe and Chubb claim that two-thirds of American children have difficulty with reading comprehension. For many of these students, they write, problems stem from a failure during the primary years to gain fluency, by which they mean the ability to decode letters and sounds quickly, automatically, and unconsciously into words, phrases, and sentences. Without fluency, they more than plausibly write, "students cannot comprehend complex text because the sheer concentration required to decode leaves little mental capacity to think about what is being read."

If all were right with the world, Moe and Chubb continue, schools would figure out and remediate such problems early on. But doing so "requires attention to individual decoding issues and lots and lots of practice." Instructional programs have been developed to do precisely this via very small groups, but obviously, this is an expensive approach, requiring lots of teachers and time. That's the bad news. The good news is that in recent years, according to Moe and Chubb, "technology has provided promising solutions that appear superior to teach-led approaches."[42]

As with any proposed educational change of course, efforts to focus more on virtual education and less on other pedagogical means doubtless will work wonderfully for some children, poorly for others, while making little if any difference for others still. But for boys and girls growing up in stressed situations who can handle the relative freedom, spending less time in conventional classes taught by teachers who may not convey their subjects as well as individualized, state-of-the-art computer programs, taking greater advantage of technological marvels would seem to be a terrific idea. And as for whether some kids might take the wrong kind of advantage of the latitude, Curt Johnson cites a former state commissioner of education who contends that it's "hard to be a behavior problem in a class of one." Actually, researchers in several places around the world have found that increased use of technology has led to fewer discipline problems and more engagement on the part of boys.[43] We'll return to this potentially potent point next chapter when discussing how to better help boys in particular become better prospects for marriage. One might also note here that digital learning is one of few areas where it's realistic to talk about possibly enhancing educational offerings and performance with unchanging or even fewer dollars.

In the matter of early childhood education, stars have been aligned for a long time now for its significant expansion, slowed more recently only by weak state and other public budgets. Whatever doubts might exist about its efficacy, it's hard not to go along with advocates who contend that the massive differences experienced and often suffered by a nation of children in the first few years of life (including in utero) command that we do *something*—with multiplied and reinforced early childhood programs constituting that precise something more often than not. Yet for all the enthusiasm and faith placed in such efforts in varied quarters, do we not risk exaggerating what even a well-funded continent-wide array of early childhood programs can realistically accomplish, getting carried away in much the same way as with all the other favored educational ventures we've been talking about? There would seem hardly any doubt.

Take, for example, the frequently saluted Perry Preschool study, the most famous of all explorations in the field. Routinely cited as proof that quality early childhood works, what is generally not noted is that the number of graduates of the extra-resource-rich program in Ypsilanti, Michigan who were tracked through high school totaled *58*, an absurdly small number from which to draw so many emphatic conclusions. Also rarely pointed out is that while Perry alumni have indeed done better in various ways than members of a control group, that's not to say they've done particularly well by more universal and civically essential standards. For instance at age nineteen, 31 percent of the boys and girls in the program had been arrested, 41 percent were unemployed, and 25 young women in the group had had seventeen pregnancies.[44]

Early education supporters also frequently cite two other celebrated programs: the Chicago Parent-Child Centers and the Abecedarian Project in North Carolina. Yet routinely not acknowledged here is how Abecedarian, for example, was an acutely intensive and fulltime endeavor, involving children from four months to age five, making it exorbitantly more expensive than any wide-scale replica ever could be. As for the Chicago initiative, while Ron Haskins of the Brookings Institution has noted it was the object of the "biggest study" ever conducted to produce "impressive long-term results," he acknowledges it wasn't a random assignment investigation, thus adding an "element of uncertainty" to the equation.[45]

Then there is Head Start, of course, about which one empirical finding stands above all others: To the extent that low-income children benefit academically, such boosts in performance largely and generally fade by the third grade or so. And at the risk of leaving the impression of piling on, please add two statistics that are hardly ever reported: Over the last 40-plus years the percentage of four-year-olds in one kind of pre-school program or another has grown by a factor of more than four, while the percentage of three-year-olds has grown by a factor of nearly eight.[46] Question: Is there any semblance of a sign that any of this had led to children, especially low-income ones growing up in single-parent homes, doing better in K–12 than they otherwise might? It's very hard to see how.

But as granted and alluded to above, with so many children in so much trouble, we have no acceptable option other than concertedly seeking to help them, often to the point of rescuing, well before they turn five. For confirmation, just recall what has been learned in recent years about the immensity of gulfs in vocabulary between children growing up in low-income, disproportionately single-parent households as opposed to middle-class and disproportionately two-parent environments. As for what kinds of early childhood programs might actually work best for boys and girls most in need, economist Art Rolnick, who has conducted seminal research on what he concludes is the very sizable economic returns of such activities, argues for the importance of starting early as possible in children's lives; affording parents substantial freedom in choosing programs; relying as much as possible on dynamic markets in charting adaptations; and constantly and rigorously assessing operations and results. Some might also pointedly assert the necessity of safeguarding early childhood programs from the constricting reach of educational bureaucracies and other built-in bindings.

If early childhood education programs are in fact to succeed by some reasonable measure and as large numbers of people hope, the above criteria would seem to be near-necessary requirements. Yet even so, and for all the undermining reasons we've considered throughout, I'm afraid I remain less hopeful than many. But so as end on a lifted, which is not to say high note, there's this exchange I had a few years ago with former Minnesota Gov. Al Quie, who came to be known as "Mr. Education" during his twenty-one years in Congress. Now in his late 80s, he continues to be one of the most active and forceful advocates for early childhood education in the state.

"How confident are you," I asked one morning, "that early childhood programs will accomplish what enthusiasts like you say they will?"

"I believe," he answered, "it behooves us to try as best we can to make this work because I have *no* confidence whatsoever things will turn out okay if we don't do anything. That's just not going to happen."[47]

The KIPP website talks about how "Demographics are not destiny." Absolutely true, as it would be a mammoth and self-defeating mistake to make believe that determination, personal responsibility and other hard virtues are afterthoughts. Still that doesn't mean that demographic tough breaks don't make for powerful and nasty shoves. If having marketable skills is more important all the time, but educational achievement is not increasing commensurately if at all, how can our nation not have problems? Or how can men and women without sufficient skills not have problems of both practical and intimate sort? But improving education adequately for great numbers of young people without instilling new life into marriage, as I've argued, is in the neighborhood of impossible. Imagining and pursuing ways of reviving the state of most important unions is where we now turn.

Notes

1. The following itemization draws on *Achievement Gaps and Vouchers: How Achievement Gaps are Bigger in Minnesota than Virtually Anyplace Else and Why Vouchers are Essential to Reducing Them*, by Mitchell B. Pearlstein, Center of the American Experiment, January 2007.

2. Chester E. Finn, Jr., *The Wall Street Journal*, March 22, 2005.

3. Daniel P. Moynihan, Timothy M Smeeding, and Lee Rainwater, *The Future of the Family* (New York: Russell Sage, 2004), p. xvii.

4. Grover J. (Russ) Whitehurst, Welfare Reform Academy, School of Public Policy, University of Maryland, 2007. Whitehurst's remarks, appropriately, were made in accepting the 2007 Peter H. Rossi Award for contributions to the science and practice of evaluation. In evaluating the Iron Law itself, he did qualify it by noting that "there is more variation around the mean than Peter anticipated, and that variation may have increased in the twenty years since Peter wrote about the Iron Law. Meaning, while large-scale social programs may not work as advertised or hoped for, they're not necessarily without value.

5. Ross Parish, "From Industrial Relations to Personal Relations: The Coercion of Society," www.hrnicholls.com.au/archives/vol116–4.php.

6. Susan E. Mayer, *What Money Can't Buy: Family Income and Children's Life Chances* (Cambridge: Harvard University Press, 1997), p. 16.

7. Heather Zavadsky, *Bringing School Reform to Scale: Five Award-Winning Urban Districts* (Cambridge: Harvard University Press, 2009).

8. Grover J. "Russ" Whitehurst and Michelle Croft, "The Harlem Children's Zone, Promise Neighborhoods, and the Broader, Bolder Approach to Education," Brookings Institution, July 10, 2010; and Grover J. "Russ" Whitehurst and Michelle Croft, "The Harlem Children's Zone Revisited," Brookings Institution, July 28, 2010. Also see "Geoffrey Canada Responds to Brookings Study on Harlem Children's Zone," Brookings Institution, July 22, 2010.

9. Here's one paragraph from Canada's response: "We believe even the best schools in impoverished neighborhoods would be significantly improved if there were wraparound support services for their students, families and community. If your mission is about all the students in a community, then dealing with family crises, gangs, drugs, violence, and health all become part of your strategy to support development of the whole child, not just how they perform on standardized tests. When a community becomes too violent or the schools too lousy, family—if they have the means—will move out. Poor families don't have that option; that is why your need a comprehensive strategy." http://equityblog.org/2010/07/22/hcz-responds-to-brookings/

10. http://jaypgreene.com/2010/03/24/florida-crushes-the-ball-on-2009-naep-reading/

11. *How Well are States Educating Our Neediest Students? The Fordham Report 2006*, Fordham Foundation, Washington, DC, p. 40.

12. "Dropout Rates by Race by School, 2009–10," Florida Department of Education website.

13. Malcolm Gladwell, *Outliers: The Story of Success* (New York: Little Brown, 2008), pp. 224–49.

14. McWhorter's review of Stuart Buck's book, *Acting White: The Ironic Legacy of Desegregation* (New Haven: Yale, 2010), was titled "Guilt Trip," and was published online by *The New Republic*, June 24, 2010. McWhorter's own book a decade earlier was *Losing the Race: Self-Sabotage in Black America* (New York: Perennial, 2000). The reference to "not always rational or collegial reactions" to *Losing the Race* has to do with the fair number of times McWhorter (who's African American) was slandered as a "sellout," "not really black," and other niceties.

15. John E. Chubb and Terry M. Moe, *Politics, Markets, and America's Schools* (Washington, DC: Brookings Institution, 2000), p. 2.

16. Corey Mitchell, "A Battle of Beliefs," (Minneapolis) *Star Tribune*, December 1, 2010, p. AA1.

17. Beth Hawkins, "Letters, on Teachers' Union Letterhead from Incoming School Board Members Draw Fire in Minneapolis," *MinnPost*, December 17, 2010.

18. Gerald Grant, "Are Teachers to Blame?" *Syracuse University Magazine*, Spring 2004.

19. Gerald Grant, *The World We Created at Hamilton High* (Cambridge, MA: Harvard University, 1988), p. 226.

20. One estimate, reported in 2006, had the number of single custodial fathers at 2.3 million. http://singlefather.org/articles/honoring_single_dads_on_fathers_day.php

21. David Whitman, *Sweating the Small Stuff: Inner-City Schools and the New Paternalism* (Washington, DC: Thomas B. Fordham Institute, 2008).

22. Ibid., American Indian Public Charter School in Oakland, CA; Amistad Academy in New Haven, CT; Cristo Rey Jesuit High School in Chicago; KIPP Academy in the Bronx; SEED school in Washington, DC; and University Park Campus School in Worcester, MA;

23. Ibid., pp. 3–4.

24. Ibid., p. xi.

25. Ibid., p. 28.

26. Ibid., p. 43.

27. Paul Tough, "What It Takes to Make a Student," *New York Times Magazine*, November 26, 2006, p. 69.

28. *Sweating the Small Stuff*, p. 279.

29. Ibid., p. 177.

30. *The World We Created at Hamilton High*, pp. 120–21.

31. Ibid., pp. 174–75; 178.

32. Ibid., p. 132.

33. Jay P. Greene, *Education Myths: What Special Interest Groups Want You to Believe About Our Schools—and Why It Isn't So* (Lanham, MD: Rowman & Littlefield, 2005), pp. 147–56.

34. William G. Howell and Paul E. Peterson, *The Education Gap: Vouchers and Urban Schools* (Washington, DC: Brookings Institution, 2002; 2006), pp. 186–87.

35. Email correspondence from Martin West to Michael Petrilli, January 18, 2011.

36. Paul E. Peterson, "Graduation Rates Higher at Milwaukee Voucher Schools," http://educationnext.org/graduation-rates-higher-at-milwaukee-voucher-schools/, January 10, 2011. Peterson credits research by John Warren for these findings.

37. Paul E. Peterson, "Achievement Gaps: What Will It Take to Close Them?" Center of the American Experiment, March 22, 2007, p. 12.

38. John E. Brandl, "Choice, Religion, Community, and Educational Quality," in *Liberty and Learning: Milton Friedman's Voucher Idea at Fifty* (Washington, DC: Cato Institute, 2006.)

39. James S. Coleman and Thomas Hoffer, *Public and Private High Schools: The Impact of Communities* (New York: Basic Books, 1987).

40. Clayton Christensen, Michael B. Horn, Curtis W. Johnson, *Disrupting Class: How Disruptive Innovation Will Change the Way the World Learns* (New York: McGraw Hill, 2008).

41. Terry M. Moe and John E. Chubb, *Liberating Learning: Technology, Politics, and the Future of American Education* (San Francisco: Jossey-Bass, 2009).

42. Ibid., pp. 75–76.

43. Deborah Taylor and Maureen Lorimer, "Helping Boys Succeed," *Educational Leadership*, December-January, 2002–03, pp. 68–70.

44. Charles Murray, "The Legacy of the 60's," *Commentary*, July 1992, p. 29.

45. Ron Haskins and Art Rolnick, "Early Childhood Education: Do Enthusiasts Exaggerate What It Can Do?" Center of the American Experiment, July 18, 2006, p. 7.

46. Darcy Olsen, *Assessing Proposals for Preschool and Kindergarten: Essential Information for Parents, Taxpayers, and Policymakers*, Goldwater Institute, No. 201, February 8, 2005.

47. Mitch Pearlstein, *Riding into the Sunrise: Al Quie and a Life of Faith, Service & Civility* (Lakeville, MN: Pogo Press, 2008), p. 268.

Chapter 6

Strengthening Marriage

In the world of policymaking, shotguns have been known to target gnats. In the particular matter of strengthening marriage in the United States current and proposed public initiatives routinely resemble gnats straining to pull triggers and otherwise failing to make decent dents. It was in this less-than-utopian spirit that I conceded right at the top that *From Family Collapse to America's Decline* would not necessarily offer any recommendations for reviving marriage as robust as the familial and other problems discussed. I stand by that evasion, though there are a number of important and profitable things that can be said and deserve to be pursued.

But first, permit me to return, as promised in the Introduction, to a very difficult matter in my own family from which I've learned much, albeit painfully, to the nuanced benefit of the book.

My wife Diane McGowan and I adopted Kaila (not her real name) in 1996 when she was approaching six, though we had known her since birth, as her birth mother was one of Diane's clients when she ran a church-based homeless program in Minneapolis for more than a dozen years. Without digging into an oversupply of ugly details, imagine just about everything that can go wrong in a baby's first half-dozen years of life, including drugs in utero . . . and then double them. That was Kaila's start, including sexual abuse in foster care. Severely editing the next fourteen-plus years, she had four stays of at least seven months each in residential mental health facilities for young people; at least a half-dozen shorter stays in psychiatric units of four local hospitals; abbreviated stays (which is to say she left on her own against professional and parental advice) in numerous other programs for troubled children and young people; along with one stint in juvenile detention and two each in jail and prison. She also failed to graduate high school and despite several pledges to the contrary, failed to stick with any GED program. As for her time before coming to live with us, a first adoptive family returned her to Hennepin County because they couldn't handle her, at which point she was sent to her fifteenth placement of one kind or another. Diane and I, along with my three stepsons from Diane's previous marriage, became her sixteenth.

I touched on some of these earliest events in a few things I wrote back when Kaila was still very young, but almost completely stopped writing anything about her as she got older as to protect her privacy. But given the subject at hand, and with apologies to her for unwelcomed intrusions, it would be a dereliction if I were not to write about her pregnancy and do so in adequate context.

Diane and I had long lived in fear of Kaila becoming pregnant, as in no way would this be fair to anyone involved, very much starting with the baby. When, after several disconcerting scares, she actually did conceive, it's fair to say my wife and I viewed the news as nothing short of a disaster. But acutely germane to this book which was then nearing completion was an additional realization that didn't hit me until the following day. Upon hearing from an emergency room nurse over the phone that Kaila was pregnant, I had immediately flashed to her sad history (a daily occurrence, actually) and then, just as quickly, started mentally listing all the consequent reasons why there was much to newly worry about. Yet it wasn't until the next day that I realized a critical aspect of her situation had not struck me at the time at all: the fact that she wasn't married and had no plans whatsoever to be. Suffice it to say, it wasn't much more than a nanosecond before I more deeply appreciated that while marriage is damagingly diminished in America, it's quite frequently unadvisable nonetheless.

Put most simply, I assume I had not first thought about Kaila's nonmarital status as I implicitly recognized that neither she nor the father (whom I knew a little about) were in any way equipped to be married. For them to be husband and wife, in fact, would further complicate their lives in ways neither good for them nor it's safe to say the baby—not that such a marriage would have more than the slimmest chance of surviving more than a year or two, if that long anyway. Now, fully granted is the fact that my daughter and her former, short-term boyfriend are more challenged (to use an antiseptic term) than most of the "unmarriageable" men as well as women described by William Julius Wilson, Kathryn Edin, Maria Kafalis and other scholars in Chapter Two. Yet the situation the two found themselves in profoundly highlights the obvious but sometimes insufficiently appreciated fact—especially when discussions turn to "re-institutionalizing marriage," especially in low-income neighborhoods—how many people should not be married at all, either to each other or anyone else. This is the case both for their sake and that of any children they might have or think about having.

A quick and telling sidebar: When my wife took our daughter for her first doctor's visit after learning she was pregnant, just about everyone in the public clinic told her "Congratulations." True, they didn't have too many other gracious options. But was "congratulations" exactly the right word in a disquieting and even foreboding situation which I trust was not all that difficult for at least some on the staff to surmise?

Yet without gainsaying any of the above and essential cautions, the aim here and throughout is strengthening marriage, not further discouraging it, and in all parts of America. The goal is also assuring that as many children as possible get to grow up with both of their parents in the same dwelling. How might we make progress in these regards, remaining ever-alert to how complicated and nuanced all this can be and usually is? And what obstacles, not yet sufficiently considered, stand in the way?

By "not yet sufficiently considered," I'm referring to obstacles to marriage and two-parent families for boys and girls reflected, to start, in popular places like magazines and television.

Back in the late 1990s, for instance, *Sports Illustrated* ran what, in many ways, was a solid and useful cover story, "Paternity Ward," about the extraordinary number of children fathered out of wedlock by athletes, particularly those in the National Basketball Association. But this is how the authors, Grant Wahl and L. Jon Wertheim, chose to present the "substantive questions" raised by such behavior.[1]

First on the list was a question about whether the "distraction of unplanned fatherhood and paternity suits" had a bearing on an athlete's performance (on the court and field, presumably).

This was followed by a question about whether the "temptations" of an athlete's lifestyle encouraged sexual irresponsibility. This was followed by one about whether some women "target" athletes in hopes of scoring big-time in child support payments.

These queries, in turn, were followed by a question about how judges should determine levels of financial support for children born outside of marriage and another about how a child might "deal" with having a father he or she might hardly know, save for seeing him occasionally on television. Finally, Wahl and Wertheim wondered, given the "well-known dangers of unprotected sex," why athletes were so reckless.

What's wrong with this list? Or more to the point, what's offensive about it?

Might it be the relegation of the fate of abandoned children to number five? Might not their well-being deserve to be number one? Or if not placed at the top, then perhaps at the end—but only in the way that the most profound item in a litany is frequently cited last, for extra effect? But at a minimum, one would like to think kids in such situations shouldn't be further buried in the pack. Or more precisely for our purposes, what did that story suggest about the esteem with which a major and mainstream American magazine held marriage and the importance it saw in responsible fatherhood? Interpretations can be taken too far, though in this instance, I would argue not. Or might the sequencing of similar questions be different if *Sports Illustrated* chose to update the story? Maybe it would, but then again, maybe not.

Or take *People* magazine. I must admit to not having looked at it closely for a while, but what I do recall quite well were frequent stories, often cover stories, featuring single moms: some of whom were famous and some of whom were not; some of whom were young and some of whom were even younger. What I don't remember in any of those stories was nearly as much attention devoted to how the children were faring as opposed to how their mothers were doing. Actually, I hardly recall any real attention paid to the babies and young children at all.

Or let's try one more example, an episode from the old medical show, "Chicago Hope," which ran from 1994 to 2000. The fact that all three of these instances have some age to them provides an ongoing sense of the environment.

In the installment, a man is dying and his wife is determined to have some of his sperm harvested so that she can be artificially inseminated, thereby keeping a part of him close forever. His mother, however, is very much opposed to the idea, with the rest of the hour devoted to having them, in collaboration with hospital personnel, fight it out. Now, I may be a bit off on this; maybe it was the man's mother *and father* who resisted adamantly. But what I do recall vividly was how the dilemma pivoted entirely on issues other than what might be best for a fatherless child born of such a procedure, as all attention was completely on the preferences of the surviving adults involved. It wasn't that questions about the kid's possible well-being were relegated, as they simply were never raised in the first place.

A more recent televised example of a similar omission was an episode of "Intervention" a series in which, as the title suggests, distressed families gather, with the aid of a professional, to inform addicted and otherwise severely troubled members that while they're loved, they need to be ferried to treatment immediately. The person in need of help in the show in question was a crack-addicted woman, perhaps around 50, with two adult daughters, a teenage son, and an elderly mother. With anger and not a few other emotions thrown in, the children confronted their mother, recounting their pain about not having been parented well over the decades. The three were impressive and appealing, but intriguing was how their lamenting about never having sufficient parental love and guidance focused entirely on maternal, never paternal failings. This presumably had something to do with the fact that each of the three children had been fathered by different men. For our purposes, though, the most pertinent point to be gleaned is not simply how the family picture had been complicated by three different men at one time or another, but rather how there never was a moment in the hour-long program in which notions of "parent" or "parenting" were associated with anyone or anything other than "mother" or "mothering." "Father" and "fathering" were null; never mentioned and nowhere to be found.

Can too much be made of anecdotes like these? Sure. But it's more likely that everyday media examples like these speak loudly to how ingrained our problems are.

Taking the argument up a conceptual notch or two, it's useful to consider, in the words of historian Barbara Dafoe Whitehead and sociologist David Popenoe, how and why marriage has become less "child centered" in our country. I draw here largely on a symposium the two edited in 2000 which still rings more than true, though it never received the attention it deserves, as it was released right before 9/11 and subsequently drowned out in the media.[2] Expanding on points already made, Whitehead and Popenoe wrote of how marriage, throughout our nation's history had been "first and foremost an institution for bearing and raising children." Citing three clusters of reasons, they contended this was no longer the case, with the first and most obvious reason being the "weakening link between marriage and parenthood itself," driven by huge nonmarital and divorce rates. Their second cause was the shifting away from child centeredness *within marriage*, by which they meant the way in which Americans have come to see marriage primarily as a *couples* relationship, "designed to fulfill the emotional needs of adults rather than as an institution for parenthood and childrearing." From the standpoint of boys and girls, this has not been an entirely welcomed development as the "exacting emotional requirements of the soul-mate ideal" have intensified the "natural tensions between adult desires and children's needs," with kids often getting lost along the way. Third and most generally, Whitehead and Popenoe wrote of how children are decreasingly a presence in daily American life, insofar as adults are less likely than ever to live with them, making neighborhoods less likely to contain them.

Nearly all symposium contributors made similar points about ascendant individualism, secularism, consumerism and what participant James Q. Wilson called the "greatest accomplishment of the West: human emancipation." Sticking with an increasingly wild West, Chester E. Finn, Jr. asked if was fair to admonish men and women to marry if they intend to raise children "because that's what's best for the species." Fair or not, he acknowledged such counsel was problematic given that modern Western society especially since the 1960s has been "disinclined" to tell people how to arrange their personal affairs, very much including those of sex, childbearing, and child raising. "The word permissiveness," he argued, "doesn't begin to describe this vast cultural sea change . . . a brew of relativism, modernism, libertarianism, licentiousness, self-expression, antiauthoritarianism, counterculturism," with all of them having seeped from the far reaches of the avant-garde into the mainstream.

The risk in discussions like this one, thick with "isms," is they can stretch too fuzzily far. So let me finish off this section by spending a moment with *New Rules*, Daniel Yankelovich's now three-decade-old primer on what was already a changed sense of obligation in the country, as the book is grounded as solidly—in extensive interviews and surveys—as such interpretations generally get. From there, we will have arrived at the moment of truth, when I actually start framing ways of possibly reviving marriage and two-parent families in the United States.

A preeminent pollster and analyst, Yankelovich wrote in 1981 that Americans had become subject to many conflicting pressures, with new ones urging "fulfill thyself" and more traditional ones still saying "deny yourself for the sake of others," by whom he principally meant one's family, especially children. When asked, for example, what success meant to their parents, people thirty-plus years ago said things such as: "providing for the family"; "making a home for the children"; "giving us a chance to get what they didn't have"; and "having a stable family life." Similarly, in describing what self-fulfillment meant to their mothers and fathers, typical comments included, "I don't think they were concerned with it"; and "They didn't have time to be concerned with it," as they were "too busy making a living."

In regards to questions of "familial success," Yankelovich described the era and culture which had not long earlier expired as highly esteeming only one form of family life: the nuclear family, featuring not only clearly prescribed roles for all members, but an environment in which parents (two per household) were "expected to sacrifice for their children."[3] If asked in a mildly leading way, would most Americans still say that sacrificing for one's children is a right and proper obligation? I can't conceive of them not doing so. But with one-third of all children, for example, now living apart from their father, it's right and fair to say that "obligation" doesn't mean exactly what it used to.[4]

Exactly as with ideas for strengthening education, if there were easily replicable programs for significantly strengthening marriage in the United States to be had they would have been pounced on long ago. The same holds for the simultaneously similar and different matters of preventing teenage and other unwanted pregnancies. Actually, it's much more realistic to imagine viable ideas in education, as the term "education policies" doesn't sound the least strange, while talking about "marriage policies" borders on it, given the ways in which intimate and elusive matters of culture and faith, as well as economics, sculpt marriage more than lawmaking and rule-making. This is the case as opposed to education, where new policies and directives, effective or not, flow from governments daily (beleaguered superintendents and principals might claim hourly). Still, this is not to say policy-rooted recommendations, tepid as they almost always are, aren't perpetually offered for getting more people married and then encouraging fewer of them to separate and divorce.

Following in a minute will be a taste of such well-rehearsed recommendations. This is the edited case not because there aren't decent and helpful ideas in the mix, but because other people have expanded on them much better than I either can or choose to here.[5] Rather, it makes more sense to focus on three areas which, to one extent or another, haven't been considered as frequently, and as previewed here.

My thinking on the first of the three goes back to something I heard columnist Bill Raspberry say a long time ago. Asked if had to pick just one place out of many to start addressing problems of poverty and much else, he said he'd start with the boys. Given how great numbers of men have come to be viewed as poor and even terrible prospects for marriage (and in fact are), the better I've come to realize that unless more men get their lives in decent order, no number of implorations will adequately bolster marriage rates in the United States. And by "men," what we're really talking about is "boys," just a handful of years earlier on.

The second cluster of recommendations (or at least grist for discussion) has to do with the prevalence and power of crime, which obviously is tightly linked to the unattractiveness and shortcomings of many men. Here's a too-easy question: What is the likelihood of young and not-so-young men with long rap sheets, often including felonies, building the kinds of work histories and careers that make them interesting to employers, not to mention sufficiently appealing as lifelong partners to the women in their lives? The answer in each instance is that the odds are tough.

The third area pivots on a harder question: Who speaks for girls and boys of fragmented families *explicitly*, especially those having the hardest times? This is not an arrogant swipe at the many organizations and individuals (and I do mean many) whose missions and lives are devoted to helping children and others in need. Neither is it a slap at often wonderful and overworked men and women in child protection and foster care, as their jobs would seem precisely to be that of looking after children in distress. The distinction I seek to make instead is a subtle one. Let me tease it by suggesting that to the constrained extent that single-parenthood is publicly lamented in the United States, rarely is there sufficient attention paid specifically to how children are being hurt by it. Rather, the focus is more diffuse, having to do with how one-person parenting can be extremely rugged—albeit not necessarily damaging—for all concerned, grownups and kids alike. This is fair and expected as far as it goes, but I would suggest what's finally called for is a campaign whose singular focus is on how family breakdown can in fact be harmful to children and saying with some precision in what ways. Might this be tricky to the point of offensive to many? No doubt. And am I less than completely confident it would work? That, too, I concede.

But let's start here with educational, tax, and other ideas more regularly on the table for strengthening marriage.

The most personal tack, of course, is aimed mainly at already married couples, and is captured nicely by these six chapter headings (also called "learnings") suggested by the Cooperative Extension Service at the University of Arkansas: "Creating the Story of Your Love"; "What Do We Do about Problems?"; "Showing Love Effectively"; "Seeing Your Partner Through His or Her Eyes"; "Making Effective Use of Our Differences"; and "Finding Your Common Purpose."[6]

Spend a coffee break Googling and you'll come up with loads of lists like these, in much the same way Barnes & Noble and Borders have long stocked shelves of self-help books on the subject. A "good morning kiss," a "certified" relationship coach on the Internet urges couples, is the finest way of starting the day as it will "make your partner feel special."

A distinctively important setting, however, for more academically grounded discussions is the huge annual meeting of a group called "Smart Marriages: The Coalition for Marriage, Family, and Couples Education." Topics at their 2010 conference included its customarily broad range, including a number aligned with our concerns here, such as "Stepfamily 911: Crisis Intervention"; "Strengthening Marriage in the Black Community"; "Family Wellness: Skills for Fragile Families"; "Children of Divorce: The Tough Truth"; and "Establishing & Sustaining Community Marriage Initiatives."[7]

Closer still to the mark for our purposes are proposals by the nearly twenty scholars, writers, and activists in the aforementioned symposium edited by Barbara Dafoe Whitehead and David Popenoe.[8] Bill Galston, for example, a political theorist who served in the Clinton White House, urged tax credits for working parents and plowing ahead on workplace policies such as flextime, job sharing, and part-time work with benefits. Robert Rector of the Heritage Foundation recommended ending then-current anti-marriage rules in means-tested programs such as the Women, Infants, and Children food program (WIC) and public housing. He also advocated increasing the value of Earned Income Tax Credits (EITC) for married couples with children, as couples frequently lost eligibility when they did marry. David Blankenhorn, author of the influential *Fatherless America*, offered "six puny ideas," including tightening divorce laws by lengthening waiting periods and mandating counseling, and in regards to the U.S. tax code (which he described as "probably the nation's single most important family policy") he urged that it be reformed so that it "realistically recognizes, rather than discriminates against, married couples with children." And Wade Horn, who within two years would be named assistant secretary for children and families in the U.S. Department of Health and Human Services, where he would have lead responsibility for such programs, emphasized "helping our nation's young develop both a better understanding of the importance of marriage and the skills necessary to form and sustain healthy marriages."

In many ways the Big Daddy and Mommy of marriage education programs have been those originally funded across the country during the administration of President George W. Bush. In terms of their evaluation, however, it's necessary to divide the 200-plus programs between those resulting directly from the reauthorization of TANF (Temporary Assistance to Needy Families) in 2006, and those which HHS, under Horn's relentless prodding, had started funding less formally years earlier in the president's first term. More specifically, it was in 2002, that the administration launched three "sophisticated experiments" to test the effectiveness of marriage programs aimed exclusively at low-income couples.[9] While there previously had been some evidence that well-designed efforts could help middle-class white couples improve their relationships, there wasn't any comparable research to draw on regarding lower-income and minority couples. Final reports on two of the major experiments (or collections of programs) are expected to be released in 2012. But a first report was released in 2010, and perfectly in keeping, as discussed last chapter, with Rossi's iron as well as brass laws of evaluation, barely any good news was to be had.

The first collection, containing eight programs in seven states, is called the Building Strong Families project and offers relationship-skills education and other support services to romantically involved but unmarried couples who are expecting a baby or have just had one. A little more than 5,000 couples were randomly assigned to a BSF group or not. In shortest and starkest summary, Mathematica Policy Research concluded: "When results are averaged across all programs, BSF did not make couples more likely to stay together or get married. In addition, it did not improve couple's relationships." There were caveats, of course; for example, the program in Oklahoma City showed a "consistent pattern of positive effects" and maybe good things will take hold for other participants later on. But overall, "Fifteen months after entering the program, the relationship outcomes of BSF couples were, on average, almost identical to those of couples in the control group."[10] One clear reason for this failure was the refusal of many participants, especially men, simply to show up for sessions. Isabel Sawhill and Ron Haskins, for instance, noted in 2009, that 70 percent of couples attended less than 40 percent of the approximately 20 "curriculum sessions," with attendance by males often "especially challenging."[11]

This is not to say marriage programs, of this or some other sort, are never destined to work well. Studies of the two other experiments or clusters of programs, one of which deals with already-married couples, remain under way and maybe results will be better with them. But perhaps even more so than with elementary and secondary education, progress in this realm can be excruciatingly hard.

With all that soberness said, it's hard to think of a more statistically cold-showering introduction to the state of American boys and young men than the ways in which their well-being differs, often radically, from that of American girls and young women, and in far from good ways. Tom Mortenson (who, a long time ago worked in an office across the hall from mine at the University of Minnesota) is a prolific analyst with a deep interest in expanding postsecondary opportunities for students of all stations. You may be familiar with what might be called his "For Every 100 Girls" exercise. Here are a quick twenty examples, drawn from a 2006 edition of *Postsecondary Education OPPORTUNITY*, a research letter he publishes.[12]

- For every 100 girls who repeat kindergarten, 194 boys do so.
- For every 100 girls, ages 15 to 17, enrolled below "modal grade," 137 boys of the same ages are.
- For every 100 tenth-grade girls who play video or computer games one or more hours per day, 322 tenth-grade boys do so.
- For every 100 tenth-grade girls who perform community service at least once a week, 68 tenth-grade boys do the same.
- For every 100 twelfth-grade girls who carried a weapon on school property, 287 twelfth-grade boys did the so.
- For every 100 twelfth-grade girls who engaged in a physical fight on school property, 214 twelfth-grade boys did so.
- For every 100 girls *suspended* from public elementary and secondary schools, 250 boys are.
- For every 100 girls *expelled* from public elementary and secondary schools 335 boys are.

- For every 100 girls diagnosed with a learning disability, 276 boys are.
- For every 100 girls diagnosed with "emotional disturbance," 324 boys are.
- For every 100 girls, ages 3 to 5, diagnosed with a developmental delay, 154 boys of the same ages are.
- For every 100 girls, ages 6 to 14, who have difficulty doing "regular school-work," 176 boys of the same ages do.
- For every 100 women enrolled in college, 77 men are.
- For every 100 women who earn a bachelor's degree, 73 American men do.
- For every 100 women who earn a master's degree, 62 men do.
- For every 100 women who earn a doctoral degree, 92 men do.[13]
- For every 100 females, ages 15 to 19, who commit suicide, 549 males of the same ages do.
- For every 100 females, ages 20 to 24, who commit suicide, 624 males of the same ages do.
- For every 100 women, ages 18 to 24, living in group homes, 166 men of the same ages are.
- For every 100 girls, ages 15 to 17, in correctional facilities, 837 boys of the same ages are.
- And for every 100 women, ages 22 to 24, in correctional facilities, 1,448 men of the same ages are. (Where exactly are enormous numbers of out-of-circulation American men to be found? Often in jail and prison—if they're still alive to begin with. More on the mammoth role of crime in short-circuiting marriage shortly.)

In gulping down such data, it's perversely fascinating to recall that it wasn't all that long ago when it was simply assumed in many quarters that boys were doing better than girls in education and other ways, due in no small part to girls being discriminated against intentionally and otherwise. This was so much the case, for example, that the U.S. Department of Education, as recently as 2000, disseminated more than 300 books, working papers, pamphlets, and other publications on gender equity, with none of them aimed at helping boys do as well as girls.[14] I've tried hard most of the time in these pages to stay clear of ideologically flavored language that might be unconvincing and off-putting to one group or another. But examples of blinkered eyes like these in a Cabinet-level agency make it very hard not to conclude that politically correct strictures, once again, have significantly limited debate.

A decidedly non-politically correct observer named Judith Kleinfeld runs "The Boys Project" at the University of Alaska in Fairbanks and has argued that while problems facing boys are "serious," they are *not* in crisis. Yet she comes pretty close to belying her own assertion by writing that boys' problems "center in literacy, school engagement, low grades, placement in special education, dropout rates, enrollment and graduation in postsecondary programs, such mental health problems as suicide and conduct disorders, injuries, premature death, and criminal activities." Just imagine if they really were "in crisis."[15]

With numbers, trends, and abysses likes these, one can conceive the contours of what some might describe, in friendly ways or not, as an increasingly matriarchal country. This would especially seem to be the case in regards to America's educational elite, as it becomes, in the description of Jonathan Rauch, "as disproportionately female as it once was male." Or, for our purposes, we're talking about a place in which ever-larger numbers of women are "marrying down" educationally, if they choose to marry at all. "A third of today's college-bound 12-year-old girls," Rauch has predicted, "can expect to 'settle' for a mate without a university diploma." This seems plausible, as by 2017, according to a projection made by the National Center for Education Statistics, half again as many women as men are expected to earn bachelor's degrees.[16] (Not that that term "bachelor's" degree will fit particularly well any longer.)

"Men don't marry," a 42-year-old divorced mother from the Bronx told the *New York Times* in 2006, "because women like myself don't need to rely on them." Punchier, a woman in her 30s, also from the Bronx, asked: "Why would you want to be in a stable relationship with somebody who is unstable?"[17]

The focus for the last few minutes has been on boys in general. But how are minority boys doing, especially African Americans? The answer is even more discouraging and familiar, but another *New York Times* article, this time in 2010, suggested that academic matters were even worse than generally assumed. Headlined "Proficiency of Black Students is Found to be Far Lower than Expected," the piece noted how, according to a then-recently released report of the National Assessment of Educational Progress, only 12 percent of fourth-grade black boys were "proficient" in reading and only 12 percent of eighth grade black boys were likewise in math. Corresponding proportions for white boys were more than three times higher in the former instance, and almost four times higher in the latter.

Poverty alone, the article said, does not appear to explain the differences, as poor white boys performed just as well as non-poor African American boys, as measured by whether the two groups qualified for subsidized school lunches. Very much in keeping with aforementioned research about the way lower-income parents communicate with their babies and young children— including the hugely smaller number of words they tend to use in comparison to middle-class parents—Ronald Ferguson, director of Harvard's "Achievement Gap Initiative," pointed to growing research regarding racially based differences in what kids experience before starting kindergarten. "They have to do with a lot of sociological and historical forces," he said, and that in order to address them, "we have to be able to have conversations that people are unwilling to have." Issues such as, "How much we talk to [our boys and girls], the ways we talk to them, the ways we enforce discipline, the ways we encourage them to think and develop a sense of autonomy."

Very much related here is economist and Nobel Laureate James Heckman's well-noted assertion that families are the "major source of human inequality in American society," and his corresponding work on the potentially ameliorating contributions of strong early childhood programs—though not necessarily because they wind up improving test scores or increasing I.Q. Such programs targeted to disadvantaged children, he has said, have had their best effect on non-cognitive skills such as motivation, self-control, and what he calls "time preference." This is by no means disappointing news, he suggests, given that both social and emotional skills, often described as softer skills, are essential in "producing successful people."[18]

If Heckman looks first to early childhood education in helping disadvantaged children (and he makes his case as well as anyone), what routes might others emphasize in helping boys in general do well, which by my definition, eventually includes doing well in their relationships with women?[19] Unsurprisingly, most roads lead back to schools and school programs of one kind or another.

For instance, researchers in several countries—frankly, confirming my instincts last chapter—have found that increased use of technology and computer education has resulted in greater academic engagement on the part of boys as well as fewer discipline problems in classrooms.

One frequently hears of reading programs in which books are selected with boys specifically in mind. According to this approach, boys are likely to be more enthused by non-fiction works as well as those they choose for themselves, such as a wrestling magazine in one reported instance. It was by a "young man who insisted he hated to read," but who began reading it enthusiastically, ultimately graduating to more "sophisticated" materials.

One also frequently hears of how boys learn best when they allowed to move around a bit and handle objects, which has led some researchers to suggest that teachers "accept restless behavior as long as boys are on task." Incorporating opportunities for physical activities into lessons is likewise thought to increase motivation among other things.

And one sporadically hears of educators and parents interested in starting single-gender schools and/or classrooms, though it's fair to say they have rarely been evaluated rigorously. Perhaps this is because various governmental agencies and interest groups are routinely primed to challenge their very existence with equal rights and civil rights arguments.

As for mentoring programs, be they in or out or school, boys can benefit from having "male role models who believe in them" and help them grasp what they are capable of accomplishing. As one might guess, this kind of attention can be crucial for young men who do not receive much male attention at home.[20]

Perhaps the breakthrough book in focusing on how poorly boys have been doing in contrast to girls was Christina Hoff Sommers' *The War Against Boys*, released in 2000. One of her arguments was that Great Britain started coming to grips with such disparities, particularly in education, in the 1980s, which is to say a lot earlier than the United States did—to the extent we actually have. This is how she described some of the conclusions of educators who had unusual success in teaching boys.

"The headmasters advise schools to avoid fanciful, 'creative'" assignments, noting, 'Boys to not always see the intrinsic worth of 'Imagine you're a sock in a dustbin.' They want relevant work.'" The head teacher of a school in Winchester, a man named Bradbury, identified about 30 boys who were at risk of failure and put them in a class together, and chose an "athletic young male teacher" to lead them. Quoting Bradbury, the class was "strict and old fashioned," meaning its method was "didactic and teacher-fronted." The questioning was "sharp" and discipline "clear-cut." If homework wasn't "presented," it was completed in detention. A visiting journalist described a typical class: "Ranks of boys in blazers face the front, giving full attention to the young teacher's instructions. His style is uncompromising and inspirational. 'People think boys like you won't be able to understand writers such as the Romantic poets. Well, you're going to prove them wrong. Do you understand?'" A former president of a Scottish headmasters association is said to urge his colleagues (in Sommers's words) "to be brutally honest with boys about what life has in store for them if they continue to underperform academically."[21]

If I'm at all confident about the efficacy of any educational approach when it comes to helping (and saving) boys it's essentially this kind, which suggests at least the flavor of the paternalistic and religiously animated schools described by David Whitman and Gerald Grant last chapter. In this regard, consider two sets of data regarding the degree to which boys—in this instance, especially African American boys—trust and "feel supported" by their teachers.

The first is a survey of 537 seniors in an academic magnet school. Whereas 54 percent of the white males said they either "strongly agreed" or "agreed" that "My teachers support me and care about my success in their class," only

20 percent of black males did. (The discrepancy between white and black females, actually, was even larger: 71 percent for white girls and 28 percent for the black girls.)[22]

In a much larger survey of almost 4,000 students, 39 percent of overall said they trusted their teachers "only a little or not at all." Broken down, 47 percent of minority students said they felt that disapproving way, with the proportion for poor students even higher at 53 percent.[23]

These numbers and others like them mean something, which is not to say that the teachers in question necessarily did anything—or failed to do some-thing—that warranted the critical responses, insofar as how the students may have *felt* may have had wholly different and distant historical, psychological and other roots. Rather, an important point about these data was suggested by Pedro Antonio Noguera, an education professor who cited them in a very useful essay with the telling title of "The Trouble with Black Boys." There is research, Noguera wrote, suggesting that the "performance of African Americans, more so than other students is influenced to a large degree by the social support and encouragement they receive from teachers. To the extent this is true," Noguera continued, "and if the nature of interactions between many Black male students and their teachers tends to be negative, it is unlikely that it will be possible to elevate their achievement without chang-ing the way in which they are treated by teachers, and the ways in which they respond to those who try to help them."

Again, many excellent teachers doubtless have been treating even the most distrusting of students great and, in those instances, teachers have been the ones treated unfairly. Nevertheless, if one of the key notions here is a stu-dent's feeling of demonstrable support it's hard to think of schools better at providing it than those with "paternalistism" and "God" in their DNA. Refer-ring to just that kind of demanding and tough-loving spirit, when asked in an interview about the common traits of schools most successful in educating boys, Richard Whitmire, the author of *Why Boys Fail* spoke of the "refusal" of successful schools' "to let students slip behind." The biggest problem he sees in less effective schools is lax attitudes toward males—as in "Don't worry, Mom, boys will be boys. Your son will catch up"—because a lot of them never will.[24] Sure sounds like KIPP-type schools to me.

Another way extraordinary numbers of boys and men never recover is if they have criminal records; which, as with schooling, begets circular problems.[25] In the matter of education, getting a good one increases one's chances of attracting a mate and having a healthy and lasting marriage. Yet for children growing up outside of such healthy and long-lasting marriages the chances of their getting a good education decreases—as do the odds of subsequent generations marrying successfully. When it comes to crime, research is congruent with common sense in showing how married men are less likely than single men to break the law. Yet men already caught up in the criminal justice system are less attractive marriage partners, and not just because they may be incarcerated at the time, but because rap sheets are not conducive to good-paying, family-supporting jobs and careers. Yet by not marrying, they lose a major support and spur in their lives for staying out of jail and prison going forward. How to escape the maze? Before suggesting several ideas, and staying with a pattern of this and previous chapters, let's look at some very discouraging numbers first. (By "prison" here and throughout, as well as in regards to "incarceration," unless otherwise stipulated, the references are to actual state and federal penitentiaries; not to local jails.)

- The incarceration rate in the United States is approximately seven times the average for Western Europe and is approached only by South Africa and several former Soviet republics.[26]
- At yearend in 2009, there were more than 1.6 million inmates in federal and state prisons.[27] During the twelve-month period ending on June 30, 2009, 12.8 million inmates had been admitted to local jails.[28]
- As of the early 2000s, more than 11 percent of American men could expect to go to prison sometime in their lives.[29]
- Across the country, studies show that more than 40 percent of low-income men who father a child out-of-wedlock have already been in jail or prison by the time their first son or daughter is born.[30]
- For men born between 1975 and 1979, one in five African Americans had experienced imprisonment by the ages of 30 to 34. The comparable ratio for white men was one in thirty. For African American men who had not graduated high school their chances of experiencing imprisonment by the ages of 30 to 34 were two out of three.[31]
- As of 2000, about 25 percent of African American men between the ages of 22 and 30 were married. The marriage rate for incarcerated African American men was less than half of that, at 11 percent. This was the case even though (as of 1997–98) African American men, be they in prison or not, were similarly likely to have children: 70 percent for incarcerated men; 73 percent for non-incarcerated men. "As a result," criminologist Bruce Western has written, "African American children growing up in fragile families are likely to have fathers who have been incarcerated at some point."[32]

Statistics like these powerfully beg the question of whether the United States locks up too many people. As embarrassing questions go, it has been particularly salient for three or more decades, as prison populations have exploded over the period, in large part because of radically higher drug convictions plus mandatorily stiff sentences for crimes more generally. The latter includes life sentences and other very long sentences in many states for a third felony conviction. Expressed in multiples, over the last third of a century, the U.S. incarceration rate has grown about fivefold, from approximately 100 prisoners to 500 prisoners for every 100,000 people.[33]

In the abstract, it's hard not to agree that we do, in fact, incarcerate far too many men and (to a much lesser extent) women. Doing so doesn't seem to make sense or serve justice—*except* for the overpowering fact that drug trafficking continues to destroy almost all in its urban wake by serving as cause and ammunition in gang wars and more personal demises. Likewise, huge imprisonments in a free country would seem to make little sense and suggest even less justice—*except* for the enraging fact that too many bad actors continue prowling streets, despite having scores of police "contacts," making life miserable and sometimes deadly for city residents. It's hard, moreover, to square claims that the American judicial system is overly eager in putting people away with the fact that nearly every time a person is arrested for a particularly outrageous or heinous crime, his rap sheet is found to be pages longs, provoking justifiably angry citizens to wonder how and why such a predator had been free amongst them. It's important to point out here, and contrary to an urban myth or two, over 90 percent of inmates in state prisons are either violent offenders or convicted recidivists and not first-time nonviolent offenders.[34]

Yet no matter what bottom line or lines one might choose, an inescapable conclusion is that far too many Americans, for whatever reasons, commit far too much crime. To this fray and failure, how does marriage tend to calm things down and help? Or more commonly for our purposes, how does the absence of marriage tend to rile things up and destroy? Here's an illustrative example.

In a study of 500 chronic juvenile delinquents aimed at determining why some young men stopped their criminal behavior while others continued into their early thirties, researchers (according to demographer Linda Waite) found that a good marriage made more than a little difference. Men in the study who improved their ways were very similar to those who did not in terms of childhood characteristics like poverty rates and IQs. They also had been rated as equally "difficult" and "aggressive" and had been arrested as teenagers about as often. Nevertheless and over time, "those who entered a good marriage reduced their criminal activity sharply." More specifically, they did so by about two-thirds compared to men who did not establish good marriages or had not married at all.[35]

Not at all unrelated, the U.S. Justice Department reported back in the mid-'90s that single and divorced women were four to five times more likely than married women to be victimized in any given year (although widowed women were least likely to be victimized). Single and divorced women, in fact, were found to be three times more likely to be the victims of aggregated assault and almost ten times more likely than married women to be raped. And the evidence is "overwhelming that being unmarried puts women at special risk for domestic abuse" insofar as a large body of research shows that marriage is a much less dangerous arrangement than cohabitation.[36]

As for how children generally fare in all of this, the profoundly obvious answer is not well. In a recent review of the research, Christopher Wildeman and Bruce Western cite how parental incarceration increases the likelihood of infant mortality, homelessness, and foster care placements. Again, none of this is the smallest surprise—although this next statistic may well be a big one: One study has shown that increases in female incarceration rates explain fully 30 percent of the increase in foster care caseloads in the short fifteen years between 1985 and 2000. "[P]arental incarceration," Wildeman and Western write, "may increase not only criminality and behavioral problems more broadly, but also the risk of being severely marginalized in childhood and adolescence."[37]

Assuming that millions of Americans (mostly men) will not be going cold turkey anytime soon when it comes to going straight, what steps can we take to reduce the destruction and pain of past and future incarceration, especially in terms of increasing the likelihood of ex-offenders getting and keeping reasonably decent jobs, thereby making themselves more appealing and likely marriage partners and better parents? More specifically, what lesser-attended to steps might we take over and above those more routinely pursued like strengthening mentoring and reentry programs, as well as the kinds of large-scale jobs and anti-poverty initiatives proposed more than occasionally? The same omission applies to faith-based programs such as Prison Fellowship, for which I have great respect. Rather, let me suggest a couple of different routes by first briefly describing how several additional hard-to-sidetrack obstacles—one which has been growing only more problematic—retard chances for employment for people with records.

The terms "collateral sanctions" and "collateral consequences" refer to the legally stipulated as well as extra-legal—which is to say, much broader and insidious—collection of blockages to employment and other benefits for ex-offenders. Think of the first term, "collateral sanctions," as a "legal penalty, disability, or disadvantage" imposed on a person automatically upon conviction; for example, ineligibility for various jobs for which they might otherwise be capable of performing such as school bus driver or property manager for an apartment building. As for "collateral consequences," think of it as encompassing the full range of bad things and debilitating restrictions—both official and unofficial, codified or not—regularly confronting people after they've served their sentences. Or, in the words of one scholar, the everyday phenomenon of collateral consequences applies not only to the specific sanctions mandated by the judicial system, but also to the "degradation of social status often called the 'stigma of conviction.'"[38] An organization determined to shorten and soften the reach of such prohibitions and taints has written how "people with criminal records seeking reentry face a daunting array of counterproductive, debilitating, and unreasonable roadblocks in almost every important aspect of life."[39] Putting aside how not all of the group's concerns are equally compelling, its report does reinforce the larger point that once a person is convicted of a crime—and sometimes merely arrested without ever being convicted—life can spiral under.

Question: How to help ex-offenders, who are trying to do right things, overcome—while protecting public safety at every moment? It's a huge problem increasingly compounded by the rapid growth in the number of firms providing potential employers (as well as landlords, casual friends, et al.) with instantaneous electronic access to everything in a person's criminal record. Also increasingly accessible by this fundamental high-tech change is every scrap of incorrect information that may live in the file of a man or woman straining to play by the rules.

"While it has never been easy," a journalist wrote several years ago, "for a former convict to secure a full-time job, the rise of the electronic background check and fear of lawsuits among potential employers, are creating ever-higher barriers to work for those leaving prison."[40] Shortly before, in 2004, the *Wall Street Journal* reported that about 80 percent of big U.S. companies were doing criminal-background checks, the implications of which were huge, the two Journal reporters wrote, because if "former offenders can't find legitimate jobs, they may be driven back to crime."[41] If the percentage of big employers doing checks was 80 percent back then, it's hard not to believe the proportion is bigger now.

Given all this, what to do? Here are three quick thoughts.

Review collateral sanctions with an eye to safely reducing their number and duration. When compared to all the problems faced by former inmates in trying to turn their lives around, my sense is that specific laws and rules prohibiting them from filling certain jobs—as opposed to the barriers posed by the great gamut of everything else—are usually not the main obstacle they face. In Ohio, for example, it's just not that burdensome that people convicted of a felony, or who have pleaded guilty to a misdemeanor, are forever disallowed from serving as a police chief or even a constable. Likewise, it's no unjust calamity that no one in Ohio can be an auctioneer or apprentice auctioneer for ten years if convicted of a felony or any other crime involving fraud. And, of course, there are loads of proper and essential restrictions across the country when it comes to felons working anywhere near children and other vulnerable people. Then, again, the fact that Ohio disqualifies anyone with a "second conviction arising from two or more separate incidents" from ever getting a commercial vehicle driver's license can well mean additional shackles on an ex-offender's ability to make a living.[42]

All that said, more than a few states have more than a few collateral sanctions that can be done without, as they're more the product of overkill than necessity. For example, a group called the "Center for Cognitive Liberty & Ethics" claims that a person convicted of growing marijuana is "often subjected to the same, and sometimes greater, collateral sanctions than a person convicted of murder, rape, or robbery."[43] This is hard to believe, not that I don't believe it. But if it is, in fact, even in the vicinity of the truth, it's an absurdly disproportionate package of lifetime penalties. And while it may sound tepid to recommend that current efforts to review collateral sanctions should be accelerated and that new ones should start—with all conversations about redemption viewed through a prism of public safety—they really should.

Come to realistic grip with widespread Internet access to criminal records. Notice that this recommendation doesn't suggest actually restricting public access to criminal records. This is because I have little faith that any law written to remove certain records from public scrutiny in order to protect privacy and good name of individuals *who indeed deserve to be so protected* can withstand the onslaught of high technology. For example, it can be a crime of very different and unfair sort for people to carry around arrest records for the rest of their lives when they've never been guilty of anything beyond a parking ticket. This is especially the case when, in fact, they were wholly innocent of whatever they were arrested for. Yes, there are procedures for sealing or expunging such information, but it always takes time and often money to do so, and by the time all bureaucratic hurdles have been jumped, serious damage can already have been done, since documentation of the perhaps hollow arrest may already be deep within and, therefore, forever irretrievable from cyberspace. By serious damage, I mean unfairly being denied jobs, apartments, and other opportunities and benefits. Viewing the issue in terms of race, some share of the immense number of young and not-so-young African American men arrested every year get picked up because they really were in the wrong place at the wrong time.

One possible safety valve would be for police to make greater use of citations (which don't necessarily wind up on the Net) rather than actual arrests. The idea, which was proposed several years ago by the Minneapolis-based Council on Crime and Justice, presumably would help a significant number of disproportionately minority kids avoid life-scarring records. "[T]he police," the Council urged, "should use the citation process for low-level offenses . . . unless an arrest is justifiable because the offender presents an articulable threat to public safety."[44]

In terms of more tangible approaches and policies, where might "coming to grips" with widespread electronic records further lead? Please see the next recommendation.

Investigate safest possible ways of helping former offenders cleanse their name. Traditional means for helping individuals who have completed their sentences get on with their lives have included legal and administrative devices such as pardons and the expunging of records. These and others are flawed in one way or another. For example, expunging records requires a willingness to "rewrite history," something that is "hard to square with a legal system founded on the search for truth." Also, to the degree, it tends to hide an individual's criminal record from public view, "it tends to devalue legitimate public safety concerns."

This critique of expungements is by the same legal scholar, Margaret Colgate Love, who earlier wrote of the "stigma of conviction." While she fails to adequately appreciate the public's fear and anger at growing crime in the 1970s and 1980s, which in turn led to government at all levels coming down harder on criminals, she is compelling when she writes: "We sentence, we coerce, we incarcerate, we counsel, we give probation and parole, and we treat—not infrequently with success—but we never forgive."[45] A friend of mine once said in response to something else I had written on the subject: "I continue to be amazed that the fundamental teaching in most faiths of forgiveness is not part of the discussion in a society that considers itself so religious." How, exactly, to forgive—safely?

Drawing on a "Model Penal Code" drafted by the American Law Institute a half-century ago, Love, in a 2003 law review article, offered a route worth investigating. Her aim was and remains integrating offenders into society "not by trying to conceal the fact of conviction, but by advertising the evidence of rehabilitation." She and the model code proposed doing this in a two-tiered process. First, the original sentencing court "may issue an order relieving all disabilities after an offender has satisfied his sentence." And second, after a further period of "law-abiding conduct" (the model codes suggested five years), the sentencing court "may issue an order 'vacating' the convictions." What might this approach accomplish that others do not? Love concludes:

The resulting scheme provides the offender both incentive and reward for rehabilitation, and satisfies the need for a ritual of reconciliation. In relying primarily on the sentencing judge, it provides a more reliable and accessible process than pardon or other executive restoration devices, and a more respectable one than automatic statutory provisions. In contrast to expungement, it does not sacrifice the legitimate concerns of law enforcement or undermine respect for the value of truth in our legal system.

Would such a system, which essentially has been adopted in Illinois, help some people move on in good ways? It would seem so, and in a subsequent article, Love (what a great name under the circumstance) showed exactly how it has done so on behalf of a single-father and former drug addict in Chicago.[46] Would the reform likewise increase the likelihood of some people marrying? It would seem so again, if only modestly. Yet stepping back and surveying the larger nexus of crime and marriage, it's impossible not to recognize how miles beyond sad it is, starting with millions of young men, disproportionately of color, whose lives are crippled barely after they've begun because of criminal behavior. What a ruin for themselves, their families, and our nation.

Let me propose a third and final non-routine way for strengthening marriage in the United States; what might be considered another indirect—albeit at the same time, unusually pointed—tack.

A question teased earlier: Who speaks explicitly for the often impeded children of fragmented families? Putting matters undiplomatically, the question I have in mind is not about who might likewise speak for their parents, but rather, who might speak, and with emphasis, on behalf of the kids exclusively? Or if we were, in fact, interested in looking beyond the well-being of just little ones and adolescents, is there any organization out there whose public words and implorations could be said to also focus—not on how family breakdown can be tough on grown-ups—but instead, on how family breakdown can be tough on our country? If there are such voices, I can't think of many, if any.

Try this exercise. Presuming that you think it's generally not great for children to live with only one parent, and that it's similarly not great for the commonwealth either, what might you be tempted to say *if etiquette and manners weren't all that important and feelings were hard to be hurt* to a young woman or a man who was blasé, perhaps even eager, to bring a child into the world in which it was understood, from Day One, that one of his or her parents was essentially out of the family portrait and would remain that way? This is what I might say, although still with as much empathy and grace as I could:

> I assure you I know that life can be terribly unpredictable and difficult. In fact, it usually is. This is especially the case when it comes to the most personal and treasured things going on in our lives, starting with our children and other

people we love. It also can be especially the case when it comes to people we may not love very much anymore at all, if we ever really did. And I very much assure you as well that I'm far from the best or right person in the world to talk to you about these matters, as my own life has been jammed with mistakes and disappointments.

You might say what we're discussing are holy matters, but my interest in being holier than thou or anyone else is zero, and to the extent I may come across as presumptuous or arrogant, I'm truly sorry. But whatever the risk of intrusion on my part and discomfort on yours, we each owe it to everyone we love and are obliged protect to consider several uncomfortable facts about current American life, most of all those facing and holding back young people.

In simplest and starkest terms, the United States has one of the highest out-of-wedlock birth rates in the world. We also have one of the highest divorce rates in the world. Overall, Americans tend to move in and out of romantic relationships faster than about anyone else in the world. These patterns and trends are the opposite of good news for any group, but they're particularly bad news for boys and girls, as they diminish their well-being now and undercut their futures, as scholarly research on this has grown absolutely clear. Does single parenthood always hurt kids educationally and in other ways? Of course not, is the answer. But the fuller and unavoidable answer is that children's odds of doing well are measurably better if they grow up under the same roof with their married mother and father than if they grow up in any other setting.

Children are the most joyous of blessings. And I deeply appreciate how enormous numbers of Americans believe that siring and bearing them are the most meaningful things they ever will do in their lives. But I'm afraid we've reached a stage in which we must recognize that while the happiness and hopes of adults are surely important, the health and prospects of children must be considered more so, as far too many of them are doing poorly on their often unduly rocky road to adulthood. For millions of kids, more specifically, trying to grow up with gaps and absences where both their parents should be is a very big reason why this is the case. Or more specifically still, unless we change and start bringing far fewer babies into this world outside of marriage, and likewise, unless we divorce and separate far less often, our children will not do nearly as well as they otherwise might and as we all hope and pray.

Mothers and fathers have always sacrificed for their children. It's what they're supposed to do. But we've come to a time and place in which parents, as well as people who are not yet parents, must think first and foremost about boys and girls they're responsible for or someday may come to be. One way or another, both men and women—and especially teenagers—must better commit to not having children without first being married. And if and when married, they must better commit to building unions that are loving and respectful and lasting.

It's completely understood that plenty of organizations and other American voices see themselves speaking precisely on behalf of children in fragmented families, though none, I trust, has ever had any interest in doing so in the way I just proposed.

The Children's Defense Fund in its mission statement, for example, refers to how it "provides a strong, effective and independent voice for *all* children of America who cannot vote, lobby or speak for themselves," paying "particular attention to the needs of poor and minority children and those with disabilities." [Emphasis in the original.] CDF also advocates "preventive investments" before kids "get sick, drop out of school, get into trouble or suffer family breakdown." This is fine and conventional as far as it goes, but far from what I have in mind.[47]

A portion of the mission of the National Fatherhood Initiative is improving the "well-being of children by increasing the proportion of children growing up with involved, responsible, and committed fathers."[48] This is closer, but not nearly enough.

Then there's the National Campaign to Prevent Teen and Unplanned Pregnancy, which "seeks to improve the lives and future prospects of children and families and, in particular, to help ensure that children are born into stable, two-parent families who are committed to and ready for the demanding task of raising the next generation." The Campaign does this by supporting a "combination of responsible values and behavior by both men and women and responsible policies in both the public and private sectors."[49] This conception is even closer to what I'm proposing, but still a ways away, though I'm quick to acknowledge that all three of these Washington-area-based interest groups are unusually effective (with the term "interest group" definitely not used as a pejorative).

If I were to frame a mission statement for my proposition (until we can come up with something more felicitous, let's call it "The National Campaign to Talk Candidly about Family Fragmentation"), it might read something like this: "The Campaign seeks to significantly increase the number of American children growing up in stable, two-parent families by drawing attention to the many ways in which out-of-wedlock births and divorce hurt and limit the life chances of boys and girls. We do this by encouraging and publicly conducting unusually frank discussions about the entwined well-being of children and responsibilities of adults, as well as about how rampant family fragmentation damages and holds back our nation."

In other words, I'm suggesting the kinds of discussions in which cameras usually don't roll, recorders don't record, and participants (especially those in public life) don't clam up in fear of being pilloried either immediately or years later when a tape surfaces on some blog. A perfect metaphor for capturing such discussions is the distinction made by Barbara Dafoe Whitehead in a speech at Columbia University twenty years ago regarding how we typically talk about family issues. She called the two disparate approaches "conference table" and "kitchen table" conversations, with the former taking place "among people like us—representatives of the media, the academic world, the policy community," and with their language that of the "policy sciences—politics and economics." In severe contrast, kitchen table conversations take place among families themselves, with their language that of "cultural norms and values."[50]

David Blankenhorn, mentioned back in Chapter One as the author of the important 1995 book *Fatherless America*, has written similarly. "You will learn more about the American family from ten randomly chosen grand-mothers than you will from ten randomly chosen family experts." This is so, he continued, because grandmothers "tend to be less shy about value judg-ments," as they "tend to say things such as: 'People today care more about themselves and less about others.' 'They want everything now.' 'They are less willing to make sacrifices.'"[51]

Might a project as cursorily outlined here possibly work, with "work" defined as resulting in some measure of consequential progress in reducing nonmarital birth rates and divorce rates while simultaneously increasing mar-riage rates? Might it counteract, even very modestly, all the powerful cul-tural, economic and other forces that have been undermining marriage—and not just in the United States—over the last half-century? Putting matters in that tough way, a person's confidence has to be slim. Moreover, would any progress possibly made be worth the offense and pain a campaign like this inescapably would cause some people, probably many? These are unavoid-able questions, though I'm unwilling to abandon the idea just moments after raising it. I'm curious, for example, what a team of experts in public opinion, communications, and other relevant fields might think about it. Could such a possibility be framed and implemented in such a way as to help more than hurt? I say it's worth exploring.

I also frequently say something that I learned a long time ago from Bill Bennett, back when he was secretary of education in the mid'80s. I was an editorial writer at the time at the *St. Paul Pioneer Press* and finagled about half-an-hour to interview him, during which time, I must admit, we talked about many of the same issues we've been discussing in this book. When his aide looked at his watch, I knew I had time for just one more question, so it had to be a good one.

"Mr. Secretary," I said, "we've been talking less about policies and bud-gets and rules and things like that and more about our very culture. How *does* one go about changing our very culture?" He said it was a real good question, that he had been thinking about it a lot, and that the best answer he had was to say what was true in his heart "and to say over and over and over again." A quarter of a century later, I still don't know a better answer at root.

Notes

1. Cited by the author in *Close to Home: Celebrations and Critiques of America's Experiment in Freedom*, by Katherine A. Kersten and Mitchell B. Pearlstein (Minneapolis: MSP Books, 2000), pp. 188–90.

2. Barbara Dafoe Whitehead and David Popenoe, eds., "Marriage and Children: A Symposium on Making Marriage More Child Centered," *American Experiment Quarterly*, Volume 4, Number, Summer 2001.

3. Daniel Yankelovich, *New Rules: Searching for Self-Fulfillment in a World Turned Upside Down* (New York: Bantam, 1981), pp. 109–11.

4. Congressional Research Service tabulations of the March 2009 "Annual Social and Economic Supplement" of the Current Population Survey.

5. For example, see Joan Petersilia, *When Prisoners Come Home: Parole and Prisoner Reentry* (Oxford: New York, 2003).

6. H. Wallace Goddard, "Strengthening Your Marriage," Cooperative Extension Service, University of Arkansas (date unknown).

7. http://www.smartmarriages.com/workshops.2010.html

8. Whitehead and Popenoe.

9. Ron Haskins and Isabel Sawhill, *Creating an Opportunity Society* (Washington, DC, 2009), p. 260.

10. Robert G. Wood, Sheena McConnell et al., *The Building Strong Families Project: Executive Summary*, Mathematica Policy Research, Inc., May 2010.

11. Haskins and Sawhill, p. 261.

12. Tom Mortenson, "For Every 100 Girls . . . ," *Postsecondary Education OPPORTUNITY*, July 28, 2006.

13. Interestingly, for every 100 women who earn a first-professional degree, 107 men do so.

14. Christina Hoff Sommers, *The War Against Boys: How Misguided Feminism is Harming Our Young Men* (New York: Simon & Schuster).

15. Judith Kleinfeld, http://www.whyboysfail.com/2009/01/21/state-of-american-boyhood-paper. Girls, Kleinfeld wrote in the same abstract, "suffer from higher rates of depression, eating disorders, and suicide attempts." Achievement gaps, moreover, in the natural sciences and mathematics "at the highest levels of achievement" still haven't closed, with boys doing better. Nevertheless, she summed up: "While boys and girls both suffer from characteristic problems, those of boys are neglected and far more serious."

16. Jonathan Rauch, "The Coming American Matriarchy: The Fairer Sex Gets Ready to Take Over," *Reason Magazine*, January 15, 2008.

17. Eduardo Porter and Michelle O'Donnell, "Facing Middle Age with No Degree, and No Wife," *The New York Times*, August 6, 2006.

18. http://minneapolisfed.org/publications_papers/pub_display.dfm?id=3278.

19. The following five examples are drawn from a journal article which briefly summarizes the main lessons of a variety of sources, which they cite. Deborah Taylor and Maureen Lorimer, "Helping Boys Succeed," *Educational Leadership*, December 2002-January 2003, pp. 68–70.

20. Ibid. Taylor and Lorimer here refer to a book by William Pollack and Mary Pipher, *Real Boys: Rescuing Our Sons from the Myths of Boyhood* (New York: Random House, 1998). The actual quote is Taylor and Lorimer's; not Pollack and Pipher's.

21. *The War Against Boys*, pp. 161–62.

22. As reported in "The Trouble with Black Boys: The Role and Infuence of Environmental and Cultural Factors on the Academic Performance of African American Males," by Pedro Antonio Noguera, *In Motion Magazine*, May 13, 2002.

23. *The American Teacher*: 2000, Metropolitan Life Insurance Company, as reported by Noguera.

24. Richard Whitmire and Susan McGee Bailey, "Gender Gap: Are Boys being Shortchanged in K–12 School?" *Education Next*, Spring 2010, Vol. 10, No. 2.

25. Portions of this section on crime draws on, "Crime and Marriage: If Wedding Rings Help Break Vicious and Violent Cycles, What's Impeding Them from Doing So More Often," Mitchell B. Pearlstein, *American Experiment Quarterly*, Fall 2005.

26. Bruce Western, *Punishment and Inequality in America* (New York: Russell Sage, 2006), p. 14.

27. William J. Sabol and Heather C. West, "Prisoners in 2009," Bureau of Justice Statistics.

28. Bureau of Justice Statistics. Page last revised on February 17, 2011.

29. Thomas P. Bonczar, "Prevalence of Imprisonment in the U.S. Population, 1974–2001 (Washington: Bureau of Justice Statistics Special Report, 2003.)

30. Kathryn Edin and Maria Kafalis, *Promises I Can Keep: Why Poor Women Put Motherhood before Marriage* (Berkeley: University of California, 2005), p. 2.

31. Bruce Western and Christopher Wildeman, "The Black Family and Mass Incarceration," *Annals of the American Academy of Political and Social Science*, Vol. 621, No. 1 (2009), p. 231.

32. *Punishment and Inequality in America*, p. 137.

33. For example, see Devah Pager, "The Mark of a Criminal Record," *American Journal of Sociology*, Vol. 108, Number 5 (March 2003); and Christopher Wildeman and Bruce Western, "Incarceration in Fragile Families," *The Future of Children*, Vol. 20, Number 2, Fall 2010, pp. 157–178.

34. Joseph M. Bessette, "The Injustice Department," *The Weekly Standard*, October 17, 2005, p. 31.

35. Linda J. Waite and Maggie Gallagher, *The Case for Marriage: Why Married People are Happier, Healthier, and Better Off Financially* (New York: Doubleday, 2000), pp. 157–58. The quotes are Waite and Gallaghers'; not the original researchers.

36. Ibid., pp. 152; 155.

37. "Incarceration in Fragile Families," p. 169.

38. Margaret Colgate Love, "Starting with a Clean Slate: In Praise of a Forgotten Section of the Model Penal Code," *Fordham Urban Law Journal*, Vol. 30, July 2003, p. 2.

39. Legal Action Center, "After Prison: Roadblocks to Reentry," New York City and Washington, DC, 2004.

40. Mike Meyers, "No Bars, But Still a Prison: Fear of Lawsuits and Greater Scrutiny among Employers Make It Harder than Ever for Convicted Felons to Find Jobs" (Minneapolis) *Star Tribune*, June 6, 2005.

41. Ann Zimmerman and Kortney Stringer, "As Background Checks Proliferate, Ex-Cons Face Jobs Lock," *The Wall Street Journal*, August 26, 2004.

42. "Ohio Collateral Sanctions Project: Executive Summary," Kimberly R. Mossoney and Cara A. Roecker, University of Toledo College of Law (undated).

43. "Life Sentences: Collateral Sanctions Associated with Marijuana Offenses," Center for Cognitive Liberty & Ethics, Ver. 1, July 2, 2007.

44. Council on Crime and Justice (Minneapolis), "Low Level Offenses in Minneapolis: An Analysis of Arrests and Their Outcomes: Final Report," November 2004, p. 36.

45. "Starting with a Clean Slate."

46. Margaret Colgate Love, Paying Their Debt to Society: An Assessment of the Relief Provisions of the Uniform Collateral Consequences of Conviction Act," *Howard Law Review*, Brandon Symposium Contribution, January 1, 2011.

47. http://www.chldrensdefense.org/about-us/

48. http://www.fatherhood.org/page.aspx?pid=319

49. http://www.thenationalcampaign.org/about-us/our-mission.aspx

50. Richard Louv, "Two Debates are Raging on Family," *San Diego Union Tribune*, February 22, 1992.

51. William Raspberry, "Grandma Knows Best," *The Washington Post*, September 25, 1990.

Chapter 7

Conclusion

A few reinforced thoughts to conclude, starting with respect for "complicated family scripts," which might be considered a classier locution for acknowledging how, as we did right at the beginning, "stuff happens."

I first heard the term "complicated family scripts" several years ago as used by a scholar named Rose Brewer in summing up how African American men, participating in focus groups, understood their own families. According to Brewer, they knew that "love and care, connection and responsibility, are not always neatly or simply bound up in a nuclear family arrangement."[1] This is all true and needs to be remembered—taken to heart might be a better ways of putting it—so as to avoid unfairness and unkindness. But equally true, as preceding pages have made clear, are the many ways in which our nation's often radical break from "nuclear family arrangements" are severely hurting all involved, starting as always with children.

This is also to fully acknowledge that the many studies we have drawn on are thick with qualifications of their own. The effects of family fragmentation are rarely if ever exactly the same for girls and for boys; rarely the same for kids regardless of age; rarely the same for children born out of wedlock, as opposed to children of divorce; rarely the same for children living in stepfamilies as opposed to other households; and rarely are they identical for black, white, and Hispanic children. Rarely, moreover, are findings the same for children contending with a lone romantic transition in their mother or father's' lives as opposed to two, or three, or more; rarely are results the same in the short term as opposed to the long term; and sometimes, thankfully, hardly any bad news crops up at all.

But inevitable variations like these notwithstanding, and on more than decisive balance, the news really is bad, made that way by family lives in the

United States involving (in Andrew Cherlin's description) "more transitions than anywhere else." While appreciation for complexity in acutely personal matters like these is required, glossing over their routinely disadvantageous effects is quite the opposite. The admonition, I might add applies even if one's conception of marriage is not overly romanticized (in either sense of the term) and expectations for its contributions are smaller than mine. The same holds even if one's view of fatherhood (as discussed earlier with the help of Woody Allen) is more in line with the paternal involvement and energy of Everyman rather than Super Dad, as stakes for kids are undeniable, regardless of what some grown-ups would prefer to think.

My conception and goals for mobility are similarly modest, or at least free of very much mystery. Would we be better served, and would American life be seen as fairer in certain sour quarters, if substantially more people moved up the income and status ranks, quintile by quintile, more rapidly? Of course—not that nearly as many men and women are glued to lower rungs as current assumptions increasingly have them. Instead, my notions about mobility borrow from my own life growing up in a lower-middle-class neighborhood of Queens in the 1950s and '60s, a place where our parents may or may not have gotten out of high school, but where my classmates, in the main, took school reasonably seriously. Meaning, when we went off to college—and large numbers of us did—we frequently were either the first person or pretty close to the first one in our families ever to do so.

Yes, virtually all of us (or so it seemed) benefited from growing up in families in which birth mothers and birth fathers still reigned. Yes, college tuitions were a pittance compared to what they now are. And yes, the United States was still in the midst of its post-War dominance. But without discounting any of those large advantages, and certainly without suggesting we succeeded "on our own," the fact remains there's no deep secret why many of us eventually wound up higher on the ladder than where we began; it was schooling, often lots of it. Updating matters, I would argue that no matter what changes have occurred in American education and other areas since then, and unless a school really is inhospitable to learning and perhaps even safety, similar routes are still very much open for young people. Provided, that is, they're interested and tenacious enough in pursuing them, starting with the not-great chore and sacrifice of actually graduating from high school, an elementary step which enormous numbers of young people choose to dismiss, damn the consequences.

Does growing up in a "broken home" make it less likely that boys and girls will do well in school, including making it out of twelfth grade, and then going on and getting more training than they otherwise might? Without question, as we've seen. But if we're to do better, this is where personal initiative has the power to kick some sociological butt and needs to. And no, this is not contrary to what I've argued throughout, as I start from the premise that no matter the constraints posed by family or other situations, personal responsibility among all parties must be understood as an imperative. Think of it as the most individualized kind of "No Excuses," as too many young people simply forfeit the opportunities they do have.

If, in many instances, this is because African Americans in particular assume that the financial return on education remains as empty-pocketed as it often did when their college-educated grandparents were forced to shine shoes and wait on diners in Pullman cars, then evidence needs to be blared louder than it has that hideous disincentives like those don't exist anymore and that the premium on a good education has come to work for everyone. And by "good education," the reference is not just to college, but also, for example, the kind of technical educations that would allow more people to qualify for the kind of sophisticated and good-paying (and regularly unfilled) machinist jobs discussed in Chapter Four.

Yet it's nevertheless also fiercely true, as also discussed in that chapter, the economy is changing in fundamental ways, in this and other parts of the world, increasing the chances of "multigenerational entrapment"[2] unless many more people learn much more. Without putting too blunt an edge on it, and returning to our discussion of the effects of family fragmentation and weakened education on economic performance, recall how giant enterprises like Facebook and Google are minuscule in terms of people employed compared to earlier-day corporate titans like U.S. Steel and General Motors. This bodes less well all the time for people without requisite skills looking for good work and hoping to keep it. How potentially poorly might it all bode? I'm hoping much more facetiously than not, but a free-market friend has spoken of tipping his hat to Marx, as "surplus labor does seem to be leading to a lumpenproletariat."

Short of a social structure of the czars, what might a decreasingly mobile society on these shores look like? The best short answer is I can only guess and would rather not. But it's already the centrifugal case that Americans marry, befriend, work with, and live in closest proximity to people most like themselves, seemingly more all the time. It's also already the case (or so I would speculate) that people who wear white collars and manipulate symbols for a living have a decreasing sense of the everyday lives of men and women who wear blue collars and make and manipulate tangible *things* for a living. This is so for no other reason than increasing numbers of college-trained people have grown up in homes with college-trained parents; this, as opposed to only a generation or two ago when many more parents, even of the most up-and-coming children, worked in factories and shops.

It's hard to imagine any of this cycling much further, propelled by profound economic changes, without unwelcomed prices exacted, starting with deepening frustrations and disillusionments on the part of many Americans, especially those in the bottom half. Suffice it to say, as a political conservative, I don't get any sense that more than a few of my colleagues on the right side of the aisle adequately (and publicly) appreciate the dynamics and dangers at work. Even if bigger government checks and tax breaks for lower-income and moderate-income men and women were the answer (they're not), we've reached a stage where there are no more uncommitted stores of government money to be had. So what might help? I would respectfully and not for the first time in these pages submit that bringing more babies into this world within marriage rather than without, and staying married unless circumstances are abusive, would be of aid, even if not nearly fast or fully enough. But there is no question that if marriage rebounded in the United States, more young people would wind up doing better, first for themselves and later for those they're responsible for and love.

In preparation for an Amen, let me close with several points about religion and faith and how they fit.

I used to finish off Rotary and other speeches on family fragmentation (much better known as family *breakdown* back when I started) by saying nothing would get adequately better until enough people grabbed their heads and declared, "My God, we've been committing suicide and we can't do this anymore." It was a nice flourish in the same way that I essentially agree with Bill Bennett when he says the best way of changing a culture is to say what one earnestly believes "over and over and over again." For a coda I still resonate to throngs of scared people "clutching their heads." But that doesn't preclude a couple of other faith-filled benevolences, though a note about a blocked possibility first.

I formerly wondered why clergy didn't spend more time preaching about and otherwise stressing the importance of congregants being married before making babies. But for a variety of reasons, including spending a fair amount of time in churches with my ordained wife, I've come to better understand that if ministers repeatedly made the point, folks in the pews might grow fatigued to the point of offended. The same pattern and drawback would apply, of course, probably even more so, to just about any speaker in any setting, regardless of who might be sitting out front. This is the case as just about everyone is close to at least a few single parents (quite often their own children) and sermons and implorations on the subject run the risk of quickly growing old and irritating. This is a double shame, because if anyone earthbound is entitled to be "judgmental," I would like to think its men and women of the cloth. I do still contend that religious institutions need to be more assertive in this realm, while being no less supportive of those in need. But how, exactly, might religious leaders pursue a good balance? It's not for me to say, if for no other reason than I don't know.

I don't doubt, by the way, that my wife's ministry as a homeless shelter director for more than a dozen years, mostly in the early days of our marriage, continues to have a large effect on how I view adults and children in need, often severe need. The pertinent benefit for our purposes here is that I would like to think I have a decent sense of the multitude of problems facing people on the edge and the resulting turmoil in their lives, very much including the lives of their children. Yet I also realize that by knowing as much as I do about people who might be considered the saddest of the sad, that I risk underestimating the wherewithal of other people who might also be in tough situations, but not as tough as those who live on streets and sleep in shelters. Might this cause me, for example, to be less confident than other observers when it comes to expecting *all* children to do well academically, as in *never* accepting any "excuses" ever? I suspect it might. But do I nonetheless believe I'm on target when it comes to my main argument about how hard it is for large numbers of children, especially those in single-parent and no-parent homes to study and learn well enough? Yes, I'm afraid I still do.

A next point returns us to prison; or, more precisely, to freer times on the proverbial outside.

For a variety of reasons, I also have come to better appreciate how hard it can be for ex-offenders, or those trying to stay straight from the start, to stay clear of people who, as a protective parent or grandparent might put it, are "bad influences." The latter reference is to people with perverse talents not only for getting themselves in trouble, but also others; questionable and bad actors who prod and provoke others to fight, shoot, shoot up and do other illegal, destructive, and self-destructive things.

What might already-multitasking churches do to help in this instance? One is tempted to say "reach out," though that's clichéd, and at any rate, if anyone is obliged to do the bulk of stretching here it's those in need of what churches have to offer. They're the ones who should take the lead in reaching *back*. Yet regardless of directional arrows, the problem to be solved is how to better surround people (and not just young minority men) with better influences. This would be less of an issue if they already spent much of their week at jobs or in school, but this is not the case in loads of instances. Organizations like Boys Clubs and Girls Clubs are terrific, but obviously not apt for older males and females, particularly those who already know jail and prison routines up close and personally. Churches are safe havens, and in regards to the people I'm talking about, all they have to do in order to take advantage of them is join and commit. But might there be other things religious institutions can do in providing buffers over and above those of the Word? Quite practical things so that fewer people are tempted, dragged down, and buried in mean streets?

It's fair to say that what I've just suggested is that churches think about new or invigorated programs as one more indirect way of helping marriage along. But haven't we learned—Rossi's iron and brass laws of evaluation and all, as well as years of failed educational fixes—things called "programs" routinely don't work if the aim is changing entrenched behavior? Yes, we definitely have, though the initiatives I'm talking about here, essentially keeping guys reasonably occupied, are of a far less-heroic sort.

Matters are entirely different, however, if intentions are bolder and more straightaway in reversing decades of family fragmentation, the scope of which in the United States is unique in the industrialized world. Programmatic line items and funding streams don't begin to cut it for a job like that, as infinitely better suited are spiritual renewals leading to fundamental cultural shifts. How to call them up? In a book like this is it kosher to say only God knows?

Notes

1. Rose M. Brewer, "Family Complexities: African American Men and Black Family Structure, *Crossroads: Choosing a New Direction: Final Report,*" *African American Men Project,* Hennepin County, MN, January 2002, p. 195.

2. Clayton M. Christensen, Michael B. Horn, and Curtis W. Johnson, *Disrupting Class: How Disruptive Innovation Will Change the Way the World Learns* (New York: McGraw Hill, 2008), p. 153.

Index

About the Author

Mitch Pearlstein is president of Center of the American Experiment, a think tank he founded in Minneapolis in 1990. He has made his career in education, journalism, and government, having served on the staffs of University of Minnesota President C. Peter Magrath and Minnesota Governor Albert H. Quie; as an editorial writer for the *St. Paul Pioneer Press*; and in the U.S. Department of Education, among other assignments. His previous books include *The Fatherhood Movement: A Call to Action* (with co-editors Wade F. Horn and David Blankenhorn); *Close to Home: Celebrations and Critiques of America's Experiment in Freedom* (with Katherine A. Kersten); and *Riding into the Sunrise: Al Quie and a Life of Faith, Service & Civility*. His doctorate is in educational administration from the University of Minnesota and he is married to the Rev. Diane Darby McGowan, a Minneapolis Police Chaplain and Deacon of an Episcopal parish in St. Paul. They have four adult children, three grandchildren, and currently only two dogs. They live with the latter, Trevor and Bailey, in Minneapolis.